How to Write and Publish Papers in the Medical Sciences

Second Edition

How to Write and Publish Papers in the Medical Sciences

Second Edition

Edward J Huth, MD
Editor, *Annals of Internal Medicine*

Williams & Wilkins

BALTIMORE • PHILADELPHIA • HONG KONG
LONDON • MUNICH • SYDNEY • TOKYO

A WAVERLY COMPANY

Editor: William R. Hensyl
Associate Editor: Harriet Felscher
Copy Editor: Stephen Siegforth
Design: Wilma Rosenberger
Illustration Planner: Lorraine Wrzosek
Production Coordinator: Raymond E. Reter

Printed in the United States of America

First Edition 1982

Library of Congress Cataloging in Publication Data

Huth, Edward J.
   How to write and publish papers in the medical sciences/
Edward J. Huth.—2nd ed.
     p. cm.
   Includes bibliographical references.
   ISBN 0-683-04272-6 casebound
   ISBN 0-683-04271-8 paperback
   1. Medical writing. 2. Medical publishing. I. Title.
   [DNLM: 1. Publishing. 2. Writing. WZ 345 H979h]
R119.H87 1990
808'.06661—dc20
DNLM/DLC
for Library of Congress

89-24914
CIP

6 7 8 9 10

Introduction,
with a Note on Style in This Book

Some books on writing papers for journals in medicine and closely related fields are mostly essays on literary style that do little to help with the practical problems in deciding what to put into a paper, how to arrange that content, and how to get the paper published. Other books offer practical help, but give no more than recipes. They do not show why certain structures are needed for different kinds of papers; they do not set out what points to consider in deciding between tables or illustrations to present evidence supporting statements in the text. This guide is a short book, but I have tried to make it a broad book. It offers as much practical advice as can be put into a concise text, and it explains the basis for its advice.

Inexperienced authors may wish to read this guide from front to back. Experienced authors may wish only to dip into chapters that might expand a bit what they already know, or they may use only some chapters or appendixes for reference. The 19 chapters describe all the steps in writing and publishing a paper: conceiving the paper, writing it, and seeing it through to print. Most of what we write goes onto paper without our thinking much about how we are writing—shopping lists, routine letters, quickly scribbled clinical notes. We forget that good writing is hard work even for experienced authors. Read what an eminent gastroenterologist had to say:

> I have not found . . . writing one bit easier today than it was 30 yrs. ago. I still have to work at it very hard and make many revisions, with a rare exception—once in a while something like an editorial or thought will come into my mind, and I'll write it out and be satisfied with the first draft. That's unusual, because the saying of Francis Bacon has always been deeply impressed in my mind . . . "Writing [maketh an] exact man." And we all have a head full of thoughts floating around that have not been formulated in a way that would withstand examination if they had been set forth in writing and allowed to be scrutinized by others. And I find this invariably so; with the general thought that I have at the start, I find that some of the premises were incomplete and incorrect and that things don't quite fit, so that the task of making things flow and putting things in their place, I still find very hard work, but work that I genuinely like . . . . I find it stimulating to write, but like any other person who does quite a bit of writing, there are times when I feel stuck, and I have to put something aside and let it mature before I get back to it.

These are words (1) from Morton Grossman, a man who published 400 scientific papers, 134 editorials and other short papers, and 71 books or chapters in books. Writing will always be work if you wish to write well. But with the right approach it can become work you like.

With the suggestions in this guide, the inexperienced author can develop skills in writing through mastering the main principles, applying them in future work, and looking into books and papers recommended in Appendix 4, "References and Reading: An Annotated Bibliography". Inexperienced authors can be helped to develop skills through workshops and seminars; defects in others' writing are usually seen more readily than those in one's own. The sequence of chapters suggests a sequence for teaching sessions. For example, Chapters 5 through 8 on the various formats can be used as a text for workshop sessions in which students analyze and criticize published papers for their content and its sequence. Teachers seeking explicit help in developing a syllabus for medical writing should consult *Scientific Writing for Graduate Students: A Manual on the Teaching of Scientific Writing* (2).

The style conventions used in this book—punctuation, abbreviation, citation, formats for references, and other details—are those specified in *Medical Style and Format: An International Guide for Authors, Editors, and Publishers* (3). Some of these are widely used in medical journals while others are just being adopted; if authors wish to be sure of the conventions specified by the journals for which they are writing, they should consult their information-for-authors pages.

In accordance with the requirements for bibliographic references specified by the International Committee of Medical Journal Editors (see Chapter 15 and Appendix 2), references are cited by reference numbers within parenthesis marks on the line; the references for each chapter follow its text.

REFERENCES

1. Boyle JD. Morton I Grossman, MD, PhD: an oral history. Gastroenterology. 1982;83:285–324.
2. CBE Committee on Graduate Training in Scientific Writing. Scientific writing for graduate students: a manual on the teaching of scientific writing. Bethesda, Maryland: Council of Biology Editors; 1968. Reprinted 1983.
3. Huth EJ. Medical style and format: an international guide for authors, editors, and publishers. Philadelphia: ISI Press; 1987. Available from Williams & Wilkins, Baltimore, Maryland.

Acknowledgments

I continue to be grateful to those persons who reviewed an early draft of Chapter 2, "Searching the Literature", for the first edition; the present Chapter 2 carries forward many points developed from their recommendations: Estelle Abrams, Clifford A Bachrach, William K Beatty, Carol Hansen Fenichel, Eleanor Goodchild, Betsy L Humphreys, Doris A Jaeger, Charlotte Kenton, Susan Knapp, Robert Mehnert, Harriet R Meiss, Marianne M Meyer, Karen Patrias, Theresa Rosen, Nancy Vaupel. Any remaining errors in Chapter 2 are my errors, not theirs. Many persons helped me greatly with information needed for revision of Chapter 2 for this edition; I am deeply grateful to them for their help: Leo P Chall, Steven DiMeo, Carolyn Gosling, Sue Jones, Sally Kilby, Sheldon Kotzin, Aletha Kowitz, Robert B Mehnert, Fred Pattison, John W Rupp, Dwight R Tousignaut.

My work on the first edition was greatly helped by the perceptive, detailed, and helpful criticisms of its first draft from Kathleen Case, Robert Day, and 4 anonymous manuscript reviewers.

In writing this second edition I have tried to take into account criticisms in published reviews of the first edition. Notably helpful reviewers were the late William B Bean, Robert E Bjork, Peter P Morgan, and the late Erwin Neter. Other helpful recommendations came from Nicholas E Davies, Michael G Fisher, Doris E Fletcher, and Anne Just.

Contents

The Paper, the Audience, and the Right Journal

Before sitting down to write or even to plan a paper in detail, you should answer 6 questions.

Question 1: What do I have to say?
Question 2: Is the paper worth writing?
Question 3: Have I already published such a paper?
Question 4: What is the right format for the message?
Question 5: Who are the audience for the message?
Question 6: What is the right journal for the paper?

You may be able to answer some of these questions yourself, but there is safety in also putting the questions to a more experienced colleague. Some authors tend to overestimate the importance of what they have to say and the size of the audience for the message. These overestimates may lead to preparing a paper for a journal unlikely to publish it.

In working out a complete answer to question 1, you may move toward writing the first draft but a first-step, short answer is a powerful test of whether you have a message and are really ready to write.

WHAT DO I HAVE TO SAY?

What is the message of the paper? Papers likely to be read are those that are useful to readers because they answer questions for them. An effective paper deals with an important question clearly answered with adequate evidence for the answer. Your being able to state the answer in a single short sentence is a powerful test of whether your paper will have a clear and strong message.

The Research Paper

You have carried out a study properly designed to answer a specific question: Is antibiotic A more effective than antibiotic B in treating disease X? The study has yielded a clear answer amply supported by statistically sound data:

> "Treatment with antibiotic A is more effective in reducing mortality in disease X than treatment with antibiotic B".

The paper with that message will make a single point; you know what you have to say.

The chief of your surgical service has been reviewing his last 50 cases of total colectomy for treatment of severe ulcerative colitis. He asks you to join him in writing a paper on his findings. You ask him what point the paper is going to make. He gets irritated. He is not "trying to make a point", he is just going to "report his experience" because his "colleagues elsewhere will be interested". Your surgical chief does not have a clear message in mind for his paper, he does not know what he has to say.

Data gathering posing as research may or may not lead to papers worth writing. The probability that a paper with a clear message will emerge from research is determined more by how the research was conceived, planned, and executed than by how well the paper is written. A clear question must be posed before the research is planned, the design of the research plan must be adequate, and the data must be properly collected and appropriately analyzed.

Well-conceived and well-executed research does not necessarily lead, however, to an answer important to a large audience; that assessment is covered by question 5.

The Case Report

Exactly what message a case report will carry is usually not clear until the literature has been searched for reports of similar or closely related cases. A clinician's feeling that a case is unique or so uncommon as to merit description may impel him to describe it in a case report. But the uniqueness of a case is rarely the message of an important case report; the importance lies more in the extent to which the report will enlarge our concepts of disease and our skills in practice. These judgments should determine the exact message of the case report, and they cannot be reached without a search of the literature for similar cases.

The Review Article

An author of a research paper is ready to consider questions 2 through 6 posed above after having concluded that it will have a clear message: The investigator examined data and came up with an answer to the question for which the research was designed. But a decision to write a review article, like the decision to write a case report, usually follows a search of the literature that has turned up no similar paper. That literature search will not necessarily lead to an exact message for the review until the relevant literature found has been thoroughly digested. The initial search of the literature will have to be guided, however, by a tentative decision on what question or questions the review might answer.

A review may not be worth writing if you cannot frame one or more important questions it will try to answer. What if the chief of your medical service suggests that you join him in writing a review on the neurologic manifestations of lupus erythematosus? The two of you must discuss exactly what questions such a review might answer. What are the various neurologic manifestations that may develop in patients with this disease? How can these be identified as due to the disease rather than to treatment? What is the effect of treatment on these manifestations? With these questions you can consult some up-to-date textbooks and search the literature for reviews of lupus erythematosus to see what answers they give.

IS THE PAPER WORTH WRITING?

Writing is hard work. Why write a paper if it is not going to get published?

What Is in the Literature?

Whether a journal accepts a paper often hinges on whether its message is new to the medical literature, or at least new to a particular audience. Even if the message is not new, the paper may get published because it expands on, or firms up, a previously published message. So deciding to write a paper may depend in part on what you find in the search of the literature. Research you started 3 years ago may have reached conclusions already reported in 5 papers published in the past year. The unusual, perhaps unique, case you think of describing in a case report has already been described in 10 papers published in 3 countries. The kind of review article you think is needed has already been published as 2 only slightly different reviews in 2 major journals.

If your search of the literature turns up no paper of the kind you are planning, you have a green light. Or the search may tell you that the findings in an apparently unique case you wish to report have been described in a French journal but not in an English-language journal. You may find a review on the topic you have in mind, but it is insufficiently critical. So a search of the literature can also tell you much about the factors determining the odds that your paper, if you write it, will be accepted for publication: the newness and importance of its message in the entire medical literature, or for particular audiences.

The "So-What" Test

How important will the paper's message be? One editor of a major journal frequently applies the "so-what" test. What if the paper's message is correct? "So what"? The "so-what" look at your message is a powerful, if crude-sounding, measure of its importance. What effect will the message have? Will it change concept or practice? How?

HAVE I ALREADY PUBLISHED SUCH A PAPER?

Scientific publishing is costly, and many editors do not wish to give space to papers representing content already published elsewhere (1), whether only in essence or in exactly the same form. And authors are ethically obliged not to waste space in the journal literature. For many years the difficulties in becoming aware of new developments in fields other than one's own may have justified repetitive publication in journals with different audiences. No longer; electronic bibliographic databases now make rapid searches for new information easy. New data added to already published data may yield new conclusions and justify a new paper, but resist temptations to trying repetitive publication. The odds are going up that the repetition will be detected by peer reviewers and that at best you have wasted your time. If the paper is accepted and published, the repetition will probably be discovered and your reputation sullied.

WHAT IS THE RIGHT FORMAT?

Your message and the materials your paper will carry for its support may point to the right format (the structure of a paper). The clinical trial comparing antibiotic A with antibiotic B for treatment of disease X has yielded a new message (the conclusion reached from the trial) that is new or, if not entirely new, important to a large audience. Critical readers will want to know many details about the trial so they can judge whether the conclusions are sound. They will want to know the criteria for case selection, how patients were assigned to treatment, and other details of study design and data assessment. They will expect a formal report of the research (see Chapter 5, "The Research Paper").

The best choice of format may not be immediately apparent. The surgeon who reviewed his 50 cases of total colectomy for severe ulcerative colitis without first asking himself what question he expected his case review to answer wound up with no clear message. Without a message that is new or valuable in some other way, he is unlikely to get his paper published in a high-ranking journal. But the surgeon may be able to use a format other than the case-series analysis (see Chapter 7). Analysis of the large body of data from his 50 cases does not yield any new important findings, but the data do firm up previously published views. Further, while analyzing his cases, the surgeon reviewed the relevant journal literature. He probably has as much information on this subject as any other surgeon and perhaps more. If the subject has not been comprehensively surveyed in a review article in the past 5 years, many younger surgeons and surgical residents may find a new review useful. With this line of thinking, the surgeon may be able to develop a plan for a comprehensive review article incorporating his case data that he could not get published standing alone in a "me-too" paper.

Choose the shortest format for what you have to report. A case report of a new, but probably uncommon, adverse effect of a drug may be accepted by a large-circulation journal despite intense competition among authors to get their papers into it if the report is very concise, prepared as a letter-to-the-editor or in other short but formal formats known variously as "brief reports", "clinical notes", or "short communications".

WHO ARE THE AUDIENCE?: THE "WHO-CARES" TEST

A powerful test of audience is "who cares", a close relative of "so what". You should look at the message of your paper and ask, "Who will care?" when they see it in print. Who will want the answer the paper offers for the question it tackled? Will it be most practitioners, or specialists in a small field, or a handful of technicians?

Any author is likely to think that his or her paper will merit the attention of far more readers than in fact it will get. This very human trait can lead to tactically poor decisions in writing a paper and selecting a journal to which to send it. If you are satisfied that the paper will have a definite, valuable message, ask yourself who are really likely to read it, not who in your opinion should read it. Remember that papers are read mainly by persons who need answers to questions. Your decision can be crucial for prompt publication. If you overestimate the probable audience, you may prepare the paper for, and send it to, a prestigious large-circulation journal likely to reject it; you will have lost valuable time.

Do not confuse probable audience with the audience you feel "need" the paper. Practitioners and investigators are busy persons with heads already full of facts. Just because your paper will carry facts unknown to them does not mean that they will make room in their brains for its message.

WHAT IS THE RIGHT JOURNAL?

Choosing the right journal is a critically important early step in planning the paper. Journals differ widely, even within the same scientific discipline or clinical specialty. They differ in scope, in balance of topics, in their variety of formats, and in the balance of research reports and synoptic papers like reviews and editorials.

If you work in a narrow specialty or a subspecialty of your field, only a few journals may be appropriate choices. But most of the medical sciences are represented by large numbers of journals. The author should draw up a list of journals that seem to be suitable choices. The list should be short enough to allow for considering each journal carefully. Apply these questions to each journal.

1) Is the topic of my proposed paper within its scope?
2) Is the topic represented in it frequently or only rarely?
3) Would it offer the best match of audience with that topic?
4) What formats does it accept?
5) Does it publish an information-for-authors page or issue a similar sheet or booklet that may give better answers to these questions?

MATCH OF TOPIC, JOURNAL, AND AUDIENCE

You may know all the journals appropriate to your topic. But if you are in a young and quickly growing field, you may profit from getting more information on possible choices before you try to answer the questions posed above. Colleagues may be able to suggest new journals not known to you. You may be able to get suggestions from a librarian in your medical sciences library. Some compilations of biomedical journals list them by fields; some also describe their scope and other characteristics.

Journal Citation Reports (2), an annual volume in *Science Citation Index,* lists in its "Section 8" the indexed journals grouped by subject field.

List of Journals Indexed in Index Medicus (3) includes a list of over
2600 journals grouped by subject field.

The Medical and Scientific Authors' Guide (4) lists more than 500
journals by subject; the main section reproduces their information-
for-authors pages.

*A Guide to Writing and Publishing in the Social and Behavioral Sci-
ences* (5) includes a list of 540 journals, many of which are potential outlets for papers in medical sociology, psychiatry, and clinical
psychology.

How can you judge a journal's quality? *Journal Citation Reports*
(2) provides several kinds of data useful for assessing the intellectual
importance of journals and the range of that influence. Journals are
ranked by their "impact factors", which indicate how many times, on
average, a journal's papers are cited. The impact factors for 2 or more
journals in a particular field give a quantitative clue to their relative
intellectual influence. What if, for example, you are preparing to write
a paper about a study on an aspect of diabetes mellitus? If you consult
Journal Citation Reports you will find the "impact factors" for 3 leading journals that report research on diabetes; in 1987 the "impact factors" were *Diabetes*, 3.826; *Diabetes Care*, 2.263; and *Diabetologia*,
3.308. These "impact factors" are close so the 3 journals differ only
slightly in intellectual influence. Your choice among the three will
probably be determined mainly by their apparent preferences for papers on basic research or clinical problems. The ranks of journals by
impact factor is not necessarily the same as the ranks by circulation.
Some journals with high impact factors have relatively small circula-
tions; they are usually journals that publish important papers, each of
which is of interest mainly to a small group of investigators.

Are some journals apparently out of your field worth considering
as possible outlets for your paper? How can you identify them? *Journal Citation Reports* (2) offers a compilation, "Cited Journal Listing",
that gives the number of citations of a journal's papers in a calendar
year. This total is broken down by journals carrying the citations and
the number of citations in each journal. Impact factors are given
before each journal. The example below represents part of the entry
for *American Journal of Hospital Pharmacy* in the 1987 "Cited Journal Listing".

AM J HOSP PHARM		2110
.90	AM J HOSP PHARM	654
.87	DRUG INTEL CLIN PHAR	65
	HOSP PHARM	51

19.31	NEW ENGL J MED	49
3.08	ANTIMICROB AGENTS CH	34
	HOSPITALS	29
4.43	JAMA-J AM MED ASSOC	29
2.51	J PEDIATR	26
	TOP HOSP PHARM MANAG	26
8.48	ANN INTERN MED	20
	DRUG TOP	17

In 1987, papers published by *American Journal of Hospital Pharmacy* in 1986 and 1985 were cited 2110 times in the journals covered by *Journal Citation Reports*. Of these citations, 654 were in its own papers. Most of the other citations were in other journals in pharmacy. But note that 4 of the journals are not in pharmacy but in clinical medicine: *Annals of Internal Medicine, Journal of the American Medical Association, Journal of Pediatrics*, and *The New England Journal of Medicine*. All of these have relatively high impact factors. A clinical pharmacist is certainly familiar with *American Journal of Hospital Pharmacy*, which dominates his field, and with closely related journals but might not be aware that the 4 clinical medicine journals publish enough papers on topics related to clinical pharmacy (presumably papers on drug therapy) to be considered as possible vehicles for papers in clinical pharmacy. Do not be timid about considering journals outside your field. Journals in clinical medicine once rarely published papers by authors not trained in medicine or the basic medical sciences, but some of them are now accepting papers on the basis of importance to their journal's audiences, not the academic degrees of the authors. An important paper by a clinical pharmacist on pharmacokinetics of a new drug in the setting of an abnormal function such as renal failure may be readily accepted by a journal with a majority of contributors drawn from clinical medicine.

Do not feel compelled to choose the most prestigious journal. A normal and leading motive for publishing is to build one's reputation among peers. Getting a paper published in a journal with a high rank raises your reputation. But submitting a paper to the most prestigious journal in your field also raises the risk that the paper will not be accepted and that you will have lost the weeks, and sometimes the months, the journal needed to process the paper, sometimes with peer review, before rejecting it. High-prestige journals also have high rejection rates. Because they receive 1000 to 4000 manuscripts per year and can publish only a small fraction of these papers, their rejection rates run as high as 90%. Should you aim lower in the ranks of relevant journals and swap some prestige for faster publication?

If you have scanned the journals worth considering and find in one of them very few papers related to your topic, does this fact raise or lower the chances that your paper might be accepted by this journal? The journal may have received very few papers from your field in recent years. Perhaps the editor has a prejudice against papers from your field or thinks it is peripheral to the main interests of the journal's audience. The 2 choices for you are to shift your preference to journals with more papers from your field or to ask the editor about the journal's policy (see below, "A Query to the Editor").

Match of Format and Journal

The journals of your choice may be right for the topic, but do they publish papers with the format you have chosen? You are planning to write a detailed, critical review of diagnosis and treatment of gonococcal urethritis. Gonorrhea is a widespread clinical problem; surely a good choice would be a journal with a large audience of practicing physicians. Why not *Journal of the American Medical Association*? This choice would probably be wrong; this journal occasionally carries short summaries of diagnosis and treatment but not long, detailed, heavily referenced reviews. Scan many issues of the journals you are considering. Also check the journals' information-for-authors pages to see if your format is mentioned. Such a page is likely to be listed in the table of contents of a monthly journal; some journals, notably the weeklies, publish such pages only once per volume, usually in the first issues of January and July. Without thus assuring yourself about this question of format, you could spend 6 weeks writing a paper in a format not used by the journal to which you send the paper. You would then have to put in more time in revising it to another format for that journal or in sending it to a second-choice journal that may require revision of it to yet another format.

Even if the journal publishes papers on the topic and in the format you have chosen, the journal may carry other clues that the odds are high against acceptance of your paper. A PhD candidate in clinical psychology wrote a long term paper on the usefulness of psychological tests in assessing emotional problems in women with breast cancer. Her faculty adviser praised the paper and urged her to try to publish it as a review article. The student picked out 6 journals in her field. Two of them publish only original research papers, 2 publish some reviews, but mostly research papers, and all the reviews they had published in the preceding 3 years were by authors preeminent in their field, not academic nobodies. She concluded that her review probably would not be accepted because she was then an academic nobody. This left 2 journals. Of the 2, 1 publishes short, relatively informal reviews of currently important topics. She chose this journal, revised her turgid and academically flavored term paper to a short, informal discussion of her topic, and got the paper accepted immediately.

A Query to the Editor

If you have gone through all of the steps discussed above and still feel unsure of whether you have picked the right journal and the right format, write or call the editor and raise the question. Be sure you frame your query the right way. The question "Will you publish a review of the diagnosis and treatment of gonococcal urethritis?" does not tell the editor whether you are talking about a 2-page concise summary of the topic or a 50-page detailed review. And when you ask, "Will you publish . . .", no editor is going to commit the journal in advance to publishing the paper; ask instead, "Are you willing to consider for publication a 50-page detailed review of the diagnosis and treatment of gonococcal urethritis?". The replies may be various. You may learn that the editor has just accepted such a review or that the journal never publishes such long reviews. Replies like that may disappoint you for the moment, but they can save you time and work later.

MULTIPLE PUBLICATION

You may be tempted to try to publish more than 1 paper from the data collected in 1 study. This impulse is understandable, given the pressure to publish for academic appointments and promotions. Some studies do justify more than 1 paper. A study of an epidemic of a serious infection caused by a newly identified bacterium could legitimately yield a paper on characteristics of the bacterium appropriate for a journal in bacterial taxonomy. A separate paper on newly developed culture methods for the bacterium might go into a journal on laboratory methods in microbiology. A clinical journal would be a suitable outlet for a third paper detailing the clinical manifestations of the infection. Each of these papers would have a clear message and a particular audience. A paper describing all of the findings would be much too long. Keep in mind, however, that papers which represent arbitrary carving up of clearly related aspects of 1 study have been called "salami science". An example is a study of the cardiovascular effects of a new drug. Is it legitimate to divide presentation of the data into 3 papers: 1 on cardiac effects, 1 on effects in the pulmonary circulation, and 1 on the peripheral circulation? The answer is "no" if all of the findings together yield a message that can be presented in a paper of normal length. The answer may be "yes" if the 3 aspects of the study yield different messages and if combined would yield a paper too long for any journal to accept.

A related question is whether to try to publish findings from a study in an informal symposium paper and then to seek subsequently to publish the same material in a formal journal paper. If you tell the editor about the symposium paper, he or she may be willing to publish the second paper. But if the editor does not have this information and the consultant reviewing the manuscript is aware of the symposium paper and points it out to the editor, the chances of rejection go up.

CONCLUSION

If you think you have a paper to write, ask yourself some questions. What is its message? Can I put the message into one sentence? What is likely to be the value of the message? Test its importance with the "so-what" test. If it passes the "so-what" test, try the "who-cares" test and ask "important to whom?"

If you still think you have a paper to write, decide on the right format: a formal research paper, a detailed review, a concise letter-to-the-editor. Inspect closely the recent issues of the journals you have in mind for the paper; consult their information-for-authors pages; query the editors if necessary. Is your topic within their scope? Do they use the format you think will be right?

If you are thinking of writing a paper as only one of several representing the same study or presenting the same data, can you justify this step as necessary for effective presentation? Or are you multiplying publication not for the sake of readers but for selfish motives?

REFERENCES

1. Huth EJ. The ethics of medical publishing: prior publication and full disclosure by authors. Ann Intern Med. 1981;94:401-2.
2. Institute for Scientific Information. Journal citation reports. Philadelphia: Institute for Scientific Information. Published annually as a volume in *Science Citation Index*.
3. National Library of Medicine. List of journals indexed in *Index Medicus*. Bethesda, Maryland: National Library of Medicine. Published annually.
4. Banes J, comp. The medical and scientific authors' guide: an international reference guide for authors to more than 500 medical and scientific journals. New York: Le Jacq Publishing; 1984.
5. Mullins CJ. A guide to writing and publishing in the social and behavioral sciences. New York: John Wiley; 1977. Reprinted in 1983.

2

Searching the Literature

If the paper you are about to write is a research report, you reviewed the relevant literature before you started the research. You probably searched the literature from time to time as the research proceeded, to keep aware of newly reported relevant papers. Reports of similar findings might influence whether you will report your research in a paper and, if so, how. You will, of course, periodically look for new reports until you prepare the final version of your paper and send it off to the journal. This chapter, then, is not likely to be useful to you; you already have a search strategy and have applied it in relevant databases.

Potential authors of other kinds of papers usually have to carry out a major search of the literature before they commit themselves to starting to write.

If you are thinking of reporting an unusual, or possibly unique, case, you must find out whether any similar cases have been described. If some have been, how close is their similarity? Is the report really worth writing?

If you are thinking of writing a review article, you must find out whether any similar reviews have been published recently. If any have been, do they give adequate answers? Are they out-of-date? Are they in foreign languages? If you do see a need for the review, you will have to search carefully for all papers that might provide the basis for your review.

This chapter cannot cover all aspects of literature searching in medicine and its related fields. For detailed guidance see the books described in Appendix 4 under "Guides to Medical Literature, Databases, and Other Sources of Information".

DECISIONS TO BE MADE FOR A SEARCH

Unless you are thoroughly familiar with search methods and tactics, do not start by rushing to the nearest medical sciences library and plunging into the latest volume of *Index Medicus*. Do not rush to sit down in front of your microcomputer to put to work your newly acquired subscription to an online database. You should first take 5 steps to organize your search.

- Decide on the subject of your search: the topics and how they relate to each other, what terms will adequately represent these topics.
- Decide on the extent of your search: how wide and how far back your search should go.
- Decide on whether you will do your own search or will seek help from a professional searcher.
- Decide on the bibliographic databases through which you will search for relevant papers (a professional searcher can offer advice).
- Decide on how you will record the references from your search.

THE SUBJECT OF THE SEARCH
Topics Representing the Subject

What topics you select to represent your subject and how they relate to each other are critically important for an effective search. The problem is akin to selecting a diagnostic test. One set of search tactics can be highly sensitive but low in specificity; it picks up all papers relevant to your subject but also too many irrelevant papers. Another set can be insensitive and miss many relevant papers while being highly specific, picking up only highly relevant papers. Different strategies may each be best for a particular need. Note that professional searchers would refer to *sensitivity* by the term *recall ratio* and to *specificity* by *precision ratio*.

High-sensitivity, low-specificity searches may be best when you do not want to risk missing possibly relevant papers, as in preparing to write a review article or a case report of a possibly unique case. You must be willing to put in the time to weed out many irrelevant papers for the sake of "complete" coverage.

Low-sensitivity, high-specificity searches may be adequate for papers such as scientific editorials, didactic articles, and textbook chapters in which you need to draw only on important papers from reliable journals.

Start by writing down the topics that will make up the subject of your paper. Suppose you want to review the clinical aspects of cytomegalovirus infection of the gastrointestinal tract in persons with the acquired immunodeficiency syndrome. Your first list may look like this.

cytomegalovirus
gastrointestinal tract
acquired immunodeficiency syndrome (AIDS)

Then you should start to think of other possible terms. Are there other related terms? Are there specific techniques that might be relevant?

AIDS-related complex?   duodenoscopy?   treatment?

What about synonyms? *Paget disease of bone* is equivalent to *osteitis deformans*. Is your subject to cover only human aspects? Might some animal research be relevant? Continue this process until you think you have exhausted the possibilities. You can help to ensure that you have developed a complete list by drafting a tentative outline of your paper (see Chapter 9). At this stage you need as full a list as you can compile; you will refine it later.

Adequate Forms of Terms

Medical vocabulary is by no means standardized in the medical literature. Variant forms of terms turn up in journals of different countries and in journals of any one country. If your list of search terms does not include variant forms, you might miss some truly relevant papers. For example, *acquired immunodeficiency syndrome* has been represented by variant forms.

acquired immuno-deficiency syndrome
acquired immune deficiency syndrome
acquired immune-deficiency syndrome

Remember that eponymic terms can appear in nonpossessive, as well as possessive, forms.

the Cushing syndrome   Cushing's syndrome

Some search systems make it easy to deal with variants like this, but some do not and you should be prepared to use all possible variants of terms.

Do not forget that many complex terms are represented by abbreviations. *Acquired immunodeficiency syndrome* is widely represented by AIDS as pointed out above, *human immunodeficiency virus* by HIV. Journals in general do not allow the use of such abbreviations by themselves without the terms they represent, but you cannot be sure that you will not miss papers relevant to these topics if you do not include such abbreviations among your search terms.

Relations of Terms

After you have compiled the terms that seem to adequately represent all possibly useful topics within your subject, assemble these terms and modify them to indicate the relations you want them to have to each other. These relations will determine how a search is specifically formulated for an online bibliographic database or its equivalent on a CD-ROM disk. Even if you are going to search a "paper-format" bibliographic index such as *Index Medicus*, you should take this step of putting together your search terms in a precise formulation. The formulation for your review on gastrointestinal cytomegalovirus infection in AIDS might look like this.

clinical aspects of gastrointestinal cytomegalovirus infection in men and women with the acquired immunodeficiency syndrome, including symptoms and signs, findings on examination, diagnostic methods, treatment, and autopsy findings.

Such a formulation will certainly be asked for by a professional searcher you engage.

Logical (Boolean) and Proximity Operators: The Combining of Search Terms

If you are going to carry out the search yourself in an online or CD-ROM database, you must be sure that you know how to combine your search terms with the possible connecting "operators".

The logical (or "Boolean") operators *and*, *or*, and *not* indicate to the computer how you want your terms treated in relation to each other during the search. (*Boolean* refers to Charles Boole, 1815–1864, the British logician and mathematician.) *And* usually indicates that both of the terms it connects must be found in each reference or document (such as an abstract) searched. *Or* indicates that terms it connects are synonymous for the search; either one must be found. *Not* excludes references and documents (such as abstracts) containing the term it precedes. How carefully you use these operators can determine the efficiency of your search. In a cytomegalovirus-AIDS search, "cytomegalovirus *and* acquired immunodeficiency syndrome" would retrieve references only to papers on both subjects, a good specific yield. On the other hand, "cytomegalovirus *or* acquired immunodeficiency syndrome" would also yield references to papers on either subject by itself, a much greater total number of papers, most of which would not have to do with these subjects together.

The proximity operators *same* and *with* used in some online systems indicate how closely the terms they connect must be linked in a document. In general the closer that 2 terms appear together in a document, for example, an introductory paragraph, the more likely the document will have major content in which both subjects are closely related. The value of proximity operators is mainly in searching full-text databases.

Professional searchers are familiar with these operators. If you are going to do your own online or CD-ROM searches, be sure you consult the manuals for the systems so that you understand their operators thoroughly; if you do not you can make costly errors in searching.

For a thorough explanation of logical operators, read "Logical Operators Used in Searching" in *Databases: A Primer for Retrieving Information by Computer* (1).

THE EXTENT OF THE SEARCH

The medical literature is enormous. No one can, or should have to, search all of it. You have not fully formulated your search until you have defined what kind or kinds of literature you are looking for, what languages you can deal with, and how far back in time you need to go.

Kinds of Literature

Most searches are for journal papers and review articles. Searches for other kinds of sources may need special strategies and specific databases. Books can be sought through card and online catalogs, but searches into what librarians call "ephemeral literature" can be difficult. Ephemeral literature is that usually judged to have a short period of usefulness and only for a small audience and hence to be not worth indexing or cataloging: public-health statistical reports, surveys of regional health problems, annual reports of organizations, and so on. Other kinds of literature difficult or impossible to find through the most frequently used indexes include technical reports and grant summaries. Several of the books described in Appendix 4 under "Guides to Medical Literature, Databases, and Other Sources of Information" discuss many varieties of this "ephemeral" literature.

Language

Are you going to look for papers in languages other than English? A truly thorough search, as for a definitive review article, calls for a review of the non-English as well as the English literature. Bibliographic indexes usually indicate the language in which papers have been published, even when the index uses English translations of titles, but are you going to pay for translations of non-English papers? Many non-English journals do publish English abstracts that give enough of the content of papers for a judgment on whether a translation is worth getting.

Period of Time

How far back are you going to search? If the paper you are planning is a report of research, you reviewed the literature before you wrote the protocol for your research. The search now needed is a check to be sure that in your routine scanning of literature in your field you have not overlooked relevant papers published since that first search. If you are planning a review on a recent development in practice—for example, a drug introduced 3 years ago—the search may not have to run more than 6 years from the present. Searches going back farther than 5 years can sometimes be avoided by finding review articles and published bibliographies that have already sifted through the older literature.

CONSULTATION WITH A PROFESSIONAL SEARCHER

Twenty years ago a search was much simpler to plan. The number of indexes was small, and online computer searches were unheard of. Today we have many indexes. Although technical improvements have greatly simplified the use of online systems, many online searches are still best conducted by persons trained in search strategies. Librarians, who are most likely to be the professional searchers whose help you can get, are not now yesterday's custodians of book and journal collections; they are experts in information sources and systems for literature searches. No matter how well you think you are equipped for a search, you are likely to benefit from consulting a librarian for suggestions on the most efficient way to find the literature you need. He or she will also be able to recommend the right person to carry out the search if you want it done for you. For most authors such a consultation is indispensable for searches into literature other than journals and books.

The searcher will need your help. One experienced searcher (2) suggests that the person requesting a search follow a checklist to be sure that the searcher gets all the help needed. The checklist below includes her recommendations.

- Work directly with the searcher, not through your secretary or laboratory assistant.
- Complete the search request form with information it calls for. Be sure you include billing information.
- Do not give the searcher just a list of keywords. Be prepared to explain all the considerations discussed above.

  How terms relate to each other

  Synonyms, variant forms of terms, abbreviations

  Subject limits on the search: human, animal, or both; age periods; any other kinds of limits

  Extent-of-search limits: kinds of literature; languages, years
- Suggest if you can a recent journal article that is the best example of the kind of paper you wish to find.
- Indicate the degrees of sensitivity ("recall ratio") and specificity ("precision ratio") you need in the search.
- Provide any relevant information not requested on the search-request form.
- Be sure the searcher knows how to reach you by telephone.
- Review the results (printout) of a search before you leave the library; raise questions and discuss any dissatisfactions immediately.

WHAT INDEXES TO SEARCH AND HOW MANY

Most authors in the medical sciences will be able to carry out searches adequate for their needs in one or a combination of the three major resources: The National Library of Medicine's MEDLINE or *Index Medicus*, *Science Citation Index*, and *BIOSIS Previews*. Even these major resources differ in scope, and some subjects may call for searches into other biomedical indexes and the indexes for other disciplines. Many bibliographic databases can, or must, be entered through "gateway" systems, the computer online systems that serve as intermediate connections between searchers and particular databases.

The remaining sections of this chapter describe the major indexing and abstract services, specialized indexes within the medical sciences, and indexes in related fields. The main gateways are briefly described and the extent to which databases overlap is summarized.

The references you collect must be maintained in a form permitting subsequent sorting and retrieval. Many microcomputer programs can provide these functions, and some can assist with searching as well. These are briefly described at the end of this chapter.

THE NATIONAL LIBRARY OF MEDICINE'S BIBLIOGRAPHIC SERVICES

The National Library of Medicine (NLM) offers 2 main groups of bibliographic services.

The MEDLARS online databases (MEDLINE and related data bases)
Print indexes, including *Index Medicus* and other narrower-scope indexes

The MEDLARS Databases

The National Library of Medicine database and computer system is MEDLARS (**MED**ical **L**iterature **A**nalysis and **R**etrieval **S**ystem). The MEDLARS system, searchable online, includes a number of separate databases, most of which can be useful to authors.

MEDLINE (**MED**LARS on**LINE**): References to articles in roughly 3200 journals. Seven files cover articles published from 1966 to the present. References to English-language journals are 75% of the total. Updated monthly; references for each update are searchable separately in SDILINE (**S**elected **D**issemination of **I**nformation on**LINE**), useful for "current awareness" needs. Abstracts are available for many of the post-1975 referenced articles. MEDLINE can be searched via terms in article titles and not only via Medical Subject Headings (MeSH) terms.

MEDLINE is the main database of the Library. It is searchable by novice searchers using *Grateful Med* (see "*Grateful Med*" below) or searching through one of the gateway systems (see "Gateway Systems" below). It includes all references in *Index Medicus* and includes many references also found in *International Nursing Index* and *Index to Dental Literature.*

Files from MEDLINE are becoming available in many libraries on disks of the CD-ROM format ("**c**ompact **d**isk-**r**ead **o**nly **m**emory") for local, offline searching in the library or through local-area computer **n**etwork ("LAN"). These CD-ROM files from MEDLINE reduce the cost of searching and make searches easier for novices.

The full potential of MEDLINE is usually only realized through the services of professional searchers in the Regional Medical Libraries, libraries in health-science centers and independent hospitals, and companies in the health-science industries. Further information can be obtained from the Regional Medical Libraries, listed at the front of each issue of *Index Medicus*; inquiries on MEDLINE and other NLM online databases can also be directed to MEDLARS Management Section, Room 4N421, Building 38A, National Library of Medicine, Bethesda, MD 20894, USA ([301] 496-6193 or [800] 638-8480).

Other NLM databases serve more specialized needs.

BIOETHICSLINE: References in medical and nonmedical (including popular) literature) on topics in ethics (law, religion, philosophy).

CANCERLIT (**CANCER LIT**iterature): References on cancer in journals, monographs, meeting papers, reports, and dissertations. All records from non-MEDLINE sources include abstracts.

CHEMLINE (**CHEM**ical Dictionary on**LINE**): A file of names and data for chemical substances; can be searched by many data elements, including chemical, generic, and trivial names; fragments of chemical names; ring structure information; and Chemical Abstracts Service registry number.

CLINPROT (**CLIN**ical Cancer **PROT**ocols): summaries of current clinical investigations of new anticancer agents and treatment methods.

DIRLINE (**D**irectory of **I**nformation **R**esources on**LINE**): A directory of centers with specialized information, including organizations supplying medical information to the public.

HEALTH (**HEALTH** Planning and Administration): References to journals and other sources indexed for MEDLINE and *Hospital Literature Index*; includes financial, management, man-power, policy, service topics.

HISTLINE (**HIST**ory of Medicine on**LINE**): References to articles, monographs, symposia, and other publications on the history of medicine; the basis for the annual *Bibliography of the History of Medicine*.

POPLINE (**POP**ulation Information on**LINE**): References to journal articles, monographs, and technical reports on reproductive biology, contraceptive technology, family planning, demography, and other related fields.

PDQ (**P**hysician **D**ata **Q**uery): Summaries of tumor types, with prognosis, staging, histologic classification, and treatments; information on oncologic physicians and institutions; information on active treatment protocols.

TOXLINE (**TOX**icology Information on**LINE**): References on adverse drug reactions, human and animal toxicity studies, environmental chemicals, pollutants, and other pharmacy and toxicology subjects. Other toxicologic databases include CCRIS (Chemical **Car**cinogenesis **R**esearch **I**nformation **S**ystem), HSDB (**H**azardous

Substances Data Bank), RTECS (Registry of Toxic Effects of Chemical Substances), and TOXNET (TOXicology Data NETwork).

Five other databases meet special needs of libraries but may also help the researcher: AVLINE (AudioVisuals on**LINE**) is a catalog of audiovisual teaching materials. CATLINE (**CAT**alog on**LINE**) includes references to books and serials in the National Library of Medicine's collection; this data base is particularly useful for locating monographic materials, some government documents and statistical sources, historical items, and other literature hard to find through other routes. MESH VOCABULARY FILE is the online equivalent of *Medical Subject Headings*, the compilation of the NLM's controlled vocabulary used to index its databases and construct *Index Medicus*; it carries additional useful information. NAF (**N**ame **A**uthority **F**ile carries authority data on names, series, and uniform titles used in bibliographic records. SERLINE (**SER**ials on**LINE**) gives bibliographic information on journals and other serials cataloged or on order for the National Library of Medicine's collection.

Grateful Med

The easiest direct access to MEDLINE for novice searchers is with *Grateful Med*, the easily-run software program that can be used with most IBM PC-type computers; the Macintosh version was released in late 1989. *Grateful Med* can also be used to access CATLINE for book references. Its advantages over *Index Medicus* are many: speed of retrieval, access to 550 more journals, availability of abstracts for many references, searching by non-MeSH terms in titles and abstracts, linkage of terms to raise the specificity of references retrieved. Experienced searchers can use *Grateful Med* to access NLM databases with the standard MEDLINE procedures.

Purchase of *Grateful Med* brings a detailed manual as well as the software diskette itself. Additional insight into efficient use of the program can be found in some of the manuals on MEDLINE searching described in Appendix 4 under "Guides to Medical Literature, Databases, and Other Sources of Information'.

Further information on *Grateful Med* can be obtained from MEDLARS Management Service, Room 4N421, Building 38A, National Library of Medicine, 8600 Rockville Pike, Bethesda, MD 20894, USA ([301] 496-6193 and [800] 638-8480).

Index Medicus

The general NLM index for authors who cannot use *Grateful Med* or buy the services of a professional searcher is *Index Medicus*, a

---

ACQUIRED IMMUNODEFICIENCY SYNDROME
C2.782.815.483.23+   C2.800.801.100+
C20.673.483.23+

83

see related
    AIDS SERODIAGNOSIS
    HIV ANTIBODIES
    HIV ANTIGENS
    HIV SEROPOSITIVITY
X   AIDS
X   HIV INFECTION
X   HTLV-III INFECTION
X   HTLV-III-LAV INFECTION
X   HUMAN T-LYMPHOTROPIC VIRUS TYPE III INFECTION
X   IMMUNODEFICIENCY SYNDROME, ACQUIRED
X   IMMUNOLOGIC DEFICIENCY SYNDROME, ACQUIRED
XR HIV-1
XR T4 LYMPHOCYTES

ACQUISITION, HEALTH FACILITY see HEALTH FACILITY MERGER

Figure 2.1. Sample entries in the *Medical Subject Headings* (MeSH) compilations issued annually as a guide to terms for searching the subject index of *Index Medicus*. Under ACQUIRED IMMUNODEFICIENCY SYNDROME are the numbers indicating where this term is found in the tree structure of MeSH. "83" indicates that the term was introduced into MeSH in 1983 and hence will not be found in subject indexes in the preceding years and that other equivalent terms must be used in searching before 1983. The *see related* direction indicates other related terms that may be useful in a search for references relevant to the entry term. The terms preceded by *X* are synonyms of the entry term from which the searcher is referred to this term. The terms preceded by *XR* are related terms cross-referring to this entry term. The bottom line indicates that searchers considering using ACQUISITION, HEALTH FACILITY should search with HEALTH FACILITY MERGER. (This MeSH entry has been simulated from its original.)

printed subject and author index to almost 2800 journals and other periodicals. It began publication in its present form in 1960 and thus covers a big fraction of the medical science literature that most authors are likely to wish to search. *Index Medicus* is issued monthly; the monthly issues are cumulated for each calendar year in *Cumulated Index Medicus*. Each issue includes 2 main sections, the subject index and the author index. Other sections should also be known by authors, notably the introductory pages on how to use *Index Medicus* and the index to review articles.

Subject Index Terms. Entries in the subject index are arranged under the standard terms known collectively as MeSH (**Medical Subject Headings**). Searches for papers by subject must, therefore, be carried out using the MeSH terms. To start your search, take the topic terms you have assembled (as discussed above) and go to the MeSH compilation that should be on the library shelf with the *Index Medicus* volumes. *Medical Subject Headings* is published annually as part 2 of the January issue of *Index Medicus* and as a separate publication. You should be able to find most of the terms you have jotted down, either in the form you used or in inverted form. If the term appears in large type with a classification number beneath it, this is the term as it is used in the subject index (see Figure 2.1). If the term appears in small type followed by "see" and a synonym, the synonym is the term that is used in the subject index. Under each MeSH term appear synonymous and related terms preceded by X; these are the terms from which cross-reference has been made to the MeSH term. If, for example, you plan to use *AIDS* for your search, you will find from the MeSH compilation that *AIDS* refers you to *acquired immunodeficiency syndrome* as the MeSH term under which to search.

Tree Structure for MeSH. All MeSH terms are arranged in subject groups and hierarchical levels within groups known as "tree structures", included as part of each annual *Medical Subject Headings*. After you have found the MeSH terms that correspond to the topics for your search (identical terms, inverted versions of the terms, or synonyms reached through "see" or "see under" cross-references), inspect the terms in the tree structure around each term you have selected to find other closely related terms which you might also wish to use in searching. Figure 2.2 illustrates terms closely related in the tree structure to *acquired immunodeficiency syndrome*. Sometimes these closely related terms may yield search results more specific for your needs.

Keep in mind that the indexers always use the most specific term available in MeSH. For example, a paper on cardiogenic shock will be indexed under *shock, cardiogenic*, not under *myocardial infarction*.

Additional Information on MeSH Terms. Each annual MeSH compilation includes, in addition to the terms and the tree structures, valuable explanatory introductions that list headings (terms) introduced in that year (Figure 2.3) and terms deleted, with indications of the equivalents (if any) used for the new terms in preceding years. You need to know these changes in indexing and should not assume that current MeSH terms were used for the concepts of your search since the concept first appeared in indexed articles. Other pages explain use of MeSH terms for searches in the *National Library*

IMMUNOLOGIC DISEASE	C20	
...		
IMMUNOLOGIC DEFICIENCY SYNDROMES	C20.673	
AGAMMAGLOBULINEMIA	C20.673.88	
ATAXIA TELANGIECTASIA	C20.673.290	
DIGEORGE SYNDROME	C20.673.340	
DYSGAMMAGLOBULINEMIA	C20.673.430	
HTLV INFECTIONS	C20.673.483	
ACQUIRED IMMUNODEFICIENCY SYNDROME	C20.673.483.23	
AIDS-RELATED COMPLEX	C20.673.483.23.80	
HIV SEROPOSITIVITY	C20.673.483.23.452	
HTLV-I INFECTIONS	C20.673.483.470	C2.782.815
LEUKEMIA-LYMPHOMA, T-CELL, ACUTE, HTLV-I-ASSOCIATED	C20.673.483.470.300	
HTLV-II INFECTIONS	C20.673.483.480	
LEUKEMIA, T-CELL, HTLV-II-ASSOCIATED	C20.673.483.480.350	
LYMPHOPENIA	C20.673.627	
...		

Figure 2.2. A simulated abridged part of the *Medical Subject Headings Tree Structure* showing ACQUIRED IMMUNODEFICIENCY SYNDROME with the closely related terms. They are in Section C20, DISEASES-IMMUNOLOGIC, of the tree. The "C numbers" to their right are the numerical designations of their positions in the tree; the additional "C number" to the right of C20.673.483.470 indicates that HTLV-I INFECTIONS is also found in another part of the tree; note that similar additional "C numbers" have been omitted from this figure to simplify this presentation, which has been adapted from the original tree.

New Heading	*Previously-Indexed-Under Heading*
AIDS SERODIAGNOSIS	ACQUIRED IMMUNODEFICIENCY SYNDROME (84-88)
	ANTIBODIES, VIRAL (83-88)
	HIV/immunology (88)
	HTLV-III/immunology (87)
	HUMAN T-CELL LEUKEMIA VIRUS/immunology (84-87)

Figure 2.3. The *Medical Subject Headings* annual compilation includes a section that lists added *MeSH* terms that are new or replace previously-used headings. This simulated part of this section indicates that AIDS SERODIAGNOSIS was added in 1989 (the year of this compilation) and that references relevant to this topic were previously indexed under the headings shown in the right-hand column. The dates within the parenthesis marks indicate the years in which these terms were used to index the concept represented by the new term.

GOLD

A new lectin-gold complex for ultrastructural localization of galacturonic acids. Benhamou N, et al.
J Histochem Cytochem 1988 Nov;36(11):1403-11
Colloidal gold immunostaining on deplasticized ultra-thin sections. Mar H, et al. **J Histochem Cytochem** 1988 Nov; 36(11):1387-95

ADVERSE EFFECTS

Some extra-articular manifestations of arthritis and complications of therapy. A pictorial essay. Kattan KR, et al. **Radiol Clin North Am** 1988 Nov;26(6):1277-93 (65 ref.)
[Subacute cutaneous lupus erythematosus caused by chrysotherapy in rheumatoid arthritis (letter)] Balsa A, et al.
Rev Clin Esp 1988 May;182(9):505-6   **(Spa)**

Figure 2.4. Simulated typical entries in the subject index of *Index Medicus*. ADVERSE EFFECTS is a subheading for GOLD. The first entry under this subheading is for a review article and "(65 ref.)" indicates the number of its references; the next entry is to a letter in a Spanish journal, as indicated by "(Spa)", and the title is within square brackets to indicate that it is a translation. Searchers of *Index Medicus* should be familiar with these and other conventions if they are to use it efficiently and effectively.

of Medicine Current Catalog (lists books and serials cataloged by the Library) and the *National Library of Medicine Audiovisual Catalog*.

Using the Index Medicus Subject Index. You will probably start your search with the most recent monthly issues of *Index Medicus*. Some knowledge of how entries for journal articles are presented under each MeSH term can be useful (Figure 2.4).

Articles that are of broad interest in relation to the MeSH term or that cannot be subclassified are listed first under the term, followed by article entries classified under subheadings such as COMPLICATIONS, PATHOLOGY, THERAPY. Under each heading and subheading, articles in English-language journals are listed before those in foreign-language journals, and within these 2 groupings entries are listed alphabetically by journal title. The foreign-language grouping is sorted by language.

Articles in foreign-language journals are indicated by square brackets around their titles (presented in English translation), and parenthetical statements indicate the language in which the article is published and whether the article includes an English abstract.

Journal titles are given in the *Index Medicus* abbreviated form; the full titles are given in the introductory pages of each *Cumulated Index Medicus*. A separately issued list, *List of Journals Indexed in Index Medicus* (3), also includes titles of the journals covered by *Index Medicus* arranged by subject and country in which published.

After you have worked your way through the monthly issues of *Index Medicus* for the current year, you will switch to the annual *Cumulated Index Medicus* for the previous year; its subject index is organized as in the monthly index.

Understanding how articles are indexed for *Index Medicus* is a great help to the searcher. The preceding paragraphs have pointed out principles to be kept in mind. The hints below summarize these and additional useful points; these are drawn from a short guide prepared by the National Library of Medicine (4).

1. Look for a subject using only the MeSH terms specified in the MeSH list published with each January issue of *Index Medicus*.
2. Consider also using MeSH terms related to those you have already selected by examining the categorized list of terms (tree structures) also published with each January issue of *Index Medicus*.
3. Look in an alternate location for a subject expressed as a compound concept if you do not find it initially. Some terms are direct; some are arbitrarily inverted. An article on cutaneous tuberculosis is not found under *CUTANEOUS TUBERCULOSIS*, but under *TUBERCULOSIS, CUTANEOUS*. Vinyl ether is under *VINYL ETHER*, not under *ETHER, VINYL*.
4. Subjects are divided into more specific breakdowns by subheadings. Look for specific aspects of subjects under the subject as divided by its subheadings. Do not look under a heading that is an exact duplicate of a subheading. An article on the radiography of the pancreas is found under *PANCREAS -radiography*, not under *RADIOGRAPHY*. An article on the metabolism of glucose is found under *GLUCOSE -metabolism*, not under *METABOLISM*. An article on amino acids in the blood is found under *AMINO ACIDS -blood*, not under *BLOOD*. An article on urinalysis in gout is found under *GOUT -urine*, not under *URINE*.
5. Look for the most specific term. An article on leishmaniasis is found under *LEISHMANIASIS*, not under *TROPICAL MEDICINE*. An article on neomycin is found under *NEOMYCIN*, not under *ANTIBIOTICS*.
6. Look for organs, diseases, and physiologic processes in persons of various ages under the organ, the disease, or the physiologic pro-

cess, not under the age group. An article on gout in infants is found under *GOUT*, not under *INFANT*. An article on hand injuries in the aged is found under *HAND INJURIES*, not under *AGED*.

7. Look for research with laboratory animals under the subject of the research, not under the term for the animal. An article on arthritis induced in rats is found under *ARTHRITIS*, not under *RATS*.

8. Look for specific research methods under the specific disease, substance, and so on, not under a term for the method. An article on the chromatography of amino acids is found under *AMINO ACIDS -analysis*, not under *CHROMATOGRAPHY*. An article on the electrophoresis of gamma globulin in syphilis is found under *GAMMA GLOBULINS -analysis* or *SYPHILIS -immunology*, not under *ELECTROPHORESIS* or *BLOOD PROTEIN ELECTRO-PHORESIS*.

9. Look for diseases of various organs under the organ-disease term. If an organ-disease term is not in MeSH, look under the term for the organ. An article on diseases of the cecum is found under *CECAL DISEASES*, not under *CECUM*. An article on diseases of the appendix is sought under *APPENDIX DISEASES*, but because this term is not in MeSH, it is found at *APPENDIX* (specific) and not under *CECAL DISEASES* (general).

10. Look for diseases caused by various organisms under the organism-infection term. If an organism-infection term is not in MeSH, locate the organism in the tree structure for MeSH, observe the next level of the hierarchy above it, and then look in *Index Medicus* under the corresponding organism-infection heading. Sometimes an organism-infection term is disguised as a classic disease term. An article on infection with *Escherichia coli* is found under *ESCHERICHIA COLI INFECTIONS*, not under *ES-CHERICHIA COLI*. Articles on infection with bacteria not represented directly in MeSH by a genus or species name may be found under a higher taxonomic name, such as a family name. An article on infection with *Clostridium botulinum* is not found under *CLOSTRIDIUM INFECTIONS*, but under *BOTULISM*.

11. Look under -ology or -iatrics terms only for articles on the field or specialty of the -ologist or -iatrist. Articles on diseases, organs, or patients will not be found here. An article on dermatologic therapy found under *SKIN DISEASES -therapy*, not under *DERMA-TOLOGY*,which covers only articles on dermatology, the field of dermatology, or the dermatologist.

12. Look for general pathologic processes of various organs under the organ with the subheading -*pathology*, not under the general patho-

logic process (*NECROSIS, GANGRENE, INFLAMMATION, HYPER-TROPHY, ATROPHY*). An article on necrosis of the pancreas is found under *PANCREAS-pathology*, not under *NECROSIS*.

Abridged Index Medicus.   If you do not need to carry out an exhaustive search and will be satisfied with references to the major English-language clinical journals covering human medicine, *Abridged Index Medicus* (AIM) will be a timesaving substitute for *Index Medicus*. AIM indexes about 125 journals published in the United States, Canada, and a few other primarily English-language countries. The AIM subject index also uses the MeSH terms and arrangement of entries of *Index Medicus*. AIM is more likely than *Index Medicus* to be available in community-hospital libraries.

Bibliography of Medical Reviews.   *Index Medicus* entries for review articles are also gathered in a separate section at the beginning of each issue and in the first volume of *Cumulated Index Medicus*. References in review articles often provide a timesaving route to articles already selected by other authors for their importance.

Information on National Library of Medicine Services

Authors uncertain as to the location of the nearest Regional Medical Library and without convenient access to its listing in the front of *Index Medicus* can get help from Office of Inquiries and Publications Management, National Library of Medicine, 8600 Rockville Pike, Bethesda, MD 20209, USA; ([301] 496-6308).

Additional guidance to National Library of Medicine publications and services can be found in the references under "Guides to Medical Literature, Databases, and Other Sources of Information" in Appendix 4.

USING *SCIENCE CITATION INDEX*

Another major and valuable bibliographic resource for authors in the medical sciences is Science *Citation Index*, published by the Institute for Scientific Information. *Science Citation Index* differs markedly from *Index Medicus* in its approach to subject searches. It can be searched as *Index Medicus* is searched, that is, backward year by year by subject for papers published immediately before each yearly compilation. It differs from *Index Medicus* in that you can start with an important paper published in the past and find more recently published papers that cite it. Thus you can readily trace and consider the evolution of concepts and findings from their origin and early development.

```
SOX  HC
   73  NEW ENGL J MED   288   818
       SEE SSCI FOR 1 ADDITIONAL CITATION
       GLENN JK          MED CARE      N     25   570   87
       MARGOLIS CZ       J PEDIAT      E    110   417   87
   79  ANN INTERN MED    91   459
       SEE SSCI FOR 1 ADDITONAL CITATION
       BOTTOM WD         J FAM PRACT         24   639   87
```

Figure 2.5. A simulated entry in *Citation Index* of *Science Citation Index* for papers by HC Sox published in *The New England Jounal of Medicine* in 1973 and in *Annals of Internal Medicine* in 1979 and cited in 1987 issues of *Medical Care, Journal of Pediatrics,* and *Journal of Family Practice.* The subjects of the citing articles are presumably related to the subjects of the 2 Sox papers.

Science Citation Index has four parts: the *Citation Index,* the *Source Index,* the *Permuterm Subject Index,* and the *Corporate Index.* The *Citation Index* lists articles and other documents referred to (cited) in the bibliographies of just-published articles, with sublisting of the current citing articles. Thus it links current subjects of articles to their conceptual predecessors. The *Source Index* lists the just-published articles analyzed for citations indexed in the *Citation Index* and gives full bibliographic identification for these articles. The *Permuterm Subject Index* uses pairs of terms from the titles of articles indexed in the *Source Index* to index the articles by subject. The *Corporate Index* lists publications by institutions of origin.

Science Citation Index can be searched by subject through 2 primary routes. If you are aware of an author whose past work is important for the subject of your search, you can start the search by looking for that author's name in the *Citation Index.* If you find the name, it will be followed by brief identifications of the author's articles cited in recently published articles and the names of the citing authors (Figure 2.5). These recently published articles that cite the earlier articles relate in subject to the earlier articles and can be identified with more detail in the *Source Index.*

The second primary route by subject to articles recently published is through the *Permuterm Subject Index.* You will probably find in it almost any of the terms jotted down in your list of subjects for your search. Beneath the terms given as primary terms are co-terms that appeared with the primary terms in the titles of index articles. Beside the co-terms are listed the authors of indexed articles. These author names can then be found in the *Source Index* with their articles fully identified.

Any term that occurred to you when you jotted down topics for your search is likely to be found in the *Permuterm Subject Index* because the index is built up from words in the titles of articles indexed, not from a standard vocabulary. You should be sure, however, to search with all the synonyms you can think of; articles on the same subject may use different synonyms or near-synonyms. Failure to search under all terms (and their variants) likely to be used in the modern medical vocabulary can cause you to miss relevant articles.

Aids to Use of *Science Citation Index*

The pages on the inside of the covers of *Science Citation Index* illustrate tactics for searching by subject and by author and explain the structure and content of entries on the indexes. These explanatory pages are especially helpful if you think you know how to use *Science Citation Index* but forget some details of its structure.

Other Services Related to *Science Citation Index*

The Institute for Scientific Information offers other computer-based services useful to authors.

Automatic Subject Citation Alert (ASCA) and *ASCA Topics* are search services that provide weekly reports on new articles in your field of interest that have just been processed by the Institute for Scientific Information. *ASCA Topics* provides these new references selected for their relevance to the topics you select from a specified list; the topics include subjects such as "antifungal agents", "blood coagulation and hemorrhagic disorders", "cancer epidemiology", "hepatitis", "hypertension", "prostaglandins", and "renal function". ASCA provides compilations of new references selected more narrowly for your specified interests. Both of these services canbe especially useful to authors who have completed major literature searches in *Index Medicus* or *Science Citation Index* before starting research and want to keep up-to-date on relevant papers as they proceed with their research.

SciSearch, the online computer-based service that is the counterpart of *Science Citation Index*, covers more than 4500 journals in the natural and physical sciences; more than 50% of indexed articles are related to biomedicine. This online index offers access to research-front specialties via a unique indexing method that groups papers into active areas of research identified through their citation and co-citation patterns.

The Compact Disc Edition of *Science Citation Index* makes it available in a CD-ROM format for local searching. This format enables both experienced and novice searchers to take advantage of unique accession methods.

Current Contents Search, the online version of the 5 *Current Contents* editions (including *CC/Clinical Medicine*) provides online access to tables of contents of more than 4500 biomedical and other scientific journals. This database consists of a 3-month rolling file that is updated weekly.

Information on *Science Citation Index* and Related Services

Further information on its services can be obtained from Institute for Scientific Information, 3501 Market Street, University City Science Center, Philadelphia, PA 19104, USA; ([215] 386-0100; cable, SCINFO; Telex, 845305).

EXCERPTA MEDICA SERVICES

The Excerpta Medica system will be searched by most authors for article references in one or more of its many separate abstract journals and literature indexes. The abstract journals are issued in over 40 sections, most covering a clinical or basic-science field of the medical sciences—for example, *Arthritis and Rheumatism, Cancer, Endocrinology, Psychiatry, Surgery*. Other sections cover areas more peripheral to clinical and basic medical science—for example, *Health Economics and Hospital Management*. Each volume of a section includes abstracts arranged by relatively general subject groupings indicated by a table of contents and an alphabetical subject index. The subject-index entries are opened by a boldface entry term, followed by other entry terms that, with the first entry term, give an indication of the scope of the indexed article; the reference number for the abstract of the indexed article completes the entry. Each of the abstracts referred to by the index is headed by the abstracted article's title, its authors, the institutional origin, the journal title, year of publication, volume and issue number, and inclusive page numbers.

Excerpta Medica also has a database, EMBASE, available for online searching.

Excerpta Medica services are notably good for searches for drug and toxicologic information. Its provision of abstracts is much wider than that of MEDLINE, but this aspect of its services is responsible for its greater delay in indexing.

Excerpta Medica publishes a number of aids that provide guidance in how to use both its print and online products. A list of these aids and their prices can be obtained from Excerpta Medica, User Aids Department, 52 Vanderbilt Avenue, New York, NY 10017, USA ([212] 916-1161; Telex 420643).

SPECIALIZED INDEXES AND ABSTRACT SERVICES

The services described above are all useful in the many fields of the medical sciences, but additional specialized services are available.

Bioengineering

Many aspects of bioengineering are covered by MEDLINE, *Index Medicus*, and the services of BIOSIS and Chemical Abstracts (see descriptions below). Specialists in bioengineering may find most of their needs satisfied by *The Engineering Index*, *Bioengineering Abstracts*, and the related online system COMPENDEX. *Bioengineering Abstracts* is a monthly abstract and index journal that covers a wide range of topics, including cybernetics, genetic engineering, nuclear medicine, and waste disposal. COMPENDEX is the online equivalent of *The Engineering Index* and is available through a number of gateway systems including BRS, DATA-STAR, DIALOG, and DIALOG's KNOWLEDGE INDEX. *The Engineering Index* is cumulated annually as a casebound publication. Aids in the use of these services are available, including the *COMPENDEX Search Manual*. For detailed information, write or telephone Engineering Information, Inc, 345 East 47th Street, New York, NY 10017, USA ([800] 221-1044 or [212] 705-7616).

Dental Medicine

The main index to dental journals and relevant non-dental journals is *Index to Dental Literature*, produced from the National Library of Medicine MEDLARS system and published quarterly by the American Dental Association, 211 E. Chicago Ave., Chicago, IL 60611, USA ([312] 440-2500), with citations also available through MEDLINE. Issues are cumulated annually. The format is like that of *Index Medicus* and includes subject and author sections. The preface explains construction and use of the index. *Dental Abstracts*, also published by the American Dental Association, provides abstracts in each monthly issue to about 750 journal articles. The name and subject indexes appear in the December issue.

The American Dental Association publishes a useful short guide to reference works, *Basic Dental Reference Works*; it is described under "Guides to Medical Literature, Databases, and Other Sources of Information" in Appendix 4.

History of Medicine

A print by-product of the MEDLARS indexing of the literature of the history of medicine represented in HISTLINE is *Bibliography of the History of Medicine*, published by the National Library of Medicine annually and cumulated every 5 years.

Hospital Administration and Services

Hospital Literature Index covers journal literature on the administration and economics of hospitals and other health care institutions. It is issued quarterly, with a format like that of *Index Medicus* and subject headings based on the MeSH system. The Index is produced in cooperation with the National Library of Medicine but is published by the American Hospital Association, 840 North Lake Shore Drive, Chicago, IL 60611, USA ([312] 280-6000).

Nursing

International Nursing Index, published by the American Journal of Nursing Company, 555 W 57th Street, New York, NY 10019, USA, is produced in cooperation with the National Library of Medicine. It covers not only the journals indexed for *Index Medicus* and the Health Planning and Administration database (HEALTH), but also more than 270 nursing journals and additional sources and types of documents. The format is like that of *Index Medicus*; MeSH terms are used for the subject index. Searches can be carried out through MEDLINE. The Index also includes ISI's *Nursing Citation Index*, which indexes citations in a selected number of nursing journals and has a structure like that of *Science Citation Index* described above. *Cumulative Index to Nursing and Allied Health Literature* (CINAHL) covers over 300 journals (including many not covered by *International Nursing Index*) and many popular-type magazines. Thus, CINAHL and *International Nursing Index* overlap in coverage, but both should be used for the widest search. The CINAHL is published by Cumulative Index to Nursing and Allied Health Literature, Post Office Box 871, Glendale, CA 91209-0871, USA ([818] 409-8005). CINAHL is available for online searching through 3 gateway systems, BRS, DIALOG, and DATA-STAR; a search guide is available from the publisher, *Nursing and Allied Health (CINAHL) Subject Heading List with Online Search Guide to BRS and DIALOG*. This publisher also produces *Nurse-*

Search, an index carried on diskettes readable with 100%-compatible IBM PC-type computers.

Pharmacy

Both *Index Medicus* and *Science Citation Index* cover literature relevant to clinical pharmacy. Only generic and drug-class names can be used to search *Index Medicus* because its MeSH vocabulary does not include trade names; MEDLINE can be searched for trade names used in article titles and abstracts. The Excerpta Medica abstract journals include the sections *Pharmacology and Toxicology* and *Drug Dependence*; other sections such as *Internal Medicine*, include abstracts on drug therapy and drug effects in the various clinical fields. Excerpta Medica gathers citations of drug-related articles in *Drug Literature Index*, which can be searched with various entry terms not found in the other major indexes, including deep subject indexing (MALIMET), classification codes, and trade names as well as generic names. Coverage of many topics relevant to pharmacy but not covered thoroughly in the indexes described above can be found in *International Pharmaceutical Abstracts* (IPA), issued semimonthly by the American Society of Hospital Pharmacists (ASHP), 4630 Montgomery Avenue, Bethesda, MD 20814, USA ([301] 657-3000). Such topics include drug analysis, pharmaceutical manufacturing and chemistry, the practice of pharmacy, and the economics of the pharmaceutical industry. IPA covers over 600 journals, including many, such as state pharmacy journals, not covered in MEDLINE. IPA is available for online searching through several gateway systems, including BRS, DIALOG, Utopia (in Japan), and NLM's TOXLINE (which carries only 2 of the 3 tracks of data in IPA).

The ASHP publishes 2 guides helpful in searching both the paper and online versions of IPA, *IPA Users Guide* and *Thesaurus of Subject Terms and Cross References to International Pharmaceutical Abstracts*.

Veterinary Medicine and Science

Much of the journal literature pertinent to the biological aspects of veterinary medicine is covered by the MEDLARS system, including *Index Medicus*. But this coverage is biased toward journals oriented mainly to human medicine and does not extend into much of the journal literature on veterinary practice.

Full coverage of veterinary science and practice can be obtained only by searching online databases in addition to those of the National Library of Medicine. The 2 main additional relevant databases in the

United States are AGRICOLA (**AGRIC**ultural **O**n-**L**ine **A**ccess), a database produced by the National Agricultural Library, US Department of Agriculture, and *BIOSIS Previews* (see description below). AGRICOLA covers 6500 journals and other serials, monographs, conference papers, reports and US government publications. Information on AGRICOLA can be obtained from the National Agricultural Library, Education and Information, Beltsville, MD 20705, USA.

The widest veterinary coverage in a single database is probably that of CAB ABSTRACTS, produced in Great Britain by the Commonwealth Agricultural Bureaux (Farnham Royal, Slough, United Kingdom), the online counterpart of the 24 abstracting journals published by the Bureaux. The coverage extends to 8500 journals and to books, conference proceedings, technical reports, theses, government reports, and patents. Americans searching CAB ABSTRACTS must remember that many of its terms may have British spellings and that failure to use these alternative spellings in searches could lead to missing many relevant references; the same point applies to British preferences for some chemical and drug names. CAB ABSTRACTS is available in the United States through the gateway system DIALOG. The Bureaux also publish the important paper-version indexes, *Index Veterinarius,* a monthly and annually cumulated index with author and subject entries, and *The Veterinary Bulletin,* a monthly journal with abstracts and reviews. *Index Veterinarius* gives abstract numbers for those indexed articles represented by abstracts in *The Veterinary Bulletin.* The titles of journals covered by *Index Veterinarius* are listed in the front of occasional issues of the Bulletin.

INDEXING AND ABSTRACTING SERVICES IN RELATED SCIENCES

Biology

BioSciences Information Services (BIOSIS) abstracts and indexes literature relevant to biology and closely related sciences (including medical sciences). *Biological Abstracts,* issued semimonthly and cumulated semiannually, provides abstracts to journal research papers, book reviews, editorials, and other types of documents. *Biological Abstracts/RRM,* also published semimonthly and cumulated semiannually, provides summaries of research reports, reviews, and meetings. These 2 publications can be searched through 5 indexes.

- Author index, for searches by name of author or corporate body
- Concept index, for searches by broad concepts such as vision

- Subject index, for searches by more specific subjects such as chemicals, diseases, drugs, organisms (identified by common name)
- Generic index, for searches on an organism identified by genus-species name
- Biosystematic index, for searches by biological classifications (phyla down through families)

Other derivative services are available, including abstract collections by narrower subject-fields (such as addiction, anticancer agents, human and animal aging, pesticides) and special computer services. The online computer services are available through a number of gateway services, including BRS and DIALOG.

BIOSIS provides free courses on how to use its computer services, including a full-day Med/BIOSIS course of particular value for the medical sciences. BIOSIS provides free-of-charge several unusually detailed and helpful booklets about its publications and services and how to use them. Search manuals for the online services are available for purchase. Detailed information is available from BIOSIS User Communications, 2100 Arch Street, Philadelphia, PA 19103-1399, USA ([215] 569-4800; cable, BIOSIS; Telex, 831739).

Chemistry

Very wide coverage of all fields of chemistry, including those in the medical sciences such as biochemistry and pharmaceutical chemistry, is provided by *Chemical Abstracts* and its thorough and numerous indexes. Subject searches can be carried out through the weekly and semiannual (volume) indexes. The weekly subject index is built of keywords from article titles, abstracts, and texts. Search of the volume indexes by subject should begin with a check into the *CA Index Guide* and its supplements (issued annually) to find out whether the subject terms you have selected are in the subject indexes or whether you must use synonyms. The General Subject Index for each volume is built of main entry terms beneath which are arranged multiterm entries for the abstracts that serve in effect as miniabstracts.

The online equivalent of *Chemical Abstracts* is CAS ONLINE, available through STN International Search Service (accessible through Apple and IBM PC-type microcomputers).

Various user guides for *Chemical Abstracts* and CAS ONLINE are available, some free, some for purchase. Information on *Chemical Abstracts* and related services can be obtained from Chemical Abstracts Service, Post Office Box 3012, Columbus, OH 43210, USA ([614] 421-6940; TWX, 8104821608; cable, CHEMABS).

Psychology and Related Disciplines

Many subjects relevant to the medical sciences are covered in *Psychological Abstracts* (PA), its related publications, and its indexes: psychometrics; consciousness states, including sleep, hypnosis, and meditation; physiological states and interventions; communication; development and growth; medically relevant social processes including drug and alcohol abuse, abortion, and birth control; and physical and psychological disorders, including disease states. Most searches of PA will begin in the volume indexes for the years up to the current year. For the current year, the monthly issues must be consulted individually through the brief monthly subject index. The subject terms are drawn from the *Thesaurus of Psychological Index Terms,* a psychology counterpart to the *Index Medicus* thesaurus, *Medical Subject Headings.* Terms you have selected for your subject search should be checked against the terms in the *Thesaurus,* which offers additional guidance, with synonymous terms and terms for related but broader or narrower concepts. The *Cumulative Subject and Author Indexes to Psychological Abstracts* cover successive 3-year periods through 1983 and are more efficient for longer searches than the volume indexes. PA for 1974 to the present is available in the CD-ROM format to libraries and academic departments through subscription.

The online counterpart to *Psychological Abstracts* is PsycINFO, which is available through gateway services, including BRS, DIALOG, and DATA-STAR. The more current database is PsycALERT, available through BRS and DIALOG.

User aids include the *PsycINFO User Manual* and *PsycINFO News.* Detailed information on *Psychological Abstracts* and its related publications and services can be found in the *Guide to PsycINFO,* a booklet available from User Services, PsycINFO, American Psychological Association, 1200 17th Street, NW, Washington, DC 20036, USA ([703] 247-7829 and [800] 336-4980).

Sociology and Other Social Sciences

Similar to *Psychological Abstracts* in structure and indexing is *Sociological Abstracts* (SA). Each issue carries abstracts grouped in 30 broad and 63 narrow subject areas; among these subjects are the sociology of medicine, social psychiatry, and substance use-abuse and compulsive behaviors. Subject searches are most efficiently carried out through the *Cumulative Subject Index* for each volume. The subject index is similar in structure to that for *Psychological Abstracts*: main entry terms have listed below them grouped descriptors that serve as mini-abstracts. SA's counterpart to MeSH compilation of *In-*

dex Medicus indexing terms is the *Thesaurus of Sociological Indexing Terms.*

SA is available for online searching through the gateway systems of BRS, DATA-STAR, and DIALOG.

Inquiries should be addressed to Sociological Abstracts, Inc, Post Office Box 22206, San Diego, CA 92122-0206, USA ([619] 565-6603).

Also available for searches in sociology and related fields is *Social Sciences Citation Index* published by the Institute for Scientific Information. *Social Sciences Citation Index,* structured like its sister, *Science Citation Index,* covers journals and multiauthored books in a wide range of fields that includes not only sociology but also such fields as economics, education, geography, law, psychology, and urban studies. Its coverage overlaps with that of *Science Citation Index* through indexing for drugs and addiction, geriatrics and gerontology, health policy services, nursing, and rehabilitation. *Social Sciences Citation Index* provides 4 indexes structured like their 4 equivalents in *Science Citation Index* (see description above in this chapter).

WHICH SERVICES TO USE?

Authors who do not need an exhaustive search may be satisfied with one of the smaller-scope services or a search sharply limited to one field. *Abridged Index Medicus* covers only a bit more than 100 journals, but these are all English-language journals of relatively high quality and mainly in clinical medicine. Searches for papers in a wider range of journals (non-English-language as well as English-language) should be carried out in a larger source, such as *Index Medicus* and *Science Citation Index*, or its online equivalent. Some notably helpful guides to searching are described in Appendix 4 under the heading "Guides to Medical Literature, Databases, and Other Sources of Information."

If you work in a highly active and productive field of research, finding the most recently published papers may be a major need in your search. Of the 3 main services for the medical sciences, *Index Medicus* and *Science Citation Index* have the shortest lag times between publication of a paper and citation of it in their indexes. The online services have shorter lag times than the printed indexes.

Searches in Overlapping Services

All of the major services overlap in coverage, so searches in 2 services will usually turn up some of the same articles. Data published in 1984 (5) indicated that about 90% of articles indexed in *Index Medicus* were also indexed in *Science Citation Index* and about 50% in

Chemical Abstracts. Authors who want to carry out an exhaustive search should use both *Index Medicus* (or MEDLINE) and 1 or more of the other services, preferably 1 covering journals not indexed by the National Library of Medicine. A search on a subject in medical sociology should, for example, include *Index Medicus* and either *Psychological Abstracts* or *Social Sciences Citation Index* or *Sociological Abstracts.* A comprehensive search on a subject in clinical pharmacy might properly use *Index Medicus, Excerpta Medica,* and *International Pharmaceutical Abstracts.*

Searches in Older Literature

Index Medicus extends back only to 1960. Searches farther back will have to go into its predecessor indexes:

Current List of Medical Literature	1952-1959
Quarterly Cumulative Index Medicus	1927-1956
Quarterly Cumulative Index to Current Medical Literature	1916-1926
Index Medicus: the first three series	1879-1899, 1903-1920, 1921-1927

Other resources available in large medical sciences libraries include the *Index Catalogue of the Library of the Surgeon General's Office,* particularly valuable for the 19th century and early 20th century. Such additional resources are described in 1 or more of the books listed under "Guides to Medical Literature, Databases, and Other Sources of Information" in Appendix 4.

Gateway Systems

A number of computer services serve as "gateways" to more than 1 computer-maintained database, both reference and source (text and numeric data) databases. MEDLINE of the National Library of Medicine, for example, is available from the Library directly and through several gateway systems.

Three major gateway services would probably serve most needs in the USA and Europe for bibliographic and full-text searches in biomedicine.

BRS Information Technologies
1200 Route 7,

Latham, NY 12110, USA
(518) 7831161; (800) 345-4277; TWX 710-4444-965

DATA-STAR
DS Marketing Ltd, Plaza Suite, 114 Jermyn Street,
London SW1Y 6HJ, United Kingdom
44 (1) 930-5503

DIALOG Information Services
3460 Hillview Avenue
Palo Alto, CA 94304, USA
(415) 858-3785; (800) 334-2564; Telex 334499 DIALOG;
   TWX 910-339-9221

Information on their services can be obtained through these addresses. *Online Databases in the Medical and Life Sciences* (described under "Guides to Medical Literature, Databases, and Other Sources of Information" in Appendix 4) concisely summarizes the databases to which they offer access.

RECORDS TO KEEP IN CONDUCTING A SEARCH

Your search (and any later searches) will proceed most efficiently if you keep records of what services you have used and how.

1. Before you start, record on cards or in a computer file all the subject terms you think you will need (including synonyms, variants, and abbreviations) and the date of the record; if you add terms later, record the dates of the additions. Terms drawn from index-term compilations (like Medical Subject Headings of *Index Medicus*) should be so identified.
2. In using each service, record any synonymous terms you found were needed for its index as substitutes for your original terms. Record the services searched, the years searched; also record limitations you placed on your search, such as only English-language journals or "human only". If in using online services you record the date you searched, you will easily be able subsequently to get an updated search covering later citations.
3. In examining original articles or abstracts to which you have been directed, keep a record of those you have decided not to use so that in conducting a search with a second service you do not go back to articles you have already seen.

When you find articles you expect to use later in writing your paper, make xerographic or photographic copies of them. This precaution will enable you later to verify both the content of each article and its bibliographical details that will be needed in your references. Be sure, however, that the pages you copy have all the data you will need for the references (such as journal title, volume number, and year).

MANAGING REFERENCES

References can be managed with greater efficiency and versatility if they are kept in a microcomputer file rather than on file cards ("3 by 5s"). Most flat-file (nonrelational) programs are readily adapted for this use. If you do not wish to take time to adapt a generic file program for this use, you can use one of the numerous bibliographic management programs available for Apple, Macintosh, and IBM PC-type microcomputers. Some of these are comprehensive in functions, like SciMate *Software System* (Institute for Scientific Information, publisher of *Science Citation Index*), providing access to gateway systems as well as file management. Others combine manuscript word-processing functions and references management, such as *Manuscript Manager* published by Pergamon Software, Maxwell House, Fairview Park, Elmsford, NY 10523, USA. Specifically bibliographic programs include *ProCite* (Personal Bibliographic Software, Inc., PO Box 4250, Ann Arbor, MI 48106, USA) and *EndNote* (Niles and Associates, 2200 Powell, Suite 765, Emeryville, CA 94608-1809, USA). Some of these programs can be used to automatically assign citation numbers to references in the final version of a paper and arrange them in the order of their initial citation. A useful critical review (6) of several products of this kind has been published in *Science*.

CONCLUSION

Before you start a search of the literature, prepare a list of all the subject terms that may be relevant, including variant forms, synonyms, and abbreviations. Decide on how exhaustive a search you need, taking into account such limits as English-language journals only, years, kinds of subjects (human only, animal only), and disciplines (medical sciences only or other fields such as sociology, law, economics). Consider using the services of a professional searcher. If you are going to use the conventional on-paper indexes (such as *Index Medicus*) rather than one or more of the online database systems, be sure at the start of the search that you are familiar with the indexes. The main indexes differ greatly in their structure and, hence, in how they are searched. In addition to searching the main indexes for the medical sciences, you might profitably search indexes to literature in related disciplines, including biology, chemistry, psychology, and sociology. As you proceed with your search, keep adequate records of the terms used, the services searched, and the limits of subject.

REFERENCES

1. Humphrey SM, Melloni BJ. Databases: a primer for retrieving information by computer. Englewood Cliffs, New Jersey: Prentice Hall; 1986:53-80.
2. Calabretta N. Educating the online search requester: a checklist. Med Services Reference Quart. 1983;2:31-9.
3. National Library of Medicine. List of journals indexed in Index Medicus. Bethesda, Maryland: National Library of Medicine; [annual publication]. Available from US Government Printing Office, Washington, DC.
4. National Library of Medicine. Hints for Index Medicus users. Bethesda, Maryland: National Library of Medicine; [undated]. Available from: Office of Inquiries and Publications Management, National Library of Medicine, Bethesda, MD 20209.
5. Poyer RK. Journal article overlap among Index Medicus, Science Citation Index, Biological Abstracts, and Chemical Abstracts. Bull Med Libr Assoc. 1984;72:353-7.
6. Wachtel RE. Personal bibliographic databases. Science. 1987;235:1093-6.

3

Preparing to Write

Before you start to write the first draft of your paper (see Chapter 9), take 4 steps to prepare for that task.

Step 1. Decide on authorship: If you will not be the sole author, come to an agreement with other potential authors on who will be authors. Then come to an agreement with the coauthors on the order for authors' names on the published paper. Coauthors should also agree on who will be the author responsible for settling any later disputes on authorship, for managing any revision of the paper, and for dealing with the journal editor.

Step 2. Make sure you know the manuscript requirements of the journal to which you will submit the paper.

Step 3. Assemble research data, case records, photographs, references, and any other documentary evidence you will need to have before you in writing the first draft. Assemble documents you may need in submitting the paper to the journal, such as permissions to reproduce figures or to cite personal communications.

Step 4. Arrange for typing of the manuscript or select a word-processing program.

This chapter discusses these steps in detail.

AUTHORSHIP

Why decide so early who will be the authors? Why not wait until the title page is about to be typed for the final version? Do not wait. No failure in scholarly procedure is more likely to breed ill-will and wreck friendships than putting off decisions about authorship to a time when failure to agree may bring unpleasant consequences and even damage careers. If you are to be the sole author, you are probably ready to move on to Step 2. Be as sure as you can, however, that no one else will have a claim to authorship before you send your paper to the journal.

Criteria for Authorship

What is a fair claim to authorship? Editors wish to restrict authorship to legitimate authors but rarely have any way of knowing which authors have had legitimate claims. Decisions on authorship must be made by authors themselves. The decisions should be guided by a central ethical principle: The reader takes the authorship statement on the paper's title page as honestly representing the person or persons who can take public responsibility (1) for its content. Two points follow from this premise, in which the 2 key words are *responsibility* and *content*. First, persons who cannot take the responsibility for defending the content of the paper if it were challenged by a reader should not be authors. *Content* does not refer only to data but also to intellectual content: development of concept and interpretation of data. Second, no one is likely to be able to take responsibility for a paper's content without having taken part in writing the paper or revising it for content (2). These considerations are the basis of 3 criteria by which to judge claims to authorship.

1. An author should have generated at least a part of the intellectual content of a paper.
   a. This work could have been conceiving or designing the study reported, if the paper is a research report, or identifying the particular features of a case that justifies a case report. If the paper is a review article or editorial, the equivalent work would have been identifying the question or questions to be answered and developing a plan for the paper.
   b. This work could have been collecting reported data (including clinical observations) *and* interpreting them for the paper's conclusions. Note that interpreting data is required; collecting of data does not by itself justify authorship.
2. An author should have taken part in writing the paper, reviewing it for possible revision, or revising its intellectual content (not just its technical content).
3. An author should be able to defend publicly in the scientific community all of the intellectual content of the paper.

Only persons who qualify by all 3 criteria should be authors on a paper. Table 3.1 illustrates how these criteria can be applied for decisions on the legitimacy of what might justify authorship. For additional comment on criteria for authorship see Appendix 3.

Table 3.1. Justifications for authorship

Basis for authorship	Legitimate	Not legitimate
Genesis of the paper		
Research report	Development of a testable hypothesis or specific question	Suggestion that legitimate author(s) work on the problem
Case report, clinical observation	First notice of previously unobserved phenomenon	Physician's, nurse's, pharmacist's routine referral, care, or service.
Review	Critical interpretations of reviewed papers and assembled data	Suggestion that the review be written
Research efforts	Development of study design	Suggestion of use of standard study design
	Development of new method (laboratory, field, statistical) or critical modification of previous method	Observations and measurements by routine methods
	Personal collection *and* interpretation of data	Collection of data without interpretation
Clinical studies	New diagnostic and therapeutic efforts	"Routine" diagnostic and therapeutic efforts that would have occurred even if the paper had not been written
Interpretation of findings	Explanatory insight into unexpected phenomenona	Routine explanations such as electrocardiographic and radiologic reports
Writing of a paper	Writing the 1st draft or critically important revision of concept or interpretation in a later draft	Solely criticizing drafts and suggesting revision of presentation, not ideas
		Revision limited to technical changes, as in details of prose style or table structure
Responsibility for content	Ability to justify intellectually the conclusions of the paper, including defense of the evidence and counter-evidence weighed in reaching them	Solely attesting to accuracy of individual facts reported

Authorship for Reports of Multicenter Studies

Difficult questions on authorship can arise with research reports by large, multicenter, cooperative teams. Multicenter studies have become more frequent in the past 2 decades. Although their number may fall with declines in Federal funds for research, they are likely to continue to be organized, in part because they are often the only means for getting interpretable data on uncommon diseases and treatments of uncertain value. Editors would like to see authorship for such reports credited by group titles, such as "The National Cooperative Gallstone Study", rather than by listings of 15, 25, 50, or more "authors." The "authors" prefer having their individual names listed for visibility in tables of contents and in the reference lists of subsequent papers. The truly important claim to authorship for the sake of career is the one on the personal bibliography attached to a curriculum vitae. Unfortunately the claims to authorship in such studies may represent a continuous range of contributions from minor to major. The difficulties in discussions about authorship among participants in multicenter studies can be settled not by agreeing on which 15, 25, 50 persons, or some other fraction out of everyone in the enterprise, should be authors but by coining a group title for "author", listing the members of the group in a title-page footnote, and agreeing that persons so identified could legitimately list the paper in personal bibliographies. If a group, or collective, title is agreed on, decisions should also be made about who might be identified in an Acknowledgments section (or in a footnote on the title page) as writers of the paper, collectors and interpreters of the data, and other kinds of participants.

Division of Authors' Work

Aside from avoiding last-minute squabbles, discussing authorship early on has another practical value. When authorship has been agreed upon, the authors-to-be can then decide on how to divide the work of writing the paper. With relatively short papers the first draft is probably best written by only 1 author, but with long and complex papers the work may be shared to advantage. For example, the sections on study design and statistical analysis in a paper reporting a large cooperative study are probably best written by its statistician. With such division of work on early drafts, agreement should also be reached on their deadlines and who will pull them together for a single, integrated manuscript.

MANUSCRIPT REQUIREMENTS

If you have taken the advice in Chapter 1, you have already consulted the information-for-authors page of the journal for which you have decided to write the paper, to get information on topics and formats. The journal may set limits on the acceptable numbers of tables, illustrations, and references. There may be other restrictions. If you ignore any of these until you prepare the final version of the paper, you will face the painful job of revising at the last minute to meet the journal's specifications for manuscripts, with the risks of errors introduced by hasty revision and another retyping or more keyboarding. If you do not prepare the paper to meet the specifications, it may be published only after delay due to your having to revise the provisionally accepted version on request of the editor.

The journal's information-for-authors page may not state a limit on numbers of tables and illustrations. You can estimate what the limits might be by looking at articles in some recent issues and calculating the ratio of the numbers of their tables and illustrations to the number of words in their texts. In *Annals of Internal Medicine*, for example, the limit is 1 table or illustration to each 750 words of text (about 3 pages of manuscript text typed double-spaced). Knowing the probable limit early can spare you the distasteful work of revising tables or discarding figures late in the preparation of the paper or at the request of the editor.

ASSEMBLING EVIDENCE

Virtually all papers published in professional journals—research reports, case reports, reviews, or editorials—support their conclusions with evidence: observational data, case descriptions, photographs, citations of published papers, and other kinds of evidence. When you sit down to write, you should have the evidence before you and not rely on memory. Not all of the evidence need be in final form at this point. You may need a series of chest radiographs to illustrate how a malignant tumor of the lung regressed under treatment. Photographs of these radiographs have not been taken; you may wish to have the photographer crop the original images to emphasize the area and features of interest, or the prints may have to be trimmed so they can be assembled in a multipart, single illustration. You should at least have the original radiographs, or full copies of them, so that as you write you will be describing what you see before you, not what you think you saw a few months ago.

Citing published papers from memory is risky. If you try to recall from file cards or other notes the contents of papers you read a year ago in preparing your research protocol, you may not see points that have new relevance in view of your experience in the interval. It is safer to assemble copies or reprints of the papers you expect to cite. If you do not have copies, get them made now. Be sure you have thoroughly digested the papers you plan to cite; do not cite them from abstracts or secondary sources.

The Research Paper

Papers reporting research that get published might be said to have been written long before the first draft goes onto paper. This apparent paradox means that research with findings important enough to report in a published paper very likely has been properly conceived to answer an important question that can be framed as a testable hypothesis. The research has been carried out with appropriate design and methods, including statistical analysis. You have valid data and a conclusive answer.

The tabulated data should be complete and clearly organized before you start the first draft. Tables should include evidence of statistical analysis used to show the strength of the data as evidence for the conclusion. If statistical analysis is deferred until after you have written the first draft, you may have to revise its content heavily to accommodate changes in conclusions. At worst, you may write the first draft and then find out you do not really have an answer to the research question.

If the research was supported by a grant or at least was described in a written protocol for review by a research committee, the grant application or protocol probably contains sections describing proposed study design and methods that may be readily adapted for parts of the first draft. The list below includes these and additional kinds of evidence and documentation likely to be needed for most research papers.

- Papers to be cited (copies or reprints rather than notes): papers read before and while drawing up the research proposal; papers that came to your attention during the research; papers found in a final search of the literature immediately before you decide to report the research in a paper
- Descriptions of study design and methods: papers to be cited for methods; grant application or protocol approved by an institutional review committee
- Copies of signed informed-consent forms
- Tables of data: analyzed data, with statistical assessments
- Preliminary graphs, with statistical assessments if needed

- Case summaries
- Other kinds of illustrations: radiographs, electrocardiographs, and similar records; preliminary sketches for art work

Do not overlook the ethical need (2) to cite in your paper those pertinent reports that appeared after you started your research.

Preliminary illustrations will be adequate for the first draft. Properly drawn graphs can be prepared by you or an artist when you are sure, after the first or second draft, that you will use the graphs in the final version. The same point applies to radiographs, electrocardiographs, drawings of surgical procedures, and similar records.

Chapter 5, "The Research Paper," describes suitable structures for research papers and the principles on which they are built. You may wish to read this chapter before you start to write your first draft.

The Case Report

The documentary needs for a case report are fewer and simpler than for research papers.

- Hospital, clinic, and office records: case summaries from these records; letters
- Tables of data: data illustrating clinical course; data from special studies
- Preliminary graphs: illustrating clinical course; illustrating special studies
- Papers to be cited: copies and reprints
- Photographs and permission to use them; radiographs, electrocardiographs, and similar records

If you plan to use photographs that show a patient's identity and do not have written permission from the patient (or a responsible agent) for publication, now is the time to get permission (see below, "Permissions"). The journal accepting the case report will need to have the permission in hand before publishing the paper. If the patient has moved to another region or country, you may need a good bit of time to get that permission. Clinical records may have to be requested of other physicans or institutions; do not delay in asking for them.

Chapter 6, "The Case Report," describes the structure you should have in mind before you start to write the first draft.

The Review and the Editorial

Review articles and most scientific editorials are similar in that they look analytically and critically at currently important questions with the aim of providing justified answers. Thus the kinds of materials to be gathered before writing their first drafts are the same. Many reviews and most editorials are invited by editors; for such papers the author has special needs.

- Have a firm understanding with the editor on whether you are free to take your own position or must develop a specified position.
- Find out whether you may have one or more coauthors if you wish to have any. If the paper is to be an editorial, will it be published over your name as author?
- Agree with the editor on a deadline.
- Be sure you understand the conditions for publication—possible peer review; guaranteed acceptance or not; an honorarium?
- If the paper is an editorial to be linked to another paper in the same issue, will you be given an advance copy of that paper?

For all reviews and editorials:

- Sharpen as much as possible your concept of the central message of the editorial or review; state it in a single sentence before you outline and write.
- Find out any limit on length and on number of references, and whether tables or figures will be acceptable (and if so, what number).
- Assemble references likely to be cited and any tabulated data.

The structure of reviews is discussed in Chapter 7; that of editorials, in Chapter 8.

PERMISSIONS

You may have to use various kinds of documentary evidence in support of conclusions in your paper other than your own tables and illustrations.

- Previously published items: extensive quotations from text; illustrations; tables of data
- Photographs of patients; photomicrographs
- Letters and other "personal communications", such as unpublished papers

Some materials may be protected by copyright and cannot be used without permission of the copyright holder. You can avoid possible delay in completing your paper if you take steps to get such permission as you prepare to write. Most journal papers are copyrighted by the publisher of the journal, from whom permission should be sought even for use of single tables or figures. An example of a letter requesting permission is illustrated in Figure 3.1. If a journal article has been copyrighted by the author, his or her copyright will be indicated on the title page of the article. The copyright holder for a book is given on the page that follows the title page. Even though the copyright holder gives permission for use of copyrighted materials, it is ethically desirable also to get agreement for their use from the authors who assigned copyright to the publisher.

Previously unpublished photographs of patients, whether of their faces or other parts of the body by which they might be identified, are unlikely to be covered by copyright, but use of them without documented express permission could leave you open to legal action. A patient may have signed a blanket permission for reproduction of the photograph when it was taken, but this permission may not be adequate. It is safer to request permission for use of the photograph specifically in the article you are planning (Figure 3.2).

Letters or other "personal communications" (including informal verbal communications, talks, lectures) are sometimes cited in scientific papers, although this kind of usually unverifiable evidence is rejected by some editors. If you hold a letter or unpublished paper you plan to cite, you should ask its author for permission to cite it, whether or not you quote from it. Such a citation without permission would be highly unlikely to lead to a legal action against you, but unauthorized citations of a letter may embarrass or irritate its writer, seeking permission is a courtesy.

Use of text taken from other publications may or may not need permission of the copyright holder. In general, the factor determining the need for permission is the effect of quoting on the economic interests of the copyright holder. If the quotation is a small fraction of the original text, permission is usually not needed. If the quotation is of the entire original text—an entire poem, for example—permission clearly is needed. Uses between these limits are harder to sort out as to possible copyright infringement. A safe procedure is to request permission to quote more than 4 or 5 consecutive sentences. Most scholarly journals will give permission for generously long quotations, but some commercial publishers will charge royalty fees for even relatively short quotations from novels, biographies, and similar literary works written by professional authors and published for profit.

Persons whose names are to be mentioned in the Acknowledgments section of a paper should be asked to give permission for use of their names. The presence of such names in a paper may be taken by some readers as endorsement of its content, and the potentially named persons shoule be free to avoid such implications if the wish.

```
The Editor
Annals of Internal Medicine
Independence Mall West
6th Street at Race
Philadelphia, PA 19106-1572

Sir:                              19 July 1987

     I wish to quote a paragraph of an
editorial published in your journal in 1976.
The quotation is to be used in a paper, "The
Next 100 Years of American Medicine", I am
preparing for the Journal of American Medical
Economics and Sociology. The reference for the
editorial from which I wish to quote is as
follows:

     Smith A. Medical things to come.
     Ann Intern Med. 1985;99:921-3.

The paragraph to be quoted begins, "If H. G.
Wells were alive today ...".

     I also am requesting Dr Smith's permission
to use this quotation from his editorial.
Acknowledgment of permission to quote the
editorial will be given in the review. You may
wish to specify the form of acknowledgment.

     Thank you for considering this request.

Sincerely,


Carolyn Janavel, PhD

4321 Sequestra Street
Birch Woods, ME 01234
```

Figure 3.1. Typical letter requesting permission to use copyrighted material.

Mr John Doe
141 Wolfe Road
Nortown, MO 00001, USA

Dear Mr Doe: 23 July 1987

I am writing an article on the treatment of
burns for publication in the North American
Review of Nursing or a similar professional
journal. I would like to reproduce in the
article the pictures of your face taken by the
hospital photographers immediately after the
burns and six months later. Copies of the
photographs are enclosed.

If you are willing to let me use those
photographs in my article, please date and sign
at the indicated points below and return this
letter to me in the enclosed envelope. A copy
of this letter is enclosed for your records.

Thank you for considering this request.

Sincerely,

I L Hauser, MD

ILH:dw

DATE_____   _____
                            Signature of patient

Figure 3.2.   Typical letter requesting permission to use photographs.

SELECTING A WORD PROCESSING PROGRAM

If someone else will type your paper (on a typewriter or through
a word-processing program) you need not be concerned with exactly
how the typescript and tables will be produced. But if you are dexter-

ous at a computer keyboard, you may decide to type your own paper, both the drafts and the final version. If this is your choice, you should try to select a word-processing program that will make easier some of the more complex operations in preparing the manuscript of a scientific paper.

Manuscripts of short and simple papers like editorials and book reviews can usually be prepared easily enough with the cheaper and most simple programs. These programs can be used for longer and more complex manuscripts, but the larger programs with more features simplify some of the tasks in constructing tables, writing equations and scientific notation like subscripts and superscripts, and repeatedly revising text.

The New Writer: Techniques for Writing Well with a Computer described in the section "Guides to Writing" of Appendix 4 discusses the many advantages in writing one's own paper with a word-processing program.

CONCLUSION

Four steps will prepare you to write: deciding on authorship, getting the manuscript requirements of the journal, pulling together the data and documentary materials needed to write the paper, and either arranging for adequate typing services or selecting a suitable word-processing program. The documentary materials may include not only papers turned up in literature searches you are going to cite, but also radiographs, pictures of patients, and similar clinical evidence. Permissions to use several kinds of materials, such as photographs of patients, text from other publications, and letters, should be sought well in advance. The authors of invited reviews and editorials must be sure of the conditions accompanying the invitation before beginning to write.

REFERENCES

1. Huth EJ. Guidelines on authorship of medical papers. Ann Intern Med. 1986; 104:269-74.
2. [Huth EJ]. Ethical conduct in authorship and publication. In: CBE Style Manual Committee. CBE style manual. 5th ed. Bethesda, Maryland: Council of Biology Editors; 1983:1-6.

4

Critical Argument and the Structure of Scientific Papers

The questions most often asked in workshops on medical writing are on the right content for sections of scientific papers and its sequence. What should be in the Introduction? What should open the Discussion section? Should validation of a method be in the Methods section or in Results? Such questions are usually asked about research reports but sometimes about other kinds of papers: the sequence of sections in a review article; the arrangement of comments in a book review. This manual might simply give cookbook answers, setting out exact recipes for each kind of paper. But you will be a more resourceful author, one more able to work out your own answers, if you understand some principles that should control the content and structure of virtually all scientific papers, be they research reports, case reports, reviews, editorials, or book reviews.

Why do we read scientific journals? Most of us do not read journals closely when they arrive. We scan them as we scan newspapers, to keep aware of what is going on in our fields, to get a sense of new developments that may become important to us. But sometimes we really read papers closely. Then we are looking for more. We are looking for answers to questions; we are looking for solutions to problems. A clinician needs to know the best antibiotic for treatment of a pneumonia. A nursing instructor needs to know the best way to teach the surveillance of obstetric labor. The microbiologist wants to know what characteristics of *Legionella pneumophila* have justified creating a new genus and species in bacterial taxonomy. The physiologist wants to know how substance X mediates renal vasoconstriction. The clinical pharmacist wants to know the pharmacokinetic variables by which the dose of a new psychotropic drug can be adjusted when its renal clearance is reduced by half.

But close readers are looking for more than just answers to questions and solutions to problems. If this is all they want, they need not read entire papers; the answers and solutions are usually stated clearly in a summary at the head of the paper or at the end in a Conclusion section. What we need as close readers is to be convinced that the message of the paper—its answer to our question, its solution for our problem—is correct, is valid. We are not going to apply the message in how we think and work unless we are persuaded that we can rely on it. Scientific papers are not just baskets carrying unconnected facts like the telephone directory; they are instruments of persuasion (1). Scientific papers must argue you into believing what they conclude; they must be built on the principles of critical argument.

The "argument" in *critical argument* is not "argument" in its popular sense. It is not a Republican and a Democrat shouting at each other about the welfare state. It is not a married couple having a row about whether to squeeze the toothpaste tube in the middle or at the end. *Argument* here is "a coherent series of reasons, statements, or facts intended to support or establish a point of view" (2). And *critical* means assessing evidence for its validity, what evidence to accept and what evidence to reject. In their classic book on clear statement and the graces of prose, *The Reader Over Your Shoulder: A Handbook for Writers of English Prose*, Graves and Hodge (3) set forth "the natural arrangement of ideas in critical argument".

- Statement of problem
- Marshaling of evidence, first on main points, then on subsidiary ones—the same sequence kept throughout the argument
- Credibility of evidence examined
- Statement of possible implications of all evidence not wholly rejected
- The weighing of conflicting evidence in the scale of probability
- Verdict

At first reading, Graves and Hodge's outline of the structure of critical argument, their "natural arrangement of ideas", sounds more like an agenda for a judge conducting a murder trial than an outline of a research paper.

This "arrangement" makes more sense for the author of a scientific paper if it is restated thus.

- Statement of problem: posing of a question or stating a hypothesis
- Presentation of the evidence
- Validity of the evidence
- Implications of the evidence: initial answer or judgment on the validity of the hypothesis

- Assessment of the answer's validity in the face of conflicting evidence
- Conclusion

Consider how these elements of "critical argument" can be found in a paper reporting a study of an antibiotic treatment.

Against the infectious disease K fever, antimycin is often effective but it has a high rate of adverse effects. A new antibiotic, megamycin, has been found to inhibit the growth of the causative bacterium in vitro. But for clinicians a vital question remains to be answered: Is megamycin more effective than antimycin A in treatment of K fever? The investigators draw up a protocol for a study to answer the question. The study gets under way. Antimycin and megamycin appear for a while to have the same efficacy, but then megamycin begins to look better. The investigators carefully monitor the results of treatment statistically so that the comparative trial can be stopped when a significant answer is reached. Finally megamycin is found to be definitely better, a conclusion reached with statistically supported evidence; the trial is completed. Then the investigators write and get published a paper reporting the trial. The paper makes clear in the Introduction why the study was carried out: the question that had to be answered. The paper describes the findings in a Results section: the evidence. The validity of the findings is established through description of study design and methods, through statistical statements, and through assessment of possible alternative conclusions. A conclusion is reached; the answer is clear: "Megamycin is more effective for treatment of K fever than antimycin". The reader who needs the answer and wants to know whether the answer is reliable gets in the paper all that he or she needs. The reader is persuaded; the reader has been argued into accepting the answer.

Note that the concept of critical argument includes more than just the content of argument. Graves and Hodge's outline also specifies a sequence for the argument. The evidence is not stated first, with the question to which it is applied posed later. The question is made clear at the beginning. This principle should apply to all scientific papers, be they research reports or reviews. The reader needs to know at the beginning exactly what the paper is about, what question or questions it is setting out to answer. The sequence of its content thereafter may not follow exactly that in Graves and Hodge's outline. The sequence in a research report is likely to be that of a mainly forward narrative and in a review article, the "flashback" method. But authors must keep in mind that the sequence must be made clear to readers.

CONCLUSION

The reader of a scientific paper is looking for the answer to a question, the solution to a problem. The author of the paper must first make clear the question the paper proposes to answer. The author must convince the reader, through critically sifted evidence arranged in a clear sequence, that the conclusion of the paper is correct. This content, that of critical argument, is appropriate for other kinds of papers as well as for the research report. The sequence of the content may, however, properly differ in the several kinds of papers discussed in the following chapters.

REFERENCES

1.　Weiss EH. The writing system for engineers and scientists. Englewood Cliffs, New Jersey: Prentice-Hall; 1982:116.
2.　Gove PB, ed. Webster's third new international dictionary of the English language, unabridged. Springfield, Massachusetts: G & C Merriam; 1961:117.
3.　Graves R, Hodge A. The reader over your shoulder: a handbook for writers of English prose. 2nd ed. New York: Random House; 1979:125.

5

The Research Paper

Papers reporting research are the most frequently published kind of scientific paper. The huge number of research papers being written has forced their authors into competing intensely for space in journals. They compete most effectively when they make their papers clear and complete, but efficient, statements. The conventional format for research papers described below is not arbitrary; it is based on principles derived from the content and sequence of critical argument discussed in the preceding chapter. If you master these principles you will often be able to decide for yourself on how to build your papers and will not need to fall back entirely on recipes for the conventional format.

THE CONVENTIONAL FORMAT

Readers expect to read about your research in the sequence in which it was carried out: what question you set out to answer or hypothesis to test, how you sought the answer, what was found, and what answer you arrived at. The research paper gives this information in 4 steps.

- The question to be answered is stated at the beginning; the alternative is the hypothesis to be tested.
- How the answer was sought, or the hypothesis tested, is specified in convincing detail.
- The evidence bearing on the answer is described: your findings and other supporting evidence, counter-evidence.
- The answer to the question (or judgment on whether the hypothesis was supported) is given after assessment of all evidence.

Clearly written papers use a narrative sequence to give the "story" of the research. The elements of critical argument in the paper do not follow exactly the usual sequence in "critical argument" (see Chapter 4) but are usually divided to fit into the "story" format. The usual sequence of sections is Introduction, Materials and Methods, Results, and Discussion and Conclusions. These sections correspond to the sequence of the research (Table 5.1). You may need to vary the sequence in response to the preference of a particular journal; it may not, for example, allow use of a closing Conclusions.

Table 5.1. Structure of the research paper

Sequence of the research	Format and content	Elements of critical argument
The question to be answered	Introduction	The problem (question)
How the answer was sought	Material and Methods	Credibility of evidence
Findings	Result	Evidence (the data); initial answer
Findings considered in the light of the findings of other investigators; the answer	Discussion and Conclusion	Supporting evidence (other papers), contradictory evidence (other papers) Assessment of conflicting evidence Answer

The Introduction

When you go to an interview for a job, your clothes and behavior may determine right away whether you get hired. Likewise, the Introduction to your paper may immediately influence how the paper is sized up by an editor, a manuscript consultant, or, if the paper gets published, by a reader. If the Introduction is too long, it irritates or bores; if it is too short, it may not make clear why the research was needed. The Introduction quickly gives an impression of your skill as an investigator and writer. Four rules may help you in deciding what to put into the Introduction.

Tell the Reader Why the Research Was Started

What was the gap in knowledge to be filled by the research? By thus justifying the research, the Introduction puts a probable value on what the paper provides. Gaps in knowledge may be of several kinds. There may have been a need to account for a new phenomenon: A study of the pharmacokinetics of a new antibiotic in patients with inadequate renal function may have been launched because a serious side effect of the drug had been found to occur only in patients with renal disease. There may have been a need to reconcile conflicting previous observations: A drug for treatment of congestive heart failure has been described in 1 paper as highly effective and in another paper as effective in only about half of the patients. To what is the difference due—to different doses, to differences in the severity of the heart failure?

Do Not Explain What Can Be Found in Any Textbook in the Field

In justifying your research go back no farther in citing the relevant literature or explaining the problem than is needed by the intended audience. Do not use the Introduction to show off wide knowledge; the audience for the paper should be expected to know almost as much as you. If the paper reports a comparative trial of 2 drugs for treatment of metastatic breast cancer, you need not explain to an intended audience of physicians that metastatic breast cancer is a frequent and serious clinical problem; you need not describe its characteristics. Physicians know all of this; you start the Introduction simply by telling why a new treatment is needed and why the drugs studied were selected.

Do Not Elaborate on Terms in the Title of the Paper

If the title is "The Prevalence of Hypercalcemia in Patients with Sarcoidosis", do not start with explaining *hypercalcemia* and *sarcoidosis*. Readers of the title who do not know what you mean by these terms are not likely to be interested in going on to read the paper.

Make Clear What Question the Research Was Designed to Answer

You need not state the question as a question, but the statement of the purpose of the research should be translatable as a question. For a trial of a new multidrug chemotherapeutic regimen for metastatic breast cancer, you state, "This study was designed to compare efficacy of the new multidrug therapeutic regimen, cobracin-IL2, developed on the principles described above, with the present standard therapy, CLOPP". The reader can translate this statement into a question: "Is cobracin-IL2 a better treatment for metastatic breast cancer than CLOPP?". The statement "was designed to compare" is not, however, specific enough; the reader needs to know what yardstick was used to define "better". A more specific statement would be, "The new multidrug therapeutic regimen, cobracin-IL2, developed on the principles described above, was compared with CLOPP, the present standard therapy, for its effect on survival at 1 year after treatment". The purpose of a research study can be stated as testing a hypothesis: "This clinical trial tested the hypothesis that the cumulative mortality from metastatic breast cancer at 1 year after treatment will be lower with cobracin-IL2 than with CLOPP". A clear statement of the question to be answered or the hypothesis to be tested is indispensable in planning research; without it, the research may not yield useful conclusions (a symptom of this failure can turn up as a vague statement of purpose at the close of an Introduction). But even if you did pose a specific hypothesis at the beginning of your research and have found a clear and useful answer, readers may regard a "tested-the-hypothesis" statement as pedantic, artificial, and not in clinical idiom. Even if a hypothesis was formally proposed, most clinical readers will be more comfortable with your posing the research purpose as a question.

In closing the Introduction with a statement of research purpose, some authors include a brief summary of the study design: "The two regimens were compared in a double-blind trial with randomized assignment of patients." This kind of summary lengthens the Introduction very little; if the journal for which you are preparing your paper uses smaller type for the Materials and Methods section than for the rest of the text, a concise summary of study design at the end of the Introduction emphasizes to readers how the research was carried out.

Some authors close the Introduction with a short statement of the research findings, the paper's answer. This practice has been justified as a device to hold the reader's attention; it has been criticized as moving the conclusion from its logical place in the sequence of argument. One reason for keeping the conclusion at the end of the paper is that many journals now publish papers' full summaries or abstracts on their title pages. Why give the answer twice at the beginning of the paper?

The Materials and Methods Section

How did you carry out your research? The critical reader will want to know exactly what you did, in enough detail to be able to judge whether the findings reported in the Results section are reliable support for your conclusions.

Properly designed research has a logical sequence.

- Study design is selected (after the hypothesis is stated).
- The state or condition to be studied (disease, physiologic state) is defined.

- The subjects (patients, normal persons, animals, plants) to be studied are defined.
- Methods for selecting subjects are designed.
- Interventions (such as treatment) are decided on in detail.
- All observations to be made are specified, including the methods.
- Statistical procedures for assessment of data are selected.

The Materials and Methods section should follow such a sequence. Each part of the section must expand with relevant detail each of these aspects of the study as it was actually executed.

Content

The paragraphs immediately below do not specify all possible details relevant to a complete description of design, methods, and procedures. For thorough tabular summaries of the possibilities for reports of clinical trials see "Methods section" in Table 25.1, "Content suggestions for the study publication", in Chapter 25 of *Clinical Trials: Design, Conduct, and Analysis* by Meinert (1), and "Materials and Methods Section" in Chapter 29 of *Guide to Clinical Interpretation of Data* by Spilker (2). The desirable details for reports of drug trials are set forth in the Food and Drug Administration's *Guidelines for the Format and Content of the Clinical and Statistical Sections of New Drug Applications* (3).

Study Design and Protocol.   Some study designs are so well known that they need be specified only by a descriptive phrase. Unusual designs that have been described in the literature may be specified by a phrase but with a citation to the source. New designs should be described in detail. The study groups should be described briefly (for example, control and treatment groups) and identified, as appropriate, by kinds of intervention, including treatments. Methods for random assignment of subjects to study groups should be described. Additional details may be needed, including criteria for admission to a therapeutic trial, eligibility criteria applied before knowledge of treatment assignment, and patients' blindness to treatment.

Subjects.   Well-designed studies use subjects carefully specified and selected to minimize variations caused by subject characteristics. Results can be interpreted accurately for effects due to treatment or another kind of intervention only when other effects on results (such as physiologic effects, ethnic, or sex differences) can be excluded. Hence, subjects must be characterized as fully as possible so there will be no questions about uncontrolled variables. For animals, the sex, age, species, breed, and physiologic state should be given. For microorganisms, identify species, strain, serotype, and any other characteristics. If the effect of a drug on a disease has been studied, the criteria used in diagnosis of the disease should be specified; different diagnostic criteria can lead to including patients with different diseases or the same disease in differing states, with consequent confusion about drug effects. Ethical controls used should be mentioned: informed consent, review of the research protocol by an institutional committee, conformity of procedures to requirements of a granting agency.

Interventions (Treatment). Drugs, hormones, other chemicals, and any other agents used for experimental intervention or treatment should be described fully: the specific preparation (including details such as trade name, drug vehicle, placebo composition) and administration (dosage, route, method). Some therapeutic trials include statistical controls to prevent unjustifiable morbidity or mortality; such a control may be described with the details of treatment rather than in the description of statistical assessment.

Measurements and Other Observations. Standard methods for chemical and other laboratory procedures need to be identified only by name and citation; variations from these should be described in enough detail to enable another investigator to duplicate your results. Previously unpublished methods must be described in detail, with evidence that they have been validated. Functional tests need to be identified or described similarly. Other relevant description may include blindness of outcome assessment and of assessment of treatment complications.

Statistical Analysis. Specify the statistical methods. For methods (including computer programs) well known in your field, simply name the methods and give citations to standard sources. Unfamiliar methods should be described in detail. Information relevant to judging the power of the statistical assessment should be included. But note that data in the Results section with critical importance to the paper's main conclusions should be accompanied there by short specific statements of the methods for their statistical assessment.

Title, Placement, and Format of the Methods Section

The phrase "Materials and Methods" is widely used for the section of the research paper that describes how a study was carried out. Some more specific titles for this section may better fit what you have done: "Study Design, Subjects, and Methods" or "Study Plan, Patients, and Procedures". Do not be surprised, however, if a rigid editor forces you back to the tried-and-true "Materials and Methods"; old habits are not easily broken.

Most Materials and Methods sections indicate the author's sequence (study design, subjects, and so on) only by paragraphing each unit. If the section is long, you may wish to insert text headings for each unit. This device will also help to ensure that all of the content is appropriately placed within each headed section.

Where do you place the Materials and Methods section if your paper reports an unusual case—perhaps a new syndrome—and special investigations carried out to identify mechanisms responsible for the disorder or some of its manifestations? The case is of great interest, but so are the special studies. The paper is a hybrid: part case report, part research report. The solution? Tell the story. After the introduction, describe the case under the heading, Case Report. Then describe what you did under the heading Special Studies to distinguish them from the routine hospital studies. In this sequence, "Case Report" corresponds to "Subject"; "Special Studies" corresponds to "Interventions, Measurements, and Other Observations". "Special Studies" will then be followed logically by the next major section, "Results".

Length

What do you do if the study was long and complex and your paper needs a very long and detailed Materials and Methods section? Many of your readers may not want to read through all of the detail. One solution is to write a synoptic Materials and Methods section in which you give only the main points of design and procedure, with a more detailed description placed at the end of your paper as an appendix. You should try, however, to get the editor of the journal for which you are writing the paper to agree to this structure before you begin to write; relocating the detailed description in revising the paper might call for a complicated shift of references.

The Results Section

The evidence you need to answer the question that prompted your research may come partly from previously published work, but if your research has been concerned with a new question or has used a new approach to an old question, most of your evidence will be your own observations and data. This new evidence is what should be reported in the Results section.

New evidence should be described as efficiently as possible. Numerical data can usually be presented more effectively in tables or graphs than in text; the text should present no more than a summary or otherwise critically important data (for example, control and treatment group mean values, with appropriate statistical assessment of differences). For therapeutic trials in a very small number of cases, brief case descriptions may be convincing if the natural course of the disease is well known, but tables of case characteristics may be adequate.

The content of the Results section should follow the sequence the reader will expect. Most readers of a paper reporting a therapeutic trial will want to know, first, whether the trial was properly designed; second, whether the design was effective; and, third, the effects of the new drug compared to those of the standard of comparison, namely, the drug usually used.

Readers are assured of the proper study design by the Materials and Methods section, but did the design accomplish what was expected of it? In a therapeutic trial comparing 2 drugs, the 2 groups of patients in which they were used must be shown, if possible, to have been closely similar in all characteristics so that any differences in treatment results can be attributed to the drugs and not to patient-group differences. Therefore the first section of Results presents the data establishing the similarity of the 2 groups. If the data are in a table, the text need only call attention to the lack of statistically significant differences or point out what differences were found.

Note that the Results section must account for all subjects who actually entered the study and not only those who stayed in it as assigned. Therefore you must account for such subjects as those who dropped out even after having participated only briefly, who were changed from treatment arms, who died before completing a treatment, and those lost to follow-up. The data on results in a trial may have to include the findings when the data from all subjects who entered the study are analyzed, in addition to the findings based on all subjects who completed their part in the study.

What comes next in a paper reporting a therapeutic trial, the data from the control group (treated with the standard drug) or the data from the trial group (the new drug)? A helpful rule is to proceed from the old to the new, from the known to the unknown. In the Introduction you first summarized the state of knowledge before your research and then moved to the question to be answered. Likewise, in the Results section you should first present the data from the "known", the standard-drug group (or the control group, if no standard treatment was available). You should then move to the data from the trial group in which the new drug was used. This sequence does not necessarily call for separate paragraphs for each study group.

For detailed tabular summaries of the proper content in the Results section of a paper reporting a clinical trial, see Table 25.1 in *Clinical Trials: Design, Conduct, and Analysis* (1) and "Results Section" in Chapter 29 of *Guide to Clinical Interpretation of Data* (2).

The Results section should give as clear an answer to the question posed for the research as the data from the study will permit. Thus, statements in the text summarizing data given in detail in tables should include unequivocal statements of statistical significance or confidence intervals. You will not enhance your reputation by hiding statistically not significant results behind weaseling phrases like "tended to be greater" and "showed promising trends". Be sure to include with statements of statistical significance a brief mention of the methods by which they were derived (for example, "Fisher exact test", "Student's t test").

The Discussion and Conclusions Sections

The opening pages of this chapter emphasize that the research paper is, in essence, a special kind of argument. Usually the evidence presented is not solely that from the research being reported; the other evidence may be a major part of the Discussion section.

The opening of the Discussion should give the answer to your research question. In the first paragraph of the section, state concisely the central conclusion, or answer, to be drawn from the data presented in Results. Remember, however, that the answer may not be fully supported until you have cited additional evidence, such as research findings previously reported by you or by others. Give full credit for this evidence by citing published reports; do not omit supporting evidence from others in an effort to make your present research appear unique or more important. If a previously published paper on the same question arrived at the same answer, do not bury the citation of it in the Discussion, the "Reference 13" treatment (4). Avoid this devious practice; such citations should be in the Introduction.

Evidence from other papers supporting your own data may not be the only evidence you must present in the Discussion. There may be counter-evidence to be presented and assessed. What if another therapeutic trial led to an answer differing from that found in your trial? If you are an ethical scientist (5), you will assess this counter-evidence. Perhaps it can be dismissed because the other trial tested the compared drugs in patients at a different stage of disease, but perhaps the counter-evidence cannot be thus dismissed. The honest Discussion considers all evidence bearing on the argument.

There are several ways to close the Discussion. You may need to discuss to what extent findings in a therapeutic trial can be generalized to all patients with the disease. If you cannot resolve conflicting evidence from your trial and trials by others, you may wish to suggest how the discrepancy could be resolved in a new trial. Do not extend implications and speculations too far; readers of scientific papers are looking for firm conclusions supported by fact.

If you accept the view that a research paper is a special kind of argument, you will close it with "the verdict", the answer to your research question. For many years virtually all research papers did close with a Conclusions statement in addition to the Discussion. Today many journals do not keep readers in suspense, forcing them to go through papers to the end to learn the answer; instead they put the conclusions up front in an abstract or summary on the title page. A few journals do carry papers with a title-page abstract and a terminal Conclusions. This detail is one of the many that you should check in the manuscript-requirements statement of the journal for which you are preparing the paper.

CONCLUSION

The research paper is based on principles of critical argument. In the research you are reporting, you have raised a question, gathered evidence bearing on the question, and produced an answer. Therefore, the content of your paper should include all the elements needed for clear and fair argument, and its structure should be built on the natural sequence of question, evidence, and answer fitted into a narrative format that reproduces the sequence of steps in the research.

REFERENCES

1. Meinert CL. Clinical trials: design, conduct, and analysis. New York: Oxford University Press; 1986:264-70.
2. Spilker B. Guide to clinical interpretation of data. New York: Raven; 1986:287-91.
3. Center for Drug Evaluation and Research, Food and Drug Administration. Guidelines for the format and content of the clinical and statistical sections of new drug applications. Rockville, Maryland: Food and Drug Administration; 1988.
4. [Anonymous]. Reference 13. Br. Med J. 1985;291:1746.
5. [Huth EJ]. Ethical conduct in authorship and publication. In: CBE Style Manual Committee. CBE style manual: a guide for authors, editors, and publishers in the biological sciences. 5th ed. Bethesda, Maryland: Council of Biology Editors; 1983:1-6.

6

The Case Report

In the 19th century clinical teaching gradually shifted from lectures accounting for disease by theories and classifications more speculative than factually verified to bedside analysis of cases. Pathology increasingly based on histologic methods could demonstrate more clearly how structural changes could cause symptoms and signs. Biochemistry brought methods for detecting evidence of disease long before the eye could see it. With these new capacities for case analysis, the professor and students now could see a patient and add to the facts elicited by history-taking and physical examination such observations as protein in the urine or unusual cells in a blood smear. They could more fruitfully explain the condition of the patient and predict what treatment, if any, might alter the course of the disease.

With these changes in clinical teaching, the case report became a staple in the menu of clinical literature. The findings in a single case were usually not adequate, however, to explain and predict clinical events. Previously described cases with features in common had to be drawn on. The kind of paper that described and interpreted individual cases thus was labeled "a case report with review of the literature".

In the past 3 or 4 decades, great growth in clinical investigation and clinical pharmacology has generated a still rising flood of competing papers. Reports of single cases have become less and less acceptable for publication in major journals, mainly because of their tending to carry relatively little important new information. Four kinds of case reports still occasionally merit publication.

- The unique, or nearly unique, case that appears to represent a previously undescribed syndrome or disease
- The case with an unexpected association of 2 or more diseases or disorders that may represent a previously unsuspected causal relation
- The case representing a new and important variation from an expected pattern: the "outlier" case

69

- The case with an unexpected evolution that suggests a therapeutic or adverse drug effect

The kinds of evidence needed to support conclusions in case reports differ among these varieties. The sections below point out how these differences may call for differing structures to place them properly in the sequence of an argument that adequately supports the report's conclusion.

TYPES OF CASE REPORTS

The Unique Case

A sharp-eyed and well-informed clinician sees a patient with disease manifestations so extraordinary that they cannot be accounted for by known diseases or syndromes. In coming to this judgment the clinician initially relies on personal experience and recall of relevant medical literature. The judgment may be wrong; the clinician may not know enough to be sure that the case does not represent a previously described disease. For most cases of this kind, the best the clinician can do to establish that the case is unique is to search through bibliographic indexes to the clinical literature for previously described cases with identical or similar manifestations. Failure to find such cases may mean that the newly observed case represents a disease or syndrome not described before, but caution is in order. The failure may mean only that the search was not carried far enough or that the disease or syndrome was seen in the past but described in terms we do not use today. Previous observers may have lacked the ability of today's clinician, better equipped conceptually and technically for closer observation, to identify those features that are now apparent. All of these possibilities may have to be considered in the report's Discussion. But even if the Discussion can conclude that the case is unique, a claim such as "discovery of a new syndrome" or "the first report" ought to be eschewed and that distinction conferred not by one's self but by posterity.

The apparently unique case may have some features that give a clue to a specific chemical disorder, perhaps the result of a genetically determined defect in enzyme function. Investigation may identify the defect and establish that the case is unique. Papers describing such cases may need a format like that of research papers.

The Case of an Unexpected Association

Two uncommon diseases or disorders are found in 1 patient. The rarity of each suggests that their occurrence together may reflect some causal relation. The pathogenetic mechanism known or suspected for each may be similar (for example, an immunologic mechanism) and this implies that both may have developed from a single primary defect in the patient. Such case reports may be hard to get accepted for publication even if a review of the literature fails to turn up a similar case. The association may be coincidence. Further study may find a pathogenetic basis for the association through research; then the case report will have to have some elements of a research report. The best evidence the clinician is likely to be able to put forth against coincidental, rather than causal, association is statistical evidence on the odds of a coincidence; this line of argument can usually be developed in the Discussion.

The Case of Important Variation

An adult develops a disease or disorder previously seen only in children. Internists should know its diagnosis must now be included as a possibility for adults; the case report will change a clinical concept. Or a bacterium previously not known to be a pathogen is shown to be the cause of a case of endocarditis. The bacterium is unlikely to be found through routine culture methods. The clinician should know about this new pathogen so that appropriate culture methods can be requested. But such cases should be considered seriously for case reports only if they are likely to really change concept or practice.

The Case of Unexpected Events

Clinical medicine is not an exact science, but we do know much about how many diseases evolve and what effects of drugs can be expected. Clinicians can predict with some confidence what will happen in many cases they see. The unexpected event may be a clue to useful new information. Unexpected improvement in one or more signs or symptoms may be a clue to an unexpected, heretofore unknown beneficial effect of a drug. Unexpected deterioration of a patient's condition or an unexpected laboratory finding may be the clue to an unknown adverse drug effect. Again, unless the suspected causal association can be shown directly—by therapeutic trials in groups of patients, by rechallenge reproducing the beneficial, or the adverse, effect—the case report may be hard to get published. Critical readers of such case reports will at least expect that the postulated causal association be supported by excluding alternative explanations. The author must be sure that all data needed to consider possible alternative explanations are available before work on the report is begun.

Minor Case Reports

Some other varieties of case reports are unlikely to get published in first-rank journals.

The Everyone-Should-Remember Case

Uncommon features turn up in a case of a not uncommon disease. But what clinician will read the report, walk around for the next 10 years with it in his head, and then recall the fact to apply it? A report of the case will be particularly useless if its other presenting features were typical.

The Grand-Rounds Case

An atypical or unusually complex case lends itself to a virtuosic analysis of diagnostic possibilities or a staggeringly encyclopedic recall of relevant literature. But there is, in essence, nothing new about the case. All that can be said about it has been said before, not only in case reports and reviews but also in textbooks and from the lecture stand.

The I-Am-a-Clever-Chap Case

The lucky clinician stumbled onto a valuable clue to diagnosis in the case by accident. Or a new technical device just came on the market and gave the diagnostic answer. Good luck is not synonymous with new thought.

The Variations-on-a-Well-Known-Theme Case

A patient suffers an adverse effect from a drug that is the 10th variant of a widely used class of drugs. The adverse effect has been described for the first 9 drugs. Who did not expect the adverse effect to turn up sooner or later with any new drug of this class?

The Goodness!-Book-of-Medical-World-Records Case

A woman of age 104 develops fungal endocarditis. The last GBMWR similar case was in a man of age 94. The fact of an additional 10 years does not add 10%, or even 1%, to what we need to know for clinical work about fungal endocarditis.

Case reports of these varieties all fail to change, improve, or enlarge how we think about disease—how we interpret signs and symptoms, how we make diagnoses, how we plan treatment. Any one of us may learn something from such cases, but this possibility does not justify their publication. The question the editor faces with reports of such cases is whether they bring enough new information to warrant giving them space. Will they change concept? Will they change practice?

STRUCTURE OF THE CASE REPORT

Even though research papers usually include far more detail than case reports, they are in some ways the easier kind of paper to write. The sequence in a research paper is usually that of a story: what happened one step after another, up to and including analysis of findings. Case reports may have to have a more complex structure than research reports. The case description itself is a story, but 1 or more elements of the whole story developed in the report may have to be out of the chronologic sequence.

Reports of single cases do not arise out of searches for cases unusual enough to merit reporting. The usual sequence runs through 6 or 7 steps. The clinician

- Becomes aware of unusual case features.
- Checks memory, colleagues, textbooks, other sources.
- May get additional case data.
- Tentatively concludes that the case is unique or has unexpected features.
- Decides to write a case report.
- Formally reviews the medical literature.
- Decides whether the case is unique or is adequately unexpected to justify a report.

A case report with a format built on this sequence would be boringly long. The reader would not want to hear all the details of the author's wanderings in mind and body up to the point of writing the paper. The reader needs only 5 elements in the paper.

- A statement of why the case is worth reading about
- An account of the case, with all relevant data
- Discussion of evidence that the case is unique or unexpected
- Possible alternative explanations for case features
- Conclusion, with implications

Although in the early years of medical journalism case reports were often written entirely in narrative style and sequence, they long ago evolved into the present and more efficient conventional format summarized below.

Introduction

The reader caught by the case report's title needs to know right away what there is about the case that justifies the report. Therefore, the Introduction has to compress into 1 paragraph or 2 a concise summary of how the case came to the author's attention, its main features worth reporting, in brief what literature search or other studies were carried out, and why the case is unique or unexpected. Details on the literature search can be presented in the Discussion, where you must assess the strength of the evidence for your conclusion.

Case Description

Usually the clearest way to "tell the story" is to describe the case in a chronologic sequence, starting with the first evidence of the problem that is the focus of the report. The narrative sequence may have to be interrupted with a "flashback". If, for example, the striking feature of the case was discovered when the author first saw the patient but events in the past turned out to be important, a jump back in time may be needed to summarize them adequately. The text that follows such flashbacks must make clear that the story is returning to the present time of the case narrative.

All relevant, but only truly relevant, data should be included. Dates and times that data were collected should be specified as needed for clear sequence and adequate interpretation. A long case description that must include a large number of data can often be presented more clearly if most of the detail is set up in a table with a chronologic structure rather than strung out in the text.

Variations in Format

In most case reports, the Case Description can be followed immediately by the Discussion (see below). Occasionally other elements have to be added at this point. If the case details suggested that the syndrome could be an inherited disorder and the patient's family was studied for evidence of genetic abnormalities, a section on this family study may have to be added after the Case Description, particularly if the family study turned up evidence confirming a genetic disorder. If the initial case observations led to special detailed laboratory studies, the author may have to insert Materials and Methods and Results sections at this point, as in a research report.

Discussion and Conclusions

You will justify the case report in your Introduction, but your argument that the case is unique or unexpected belongs in the Discussion. The features of the case that justify the report are in the case description, but other evidence to support the argument is needed. Such additional evidence may be, in part, drawn from extensive case records in the author's institution. The Mayo Clinic, for example, has such large numbers of well-indexed and detailed case reports that a search of those records can produce convincing evidence that an apparently new syndrome had not been seen there before. Some drug companies keep large, detailed files that are particularly useful in searching for evidence of previously recorded cases of adverse drug effects. Most of the additional evidence is likely to have to come from a thorough search of the medical literature through one of the bibliographic services. But you cannot simply say that "a search of the literature failed to turn up any similar cases". The extent of the search should be summarized: the indexes searched, the search terms used, whether only English-language papers were reviewed, the dates of the literature covered. This information, rarely given in case reports, will help to convince the reader that you have weighed carefully the question of the case's value. The details of the search will also indicate what literature you have not searched; do not forget that in an honest critical argument in science you do not conceal any weaknesses in your evidence. And future students of the problem will be greatly helped by knowing what additional searches of the literature they may find helpful.

Clearly the needs for full and fair argument also apply to other aspects of some case reports. How credible is the evidence in the case description? If the report is of liver injury thought to be due to a drug, is the observed change in serum enzymes adequate evidence of liver injury, or could there be causes in the liver other than the drug? If the evidence for liver injury is abnormalities in histologic sections obtained by liver biopsy, are the findings specific for drug injury or could there be other causes? Counter- or contradictory evidence must be dealt with. If a case is thought to be unique but a review of the literature turns up cases with similarities, this potential counter-evidence must be presented fully and assessed.

Useful discussions of the kinds of evidence needed in case reports on adverse drug effects and drug-drug interactions can be found in many sources. Two notably concise summaries can be found in *Guide to Clinical Interpretation of Data* (1, 2) by Spilker.

As with research papers, a Conclusions section may not be needed at the end of the Discussion if the journal for which the report is being prepared places abstracts or summaries on the title pages of articles. If a formal Conclusions section is not allowed, a concluding paragraph at the end of the Discussion can suggest possibilities for further study or point to implications for clinical practice.

CONCLUSION

The case report, a format less frequently used today than in the past, has to be prepared with as much attention to the elements of critical argument as in other kinds of papers. The format, however, may not follow the sequence of critical argument as closely as research papers do; the various kinds of case reports may call for variations in format.

REFERENCES

1. Spilker B. Presentation of data on adverse reactions (Issue 13). In: Spilker B. Guide to clinical interpretation of data. New York: Raven; 1986:64-5.
2. Spilker B. Drug interactions. In: Spilker B. Guide to clinical interpretation of data. New York: Raven; 1986:245-8.

7

The Review, the Editorial, and the Case-Series Analysis

The medical literature of our time is so large that no one, clinician or investigator, can read more than small fractions of it. All of us must rely heavily on synoptic papers: review articles, scientific editorials, and other kinds of summaries. The review or scientific editorial carefully conceived to answer an important question, based on critical assessment of the literature, and written with a logical structure is a valuable document. It spares clinicians the burden of searching and sifting the literature for reliable guidance in practice. It tells investigators where their field stands on a particular problem and may suggest what directions new research should take. The other kind of synoptic paper likely to be highly useful for clinicians is the case-series analysis based on a critical review of case records in the author's practice or institution as well as on a critical review of the literature.

THE REVIEW

The review appears to differ greatly in structure from the research paper, but a well-conceived and clearly organized review is also built as a critical argument. Most of the overt structure, usually indicated by subheadings that divide parts of the text, usually has to represent the sequence determined by the subject of the review.

The Introduction

A well-conceived review answers a question or closely related questions: What do we know and not know about acute myelocytic leukemia? How should we treat constipation? What are the adverse effects of cimetidine, and what should be done about them clinically? The question should be made clear at the beginning of the review; the title may not be able to reflect fully the review's scope. The stated or implied question usually should not come first; an opening more helpful for the reader would be an indication as to why now is the time to raise the question for review. Thus, a review of adverse effects of cimetidine might start with opening sentences like these:

> Cimetidine has been available in the United States as a prescription drug for over 10 years. Because of its efficacy, it is now among the most frequently prescribed drugs. The variety of adverse effects reported since it was introduced is substantially greater than when the drug was approved by the FDA.

Such an opening justifies reading the review.

Methods

A conclusive and useful review article is likely to emerge from the review process only if the process is deliberate and thorough. (For a detailed tabular summary of the process, see "The Stages of Research Review" in Chapter 1 of *The Integrative Research Review: A Systematic Approach* (1) by Cooper.) The topic of the review must be defined and limited before the review is written. In a properly designed review, these definitions (such as diagnostic criteria) and limits (such as age limits on cases) are decided on before the literature search and selection of case material. A review on acute myelocytic leukemia should tell the reader what definition (diagnostic criteria) the author used for this disease. The reader needs this definition to be assured that he or she shares the author's concept of the disease.

The reader also needs to know how the author decided on the relevance of the reviewed papers for the review (2, 3) and the validity of their data and conclusions. In a review on adverse effects of cimetidine, the drug will not have to be defined, but the reader should be told what criteria have been applied in critically assessing case reports for "possible adverse effect", "probable adverse effect", and "proved adverse effect".

These definitions and limitations are most logically placed immediately after the Introduction, in a Methods section, which serves a function like that of the Materials and Methods section in a research paper.

The Methods section in a review should fully describe the literature search (2–4): the bibliographic indexes and databases searched, limits on years and languages, search terms. A discussion of the search terms may be critically important if there is a chance of disagreement on the diagnostic criteria given for the disease under review. Supposedly synonymous terms for diseases do not necessarily have the same meaning among different readers, and differing terms may in fact refer to the same entity. Reviewers who have gone into literature more than 5 to 10 years old may have to explain how they related present definitions and terms to the older definitions and terms.

Reviews based on papers reporting quantitative data must specify how the data from different studies were integrated for generalizable conclusions (2); this methodologic information is indispensable in a meta-analytic review (5).

The Body of the Review: Sequence of Sections

The sequence of topics (to be represented by sections of text) is usually determined by how the reader will want to look at the overall subject of the review. A descriptive review of a disease will probably follow the conventional sequence found in textbooks; the body of the review is likely to have these main sections.

ETIOLOGY
PATHOGENESIS
MANIFESTATIONS
   Clinical
   Roentgenographic
   Laboratory
DIAGNOSIS
TREATMENT
PROGNOSIS

This sequence has a logical basis. It is a chronologic sequence well known in clinical concept and experience: A disease has a cause (or causes); it develops before it becomes clinically manifest; the patient becomes aware of the disease, and evidences of it are detected by the clinician in history-taking, examination, and special studies; diagnosis also calls for differentiating the patient's disease from other possible diseases; diagnosis leads to treatment; the clinician has to estimate the outcome of treatment.

Other sequences are useful for other kinds of topics. Topics might be presented in order from the general to the particular, or from the components of a system to its integrated structure. A review of adverse effects of a drug might use a sequence proceeding from cellular effects to whole-body or systemic effects.

EFFECTS ON CELLULAR METABOLISM
EFFECTS ON MEMBRANE STRUCTURE AND FUNCTION

EFFECTS ON MYOCARDIAL CONTRACTILITY
HEMODYNAMIC EFFECTS
  Blood-pressure effects
  Congestive heart failure
SYSTEMIC EFFECTS
  Fever
  Dehydration

For another kind of topic the best sequence might run from the most frequent and important problems to the rare, as in a review of hypercalcemia.

METASTATIC MALIGNANCY
PRIMARY HYPERPARATHYROIDISM (and so on to rare causes)
IDIOPATHIC HYPERCALCEMIA OF INFANCY

Whatever kind of sequence is used, the sequence should be made clear by subheadings that correspond to an outline (see Chapter 9).

The Body of the Review: Elements of Critical Argument

As much as the author of a research report, the author of a review is obliged to present all the elements of critical argument needed to support the conclusions reached. If the Methods section suggested above as an early section of the review describes the literature search used in finding papers for assessment, the author supports the credibility of his evidence—the thoroughness of the review.

The author of a carefully prepared review critically assessed the evidence—the papers read—long before beginning to write. Papers not meeting critical standards were rejected as not-useful evidence. Most of these decisions need not be defended in the review. Sage authors of reviews do not promise the reader a "complete review of the world's literature". Certainly all papers widely known and likely to be regarded by readers of the review as having sound data and valid conclusions must be assessed in the review; the author must make clear the basis for any disagreement with their content.

In a thorough and careful review of a topic, the author may have identified certain issues and problems as unresolved and needing further study. These points can be regarded as "implications of evidence not wholly rejected". If they have to do with issues pertinent to the entire subject of the review, they may be best dealt with in a closing section of the review, perhaps designated Discussion. The reader will be able to leave the review with a view of what is *not* known about the subject (6), to accompany the view earlier in the review of what *is* known.

THE EDITORIAL

At one time the term *editorial* indicated that the editorial was indeed a message from the editor. Today the editorial in professional journals also serves other functions. Many editorials are concise critical reviews of scientific topics, particularly topics that represent recent developments. An editorial may comment on an original paper published in the same issue. The commentary editorial may critically assess the paper for its scientific validity, may differently interpret its data. It may put the paper's contribution into perspective with other recently reported findings that could not have been taken into account when the paper was written. It may speculate on what the paper implies for future concepts or practice. Some editorials take political positions; if they cite documentary evidence, they may also have some of the character of a review article.

Structure of the Editorial

Writing an editorial is in some ways more demanding than writing a research paper. The well-known usual format for research papers is a mold into which data and interpretations are set easily; at first glance the editorial has no format. The research paper usually runs to more than 2 printed pages, and an occasional slackening in its thought may not be noticed; the editorial is short, and flawed ideas and sequence stand out. So the task is to fit what you have to say into a tight space and give it a clear and logical sequence.

The task is easier if you keep in mind the steps of critical argument. The editorialist has to settle on the issue, the problem, the question; has to pose one or more possible answers; has to weigh the evidence supporting these answers; has to assess counter-evidence; and has to conclude with an answer. The answer might seem to be that there is no answer and that more information is needed, but that is itself an answer! Even such an answer is reached in a well-reasoned editorial through critical argument.

Table 7.1 illustrates how the structure and sequence of an editorial relate to the elements of critical argument. The length of an editorial and the number of its paragraphs depend on how complex a problem it considers, the amount of evidence it examines, and the number of possible answers. Some editorials might consist of only 1 paragraph and yet carry the main elements of argument in their natural sequence.

Table 7.1. A typical editorial as critical argument

Paragraphs	Elements of critical argument
Introductory paragraph	
Too many people cannot afford good medical care; we need national health insurance.	Statement of the problem; tentative answer
Middle paragraphs	
National health insurance would spread costs among industry and the wealthy.	Evidence in support
Other countries have successful national health insurance.	Evidence in support
Our country cannot afford such insurance in the face of competing demands for defense spending.	Counter-evidence
Closing paragraph	Assessment of all evidence; final
Health is more important than military spending. We should work politically to get top priority for national health insurance.	answer

The opening paragraph states the first element of argument: the problem or question. Most readers will need more than a simple statement of the problem. Experts on the subject will know what new events or new knowledge led to awareness that a problem needs an answer, but most editorials are not written for experts. The question of how much background to include in the lead-in to the statement of the problem is probably best answered as it is for the Introduction to a research paper: The editorialist should assume that readers know less than he does about the topic of the editorial but are well informed on the larger subject field within which the topic lies. The author of an editorial on the usefulness of laparotomy in staging Hodgkin disease should assume that the reader knows less than experts experienced with this use of laparotomy but is well informed in general on recent developments in Hodgkin disease and knows the meaning of "laparotomy" and of "staging". The editorialist can then open with a brief summary of the unsatisfactory methods for staging or with a summary of the current controversy on laparotomy, depending on the actual situation. This stance will guarantee an adequate, if brief, lead-in, while avoiding a long-winded and patronizing ramble to the main point to be made by the end of the introductory paragraph.

Although the middle paragraphs of an editorial carry the evidence considered in the argument, they differ from one of the counterpart sections of a research paper, the Results, in not presenting detailed data. They resemble more the paragraphs in a review article in that the evidence is likely to consist of statements supported by citations to published papers. Usually there is not enough space in an editorial to examine "the credibility of evidence"; the reader can assume that the "credibility" of papers selected for citation in the editorial was "examined" by the editorialist while reading the papers considered as possible references.

The closing paragraph should carry a clear final answer to the question posed in the opening paragraph. If the answer is that there is no answer, so be it. But then the editorialist may wish to suggest possible routes to new evidence that may dispose of the no-answer answer.

A VARIANT OF THE EDITORIAL: THE POSITION PAPER

Some journals have a section for opinion papers the editor prefers not to publish as editorials. The papers may be too long. They may take positions the editor does not wish to seem to support by giving them the authority implied in an editorial. Two such sections are "Sounding Board" of *The New England Journal of Medicine* and "Perspective" of *Annals of Internal Medicine*. Well-written papers of this kind usually have the same structure as a clear and logical editorial, although they may differ widely in their use of documented reasoning and rhetorical heat. The points made above about editorials apply as well to position papers.

THE CASE-SERIES ANALYSIS

A hybrid kind of paper is the so-called "case series", a paper based on retrospective study of case records, usually cases collected in one institution. The cases may be described in short case reports that are followed by such generalizations as can be drawn from these cases and, perhaps, from similar case reports in the literature. In this format the paper has much of the character of the single-case report (see Chapter 6).

Some papers based on analysis of a series of cases are written only after authors define questions they hope to be able to answer from their case data and cases in the literature. If the case review is carried out with enough intellectual rigor (specific questions or hypotheses are posed, entities are defined precisely, control or contrast case-data are sought, data are tested statistically), the format of a research paper (see Chapter 5) is the right structure. A third option in format for the case series is that of the review article. In this approach the cases reviewed at the author's institution are treated as a unit, "my series", as if the cases and their data had already been described in a published paper. The cases are not presented in separate reports, however; rather, the data are combined, usually in tables, along with the data from published case material. The sequence of topics is chosen by one of the criteria discussed for the body of reviews in the first part of this chapter. In the review format, the paper must include a Methods section to state the definitions and limits used in selecting the author's cases, so the case material can be judged critically, as in other kinds of critical reviews.

CONCLUSION

Although review articles usually do not have a structures closely related to the natural sequence of critical argument, they should use its elements of critical argument: clear statement of question, definition of terms and limits of subject, and assessment of counter-evidence as well as supporting evidence.

An editorial has little room in which to deliver its message. The structure must be well worked out, with the right sequence of the elements of critical argument, lest the very brevity of the editorial expose all too clearly any flaws in logic.

The case-series analysis may use the format of the single-case report, the research paper, or the review.

REFERENCES

1. Cooper HM. The integrative research review: a systematic approach. Beverly Hills, California: Sage Publications; 1984:12-4.
2. Mulrow CD. The medical review article: state of the science. Ann Intern Med. 1987;106:485-8.
3. Cooper HM. The integrative research review: a systematic approach. Beverly Hills, California: Sage Publications; 1984:115-6.
4. Huth EJ. Needed: review articles with more scientific rigor. Ann Intern Med. 1987;106:470-1.
5. L'Abbé KA, Detsky AS, O'Rourke K. Meta-analysis in clinical research. Ann Intern Med. 1987;106:224-33.
6. Morgan P. An insider's guide for medical authors and editors. Philadelphia: ISI Press; 1986:62.

8

The Book Review and the Letter-to-the-Editor

Short papers such as book reviews and letters-to-the-editor need as much care in writing as longer papers. There is no room for wasted words and wasted motion. The author must be sure that all that needs to be said is said, but no more. A wrong sequence of ideas will stand out as clearly as a misspelled word. Careful planning before the first draft is started should go into deciding what is to be said and how it should be arranged.

THE BOOK REVIEW

Book reviews are usually invited by the journal editor, who restricts invitations to reviewers qualified to render critical judgments. In spite of this practice, anyone who scans the book review sections of clinical journals is likely to be struck by the indifferent quality of most of the reviews. A dismaying fraction of reviews read like extracts from the dust jacket or the table of contents followed by some remarks about paper and price. The reader is often unsure whether the reviewer has read the book. Such reviews assess a book as if it were sitting alone on a table in the middle of the Sahara. We do not learn whether the book is the first of its kind and, if it is, whether it is needed. We are not told whether it is better or worse than similar books if they exist or for whom it may be valuable. These faults likely stem in part from reviewers' concluding from the short length usually allowed (and specified with invitations) that they need only read or sample the book, jot down a few notes on content as they go, start at the top of the sheet of paper, and write through to the bottom, briefly summarizing the book's content, writing without thinking in advance about why the review is needed and what its structure should be.

A well-thought out, thorough, and carefully written book review has no less structure (Table 8.1) than an editorial. The review opens with a question, usually implied but sometimes stated; it moves to the

Table 8.1. A book review as critical argument

Examples of points made	Elements of critical argument
Introductory paragraph	Question
Five major textbooks of pathology are available. Is this new one better? Were more needed? What need does this book meet?	
Body of review	Evidence
Text has unusual sequence of topics reflecting newer developments. Text is detailed and critical. Text reflects wide experience. Wide range of illustrations, from electron micrographs to fine color photographs of gross lesions.	
Scanty use of references; inadequate index.	Counter-evidence
Concluding paragraph	
In the balance, the virtues outweigh the defects.	Assessment of conflicting evidence
The most up-to-date general text book of pathology; recommended.	Answer

evidence and counter-evidence; and it closes with the answer. The review must develop each step fully within the length allowed by the editor; even the 1-paragraph review should proceed in these steps. Thus, in preparing to write, the reviewer should start by considering what question is going to be answered: Is this book needed? Is the book better than others of its kind? Why did I enjoy the book? For whom is the book written and is it right for that audience? Development of the evidence and counter-evidence will make up the middle sentences of a 1-paragraph review and the middle paragraphs of a longer review. The conclusion, with the answer, may be no longer than a sentence if the reviewer is willing to take a stand.

Most readers of book reviews expect to find the book assessed. An occasional review presents instead an essay of reflections touched off by the book. Such an essay can bring many readers great pleasure if the author has a rich enough view of life, personal or professional, and the skill to get that view down on paper. The author of the essay is obliged, nevertheless, to make clear to readers early on that the essay is moving from the book to other matters and that they should not expect to find an assessment of the book at the end.

THE LETTER-TO-THE-EDITOR

A chapter on letters-to-the-editor in a manual on writing papers for professional journals? People dash off letters all the time;

anyone can write a letter. Yes, but not everyone can get a letter published in a professional journal. Getting a letter published can have valuable consequences. Letters of substance in a major journal like *The Lancet* are indexed in the National Library of Medicine's *Index Medicus*. Pharmaceutical manufacturers and publishers of pharmaceutical newsletters scan letter sections for reports of adverse drug effects. A letter briefly reporting an unusual case may start the author on a fruitful exchange of correspondence with others around the world interested in the same problem. The competition to get letters published is less intense than that with formal reports, but not many journals publish letters-to-the-editor. With this competition letters should be drafted carefully.

Before you write a letter, read closely the journal's requirements. They may be stated at the beginning of the letters section in the journal, on the information-for-authors page, or in both places. If the journal does not set a limit on the length of acceptable letters, the letter writer may be able to estimate the allowable length by scanning the letters section. Most journals do not publish figures or tables with letters. There may be a limit on the number of references allowed.

Most letters are miniature equivalents of research reports, case reports, reviews, or editorials. In writing a comment on a paper that has been published in the journal, that paper should be cited near the beginning of the letter to make clear why the letter was written. The style for letters may call for identifying the paper commented on by giving its authors and title in the text of the letter; other journals may prefer a citation in the text and its reference at the end.

Letter writers should take as much care with their drafts as they would with the much longer text of a paper. Of two letters with the same message, the long, windy, and foggy one is more likely to get rejected; the short, concise, and clear letter is more likely to get accepted.

Before the final draft is typed, count the number of words in the text to make sure the letter does not exceed the allowed length. Like manuscripts of formal papers (see Chapter 15), the letter should be typed double-spaced; some journals will return a single-spaced letter for retyping or simply decide against publishing it.

Permission to publish, with an indication that it covers all authors of the letter, should be included with the submitted letter. Some letters received in editorial offices do not make clear whether they are only for the editor or are submitted for possible publication.

=========================== CONCLUSION ===========================

Book reviews and letters-to-the-editor are short forms of papers, but they should be written with as much attention to structure and sequence as formal scientific papers.

The book review should be built on the elements and sequence of critical argument: the question posed, the evidence considered, and the answer.

A letter-to-the-editor may have the structure, in miniature, of a research report, a case report, a review, or an editorial. As much care in writing is needed as for papers with longer formats. The journal's requirements for letters should be followed. Structure and prose style should be revised for clarity and brevity, and the final version should be prepared in an acceptable form.

9

Writing the First Draft

You are ready to write. If you took the steps suggested in Chapter 1, you have decided on your paper's message, defined its audience, and selected the journal to which you will send the paper. You have completed your search of the literature. You have decided on authorship, looked up the manuscript requirements of the journal, and put together all the raw materials for your paper.

Everyone who does a lot of writing sooner or later finds an effective way to get into the work of writing. And writing is work, even for professionals like novelists and playwrights. Many experienced writers in science use a methodical approach akin to that suggested below; they have found that building up a paper early in systematic steps can cut down sharply on the later work in revising first and later drafts. You will need more than 1 draft; all writers who want to write accurately and clearly revise again and again.

GETTING STARTED

The Research Paper

The Title

The method of writing a paper suggested here is the reverse of summarizing it (see Table 9.1). All journal papers carry titles, and most include abstracts. A title is a highly condensed version of the abstract; an abstract is a highly condensed version of the full text. The title may not tell what the abstract concludes, but it at least conveys what the abstract covers. In condensing the text of a paper into an abstract, the author (or professional abstractor) makes sure that every main element of the paper is represented. In preparing the title, the careful author makes sure that the title carries the irreducible number of terms needed to accurately describe the content of the paper.

Approach the first draft of your paper by first writing a title. Do not worry that it will be the final title; you will probably revise it several times before you finish revising the whole paper.

Table 9.1. Writing a paper as the reverse of summarizing

Summarizing	Writing
Read the full text, jotting down the main point of each paragraph.	Write out an informative title that states the paper's message.
List these points as a kind of outline.	Draft an abstract limited to 150 or 200 words that gives what will be the main point of each section.
From these points draft an abstract that represents the main point of each section.	In an outline state main points, add minor points and other details.
Write a title that succinctly states the paper's message (informative title) or indicates the paper's subject.	Expand the outline into a first draft of text.

Titles are of 2 kinds: indicative or informative. An indicative title tells what the paper is about: "A New Multidrug Regimen for Treatment of Metastatic Breast Cancer". The nature of the content may be amplified by adding a subtitle: "A Cooperative-Group Trial Comparing A New Regimen with Cytolysane". Note that this indicative title and subtitle do not tell what the paper says, but only what the paper covers.

An informative title is more helpful for a start in writing. The informative title tells briefly in sentence form the message of the paper: "A New Multidrug Regimen for Treatment of Metastatic Breast Cancer Produces Greater Survival at One Year than Cytolysane". Yes, this informative title is too long, and some journals might not accept it. But note that it contains words representing most of the elements that will have to be expanded into a full paper. The Introduction will have to tell the reader why "A New . . . Regimen . . ." is needed. The Materials and Methods section will have to give us the details of the ". . . Multidrug Regimen. . ." and of the comparison treatment with ". . . Cytolysane"; it will also have to give the methods for detecting and diagnostically defining ". . .Metastatic Breast Cancer . . .". The Results section will have to tell us the ". . . Survival at One Year . . ." with the ". . .New Multidrug Regimen . . ." and with ". . . Cytolysane" and will have to give the statistical assessment of ". . .Greater Survival . . . Than . . .". You might be able to write some paragraphs of the text right now, but do not start out on a full first draft. Hold to a systematic build-up; completing each step fully will add to your confidence. Move on now to expanding the informative title into an abstract.

The Abstract

Abstracts are also of 2 kinds: informative and indicative. For the research paper or case report you will need an informative abstract that, like the informative title, tells what the paper says. Do not try to write a polished final abstract at this point. The abstract, like the text of the paper, will probably have to be revised many times. In writing the first draft of the abstract, keep to the usual format for research papers. Represent each section of the paper in the abstract by at least 1 sentence, as in this preliminary abstract.

Present multidrug chemotherapy regimens for treatment of metastatic breast cancer and single-drug treatment with cytolysane improve survival to 40% at 1 year. A new multidrug regimen that includes nohistine was compared in a clinical trial with cytolysane. Ten cooperating oncology centers using a standard protocol compared the 2 regimens in 320 women, with random assignment of patients to cytolysane or the new multidrug regimen. The 2 groups were found to be adequately homogeneous with regard to histologic classification and extent of bone and pulmonary metastases. The survival rates at 1 year were 40% for cytolysane and 55% for the new regimen, a statistically significant difference. Adverse effects with the new regimen were more prolonged. These findings are similar to those recently reported from the ECCS group and suggest that the new regimen with nohistine should replace use of cytolysane.

Notice how sentences and parts of sentences in this preliminary abstract represent eventual main points in the sections of the paper.

Introduction	Present multidrug chemotherapy regimens for treatment of metastatic breast cancer and single-drug treatment with cytolysane improve survival to 40% at 1 year. A new multidrug regimen that includes nohistine was compared in a clinical trial with cytolysane.
Materials and Methods	A new multidrug regimen that includes nohistine was compared in a clinical trial with cytolysane. Ten cooperating oncology centers using a standard protocol compared the 2 regimens in 320 women, with random assignment of patients to cytolysane or the new multidrug regimen.
Results	The 2 groups were found to be adequately homogeneous with regard to histologic classification and

extent of bone and pulmonary metastases. The survival rates at 1 year were 40% for cytolysane and 55% for the new regimen, a statistically significant difference. Adverse effects with the new regimen were more prolonged.

Discussion and Conclusion
These findings are similar to those recently reported from the ECCS group and suggest that the new regimen with nohistine should replace use of cytolysane.

By writing the informative title and then a first draft of the abstract, you force yourself to state the central message coming from the research and to put on paper very short versions of some text to be developed in the first draft. After these steps you are ready to outline the proposed full content.

Note that many journals (*Annals of Internal Medicine, British Medical Journal, Journal of General Internal Medicine,* and others) are now requesting structured abstracts (1, 2) for papers reporting prospective trials and for review papers. These abstracts do not differ greatly in content from conventional single-paragraph abstracts but include headings that reflect the main elements of the papers thus represented; each section of these abstracts usually carries more explicit detail; see Figures 9.1 and 9.2 for examples. Abstracts of this type are carried in MEDLINE, and additional examples can be found in that database by searching for references and abstracts from the journals promoting their use. Even if you do not use this structure for the final version of your abstract, this approach can be helpful in that it forces you to represent all important elements of your paper in the abstract; you will be able to revise it later to the conventional format.

The Outline

Do not worry about whether you can prepare a full formal outline with the elements under the main headings being either all phrases or all sentences. Jot down your thoughts as they come. If your first outline is a hybrid, you will not have hampered progress, nor will you have to turn it in to your high-school English teacher. Your first outline might run like this.

INTRODUCTION
-present multidrug regimens and cytolysane good (40% survival at 1 year)
-we need better regimens
-new agent, nohistine, hits at critical point in cell cycle

Study Objective: To determine the efficacy of weekly pulse methotrexate in refractory rheumatoid arthritis.

Design: Randomized, double-blind, placebo-controlled, crossover trial with 13-week treatment periods.

Setting: Referral-based rheumatology clinics at two army medical centers.

Patients: Sequential sample of 15 patients with active definite or classical rheumatoid arthritis and previous treatment failure. Twelve patients (80%) completed the study; 1 patient removed because of drug toxicity (pancytopenia).

Interventions: Nonsteroidal anti-inflammatory drugs and prednisone were continued. Methotrexate 5 mg intramuscular test dose was given at week 1, increased in 5-mg steps to a maximum of 25 mg/wk if clinically needed. Intramuscular saline placebo given in control periods.

Measurements and Main Results: The following results (statistically significant findings, $p<0.05$) were in favor of methotrexate compared with placebo: number of swollen joints 6.9 (5.2, SD) with methotrexate and 19.4 (12.1) with placebo; number of tender joints 12.6 (14.2) and 26.2 (17.0); minutes of morning stiffness 78 (117.8) and 242 (131.6); joint pain (scale 0-10) 1.1 (2.1) and 4.8 (3.1); 50-foot walk (seconds) 16.1 (10.0) and 23.1 (16.3). Laboratory tests showed differences ($p<0.05$) favoring methotrexate including erythrocyte sedimentation rate and IgG. Other tests of physical and laboratory function, including immunologic tests, did not show important differences.

Conclusions: Weekly pulse methotrexate results in improvement of multiple measures of disease activity in refractory rheumatoid arthritis. The mechanism of methotrexate action is uncertain with little evidence of short-term cellular immune suppression. Larger and longer trials are needed to assess the safety of methotrexate for refractory rheumatoid arthritis.

Figure 9.1. Example of a structured abstract representing a clinical trial. (Simulated from Reference 1 with permission of the copyright holder, American College of Physicians.)

    -have substituted nohistine for plustocine in the standard multidrug regimen

    -our controlled clinical trial compared this new multidrug regimen with cytolysane

PATIENTS AND METHODS

    -standard NCI protocol

    -10 cooperating oncology clinics

    -metastatic breast cancer

    -criteria for case selection

Purpose: To ascertain the clinical benefits of digitalis treatment in patients with chronic congestive heart failure and sinus rhythm.

Data Identification: An English-language literature search using MEDLINE (1966-82), *Index Medicus* (1960-65), and bibliographic reviews of textbooks and review articles.

Study Selection: After independent review by three observers, 16 of 736 originally identified articles were selected that specifically addressed the stated purpose.

Data Extraction: Three observers independently assessed studies using explicit methodologic criteria for evaluating the quality of clinical trials

Results of Data Synthesis: Because of deficient selection criteria and study methods in 14 studies, therapeutic efficacy could not be adequately assessed. Two randomized, double-blind, placebo-controlled studies suggested that digitalis could be successfully withdrawn from elderly patients with stable heart failure, whereas patients with an S_3 gallop might benefit from digitalis.

Conclusions: The benefits of digitalis treatment for patients with congestive heart failure and sinus rhythm are not well established. To better delineate the therapeutic benefits of digitalis, investigators must conduct more rigorously designed trials involving patients with newly diagnosed failure and varying degrees of failure.

Figure 9.2.   Example of a structured abstract representing a review article. (Simulated from Reference 2 with permission of the copyright holder, American College of Physicians).

      standard lab, x-ray, and scan studies
      eliminations
   -randomization to new regimen or to cytolysane
   -new regimen: drugs, doses, schedules
   -cytolysane: doses, schedules
   -follow-up: studies and schedules
      lab methods
   -data analysis: statistical methods
RESULTS
   -effects of randomization—good homogeneity between the two groups (except for age, but 90% in each group over 50)—Table 1
   -cytolysane (Table 2): survival 40% at 1 year
   -new regimen (Table 2): survival 55% at 1 year
   -adverse effects (Table 3): nausea and vomiting, hematologic, alopecia, other
DISCUSSION

-difference in 1-year survival real advance
-similar results reported last year by ECCS (see Eur. Cancer Chemoth. Rep.)
-higher adverse-effects rate of cytolysane disturbing
-but recommend cytolysane for general clinical use
-modifying the schedule we used may reduce adverse effects

The outline is not a formal outline; it looks sloppy—none of the usual "I, A, 1" structure, a mixture of phrases, half sentences, full sentences, abbreviations. So what? Your writing is underway!

At this point, you can choose one of three options.

- Clean up this outline, putting all lines into parallel form (for example, converting all entries under each section heading into sentences) and assigning the usual Roman numerals I, II, and so on, to the headings, and A, B, and so on, to the entries. Then begin to write.
- Start writing from the present outline.
- Put the rough outline aside for a few days and then patch some more details into it, perhaps adding mention of more tables (or graphs or illustrations) that will accompany the text and making notations of other papers to be cited. After this patching, sit down to write the first draft.

I like the third option ("Put the ... outline aside ... then patch ... more details into it ..."). Perhaps you will prefer option 1 or 2.

The Case Report

The scheme described for starting to write a research report can also be used for a case report, with the outline built on the format discussed in Chapter 6.

The Review

You probably wrote a tentative outline for your review article before you started the search for relevant papers. With this step you defined and limited the scope of the review and selected the terms to be used in the literature search. You also defined the categories of notations ("histopathology", "epidemiology", "differential diagnosis") to enter on your file cards as you digest the papers you selected from the search.

Before you start the first draft of the text, prepare a second outline, fleshing it out with phrases or sentences on specific data and conclusions you found in the literature. You may also wish to patch in some notes on papers to be cited and tables you have already sketched out. Then you will be ready to write the first draft.

The Editorial

As an editorialist, you can proceed much the same way as with a review article: Decide on the message; draft an outline with attention to the sequence of argument summarized in Chapter 7; read new articles you have found and review the reprints already in your file; then redraft the outline, fleshing it out with short summary phrases or sentences for each intended paragraph.

WRITING THE TEXT OF THE FIRST DRAFT

Each author works out a preferred way to write. With a well-prepared outline and the materials recommended in Chapter 3 (preliminary tables and graphs, photographs, references), you should be able to start a first draft at the beginning and write through to the end. But almost certainly you will not try it at 1 sitting. Even professional writers rarely write for more than 2 or 3 hours at a stretch. Pick the time of the day you prefer. Write in a place where you like to work and lock the door.

Use the writing medium you feel comfortable with. Some authors type first drafts themselves. If you type fairly quickly and can run a word-processing program, you can save quite a bit of money and time in keyboarding the paper yourself. Some authors, the born talkers, like to dictate for transcription by a typist. You may prefer paper and ballpoint pen: paper, to be able to scan back now and then to see how the flow of ideas is running (harder to do with a dictating machine or with jumping through 24-line screens on a monitor); ball point pen because it gives a sharp, good-contrast line, not a weak, fuzzy line like that from a pencil.

Temporary Forms of Citations

A few practical suggestions put to use in your first draft may help you later.

The first has to do with reference citations in the first draft. You will be citing papers in the text to be identified later in the reference list (or "bibliography" or "literature cited") at the end of the paper. Most journals in medicine and the other medical sciences use the Vancouver, or citation-by-reference number, system in which the references in the reference list are numbered in the order in which they are first cited in the text (see Chapter 15). Some journals still use the citation-by-author-and-date system (also known as the Harvard system) in which the paper cited is identified by author name and year of publication. A passage in a journal using the citation-by-reference number system would read thus.

> Most of the acute injuries to the first metatarsal-phalangeal joint in ballet dancers (1) have led, in the patients we have seen, to destruction of the articular cartilages.

The paper cited with "(1)" is a paper written in 1890 by Adams and Giselle; the reference to it is reference number 1 in the references list at the end of the present paper. In the Harvard system the authors' names and the paper's date of publication are used instead of the reference number.

> Most of the acute injuries to the first metatarsal-phalangeal joint in ballet dancers (Adams and Giselle, 1890) have led, in the patients we have seen, to destruction of the articular cartilages.

Even if the journal for which you are preparing your paper uses the citation-by-reference number system, use the Harvard system for the citations in the first and other early drafts. If you assign numbers to references at this early stage, those numbers very likely will have to be changed in successive drafts as you add or delete references. The numbers can be assigned to the references; replace the name-and-date citations when you have finished revising your paper and the final version is prepared. Note that some bibliographic management programs for computers (see mention of *Pro-Cite* and *EndNote* in Chapter 2) can automatically arrange references in the order of their initial citation in the text and then convert author-date citations in text to reference numbers, a real timesaver in preparing the final version of a paper.

If you or your typist is using a word-processing program with a "search-and-replace" function, you can later speed up the finding of citations for replacement of author-and-date citations with reference numbers. In the first draft, place at the beginning of each citation a character not used elsewhere in the text, for example, an asterisk (*).

> Most of the acute injuries to the first metatarsal-phalangeal joint in ballet dancers *(Adams and Giselle, 1890) have led, as in the patients we reported recently *(Copland and del Tredici, 1985), to destruction of the articular cartilages.

You, or your typist, will be able to use the asterisk as the character to be searched for in using the "search-and-replace" function; this function will move you rapidly through the text to each citation when you have to revise citations in successive drafts, including the final version. The asterisk will, of course, have to be removed from the final version as it is completed.

Line Numbering to Facilitate Identification of Text

When coauthors, especially coauthors in 2 or more locations, have to exchange criticisms of intermediate drafts, they may have to refer to many different locations in the text. "Fred, I think you better take out those 2 sentences of lines 5 through 11 in paragraph 2 on page 7". You turn to page 7 and wonder whether he means lines 5 through 11 in the top paragraph (because it began on the preceding page) or lines 5 through 11 in the first full paragraph. In either case you have to count down the lines to get to the part of the text he is referring to.

If your word-processing program has a line-numbering function, it can automatically place line numbers in the left margin at the beginning of successive lines. The function may offer the option of numbering lines continuously through the entire text or starting numbering on each page.

```
123   and in this kind of case, we find that total extirpation offers the
124   best chance for complete relief from pain and the smallest
125   number of potential post-operative complications. This is not,
126   however, the experience of the group at the
1     and in this kind of case, we find that total extirpation offers the
2     best chance for complete relief from pain and the smallest
3     number of potential post-operative complications. This is not,
4     however, the experience of the group at the
```

Continuous line numbering through all pages offers the easiest device for quick reference to a part of the text. You may prefer the renumbering on each page if each section of the paper is maintained as a separate file on your diskette.

Identifying Drafts

As you go on from the first draft and revise the paper in successive drafts, you must be sure that you do not mix up pages from different drafts. Therefore it is wise to mark each page of a draft with a brief note of the number of the draft, the page number, and the date. If the drafts are being prepared with a word-processing program, such notes can be easily and automatically placed on each page with its headers-and-footers function. Such headers for the second draft might look like this at the top of a page in the Materials and Methods section.

[Nohistine Regimen, 2nd draft]   [14 July 88]
and the patients were alternately assigned to the nohistine group or the cytolysane group and then . . .

If you work on the first and successive drafts of the text from beginning to end, you can number the pages successively. If you write sections out of order (see below, "Writer's Block") or the various sections are worked on by different coauthors and the text is produced with a word-processing program, you may wish to maintain each section as a separate file with its own sequence of page numbers. The sections will, of course, eventually be assembled in their right order and the pages numbered from the beginning.

WRITER'S BLOCK

What if you sit down to write and cannot get started? You chew your nails, you stare out the window, you get up for a coffee, you decide to shop for groceries. You have "writer's block". A diagnosis is not much help without treatment. Fortunately, the syndrome is treatable. Professional writers usually work out a treatment—they, too, often find writing painful. You can find a treatment that suits you.

Two good discussions of writer's block (3, 4) point out that blocks come basically from 3 related causes. Writing is your work laid out plain for you and others to see. You dislike judgment by others of your work and, hence, of yourself. You are burdened by your own internal self-criticism (Freud's "super-ego") developed unconsciously to try to spare yourself the pain of being harshly judged by others and even punished. Different solutions are available, some of which are akin to what is suggested earlier in this chapter, building from a title to an outline.

One solution is called "nonstops (kitchen-sinking it)," a method (1) in which you repeatedly sit down and write nonstop for a fixed but short time, say 15 minutes, about any aspect of your topic. These bits can be revised and pieced together for a first draft that may be crude but is a start.

Another solution (2) is called "satisficing". You satisfy yourself by sacrificing the ideal of a flawless first draft. You make up your mind to get a first draft down on paper no matter how defective it looks.

Some medical authors start on the first draft by writing sections on the material they already know best: Materials and Methods, Results. They had to prepare a research protocol, perhaps for a grant proposal, when they designed their study; the protocol may be readily expanded (or condensed) to text for Materials and Methods. They have preliminary tables of data with statistical analyses, which is why they decided they were ready to write; the Results will be little more than a text summary of those data.

Keep in mind that a first draft is a first draft. It will not go to the editor, the manuscript consultants, or the printer. Do not fear criticism; learn to welcome criticism of a first draft, a second draft, a fifth draft. Embrace the fact that a first draft will have intellectual faults and flaws in prose style. You will be able to correct these later.

WHAT NEXT?

The first draft should not be the final draft. A few fine writers publish what they write in the first draft, but most go through many drafts. A close acquaintance of Dr Karl Menninger, the eminent psychiatrist who has written some classics in psychiatry for the general reader, told me that each of his books went through 10 manuscript versions. Most of the persons I know in academic medicine who have published many research papers always go through at least 4 drafts and usually 5.

CONCLUSION

Just as the full text of a paper can be condensed into an abstract and then into a title, so can a paper be developed in the reverse direction. An informative title, one that states the paper's main message, can be expanded first to an abstract, which can be expanded to an outline from which the first draft can be written. Difficulties in getting started in writing the first draft, or writer's block, can be overcome; a first draft is only a first draft, and subsequent drafts will take care of its inevitable defects.

REFERENCES

1.　Ad hoc working group for critical appraisal of the medical literature. A proposal for more informative abstracts of clinical articles. Ann Intern Med. 1987;106:598-604.
2.　Mulrow CD, Thacker SB, Pugh JA. A proposal for more informative abstracts of review articles. Ann Intern Med. 1988;108:613-5.
3.　Mack K, Skjei E. Overcoming writing blocks. Los Angeles: JP Tarcher; 1979. Distributed by St Martin's Press, New York.

4. Flower L. Understanding your own writing process. In: Flower L. Problem-solving strategies for writing. 2nd ed. San Diego: Harcourt Brace Jovanovich; 1985:21-42.

10

Revising Content and Structure

Most experienced authors expect to work through no less than 2 drafts of a paper before the final version. Indeed, the more experienced you become, the more you continue to see defects that need to be corrected, even in the third and fourth drafts. Some authors revise the content and structure of a paper and its prose style at the same time, but it is more efficient to concentrate on content and structure first. Why polish the prose style of text you may discard later?

STEPS IN REVISION

Table 10.1 lists a sequence you might like to follow in revising your paper. This sequence may not be followed fully in some circumstances. Short papers, such as "brief reports", editorials, book reviews, and letters-to-the-editor, might be readily written and revised in 3 drafts. If you have coauthors, 1 or more may not be able to respond quickly with suggestions for revising the second, or a later, draft because of a trip abroad or an illness. You should insist with coauthors, however, on a definite schedule for revision and hold them to it.

Most first drafts are not good enough for review by coauthors or colleagues. You should revise the first draft's content and structure before you ask someone else to take time to read it. Unless you have a rapidly approaching deadline, put the first draft aside for a week or 2 before you look at it again. The labor of writing the first draft often drains the energy you need for looking critically at what you have written and for preparing the second draft.

All coauthors should be expected to read at least 1 of the early drafts and recommend revisions of content and structure. If a coauthor has had only a small part in the work leading up to the first draft, he or she may be excused from reading every draft. All coauthors must be expected, however, to read and approve the final version that will be submitted to the journal; see "Criteria for Authorship" near the be-

Table 10.1. A sequence for revising content and structure

Write the first draft
  Hold the first draft 1 or 2 weeks, then revise content for sequence and structure
Work on the second draft
  Distribute copies to coauthors or to colleagues willing to offer thorough criticism
  Read this draft and make notes on revisions needed
  Get written recommendations for revision from coauthors and other colleagues
Work on the third draft: same procedure as for the second
Work on later drafts
  Confine readings to coauthors
  Continue to concentrate on structure and sequence of content
  When satisfied with content, move to revising for prose structure and style

ginning of Chapter 3 and "Principle 2" in Appendix 3. Any coauthors who foresee an obstacle to reading the final version should authorize the responsible author to submit the paper without his or her final approval, but only after giving the responsible author a statement of approval of the last draft read.

Familiarity with the content of a paper often dulls the eye. Sharper critics of your paper than your coauthors may be colleagues aware of, but not familiar with, the research you are reporting, the case you are describing, or the literature you are reviewing. Someone who does not understand every detail in a paper may be better able than the authors to see what is not clear, is out of sequence, or deviates from the subject. Pick an honest friend, not one who will pat you on the back and simply tell you how good your paper is.

AIMS IN REVISION

By the time you finish writing the first draft, you have been laboring so long in the work it represents that nausea may sweep over you when you sit down to revise. You may feel that you have done your job, that this is what you have to say, and that the reader is going to be impressed with your paper. But you have not finished your work until you have gone as far as you can to make sure:

- That you have said all that has to be said, and no more than is needed, for your message.
- That all elements of your paper are in the right sequence and every detail is clear to other readers.

Your job now is to shift from being solely a researcher or a reviewer of the literature toward being as sharp a critic of your paper as the editor of the journal to which you will send it and as those who are likely to read it for the editor, including the peer reviewers.

Editors and reviewers consider various questions in sizing up a paper. You can criticize your own paper just as sharply if you consider the same questions in reading your first and subsequent drafts. Many of these questions apply to any kind of paper.

The Title

Is the title accurate, succinct, and effective? Not all elements of the paper need be represented in the title, only those that make up the main message. For a paper that reports a double-blind trial of penicillamine for treatment of rheumatoid arthritis in which gold-salt therapy was the contrast (control) treatment, the title might simply be "Penicillamine Treatment of Rheumatoid Arthritis". But note that in some online bibliographic searches, only titles may be searched for key terms. Hence for the searcher looking for all papers with content about gold therapy a better title would be "Penicillamine or Gold Therapy for the Treatment of Rheumatoid Arthritis". The structure of the study could be described in a subtitle, "A Double-Blind Trial", if the journal allows subtitles.

Although well-edited journals do not allow unexplained abbreviations in titles, the use of abbreviations in online bibliographic searches now justifies including widely known abbreviations in titles after the full terms they represent, for example, "Peripheral Neuropathy from Infection with the Human Immunodeficiency Virus (HIV)".

Titles are more effective, more likely to catch the scanner's eye, when they begin with a key word; avoid nonspecific openings like "A Study of . . .", "An Investigation into . . .", "A Review of . . .", or "A Case Report of . . .". If the journal does not use subtitles, it may accept titles with subordinate elements after a colon: "Aspirin for Treatment of Headache: A Double-Blind Study with Placebo Control".

The Abstract

Does the abstract represent the content of all the main sections of the paper, within the length allowed by the journal? If you worked up to your first draft by preparing an abstract before the outline, the abstract may contain all that it should. Be sure that the abstract summarizes the Introduction, the central text of the paper, and the Conclusions. If the paper is reporting research, the central text to be represented includes the study design, experimental subjects (animals, human volunteers, patients), methods, results, and interpretations (Discussion). The abstract of a case report should briefly characterize the patient as well as the unusual features of the case. A review article usually has to be represented by an indicative abstract, one that tells what the review is about, rather than an informative abstract, one that represents the content in highly condensed form.

The Introduction

Does the Introduction set the stage adequately but concisely for the main question considered, or for the hypothesis tested, in the paper? Is that question or hypothesis made clear by the end of the Introduction? Research is undertaken because a question has to be answered. Is a new antibiotic a better treatment for pneumonia? Is a certain drug the cause of some cases of congenital blindness? Can bedsores be prevented by twice-daily massage of vulnerable areas of skin? The Introduction in papers reporting the studies designed to answer these questions should describe what knowledge and lack of knowledge, or new information, led to the posing of these questions: the recent treatment of pneumonia up to the availability of the new antibiotic; unusual numbers of cases of congenital blindness being reported; dissatisfaction with present treatment of bedsores. But the Introduction should not explain what is already known to readers who can understand all the terms in the title: *pneumonia, congenital blindness*, or *bedsores* need not be defined for most readers in one of the healthcare professions or their textbook descriptions summarized.

When your readers have come to the end of the Introduction, they should know why the research was prepared and carried out, what questions the review article is setting out to answer, or why the case is worth reporting. The opening paragraph of an editorial or a book review should just as clearly indicate where you are going to carry the reader in the rest of the paper.

The Main Text

Is all of the rest of the text in the right sequence? Even though you wrote your first draft from an outline, you may have strayed from the outlined sequence in your rush to get the first draft written. Or the sequence may have been defective.

Because most research papers are cast in the conventional format of Introduction, Materials and Methods, Results, and Discussion, they are less likely to have a defective sequence than papers in less rigid formats. But the careful author of a research paper will make sure that the sequence is right in each of its sections. The description of the study (Materials and Methods) should usually follow the sequence in which the research was planned and carried out. The Results section should usually proceed from the findings or comparisons directly related to the main message of the paper to any subordinate findings. The Discussion should proceed from the apparent answer to the question posed in the Introduction to considering, as necessary, the validity of the evidence supporting this main conclusion, including evidence from other studies, to considering counter-evidence, and on to resolving conflicts in evidence. If lesser conclusions also have to be developed, they should follow the same sequence. But the main conclusion should be taken up first, with lesser conclusions following. Any implications of the study's conclusions, such as needs for further research or changes in diagnosis or treatment, should come at the end of the Discussion.

Papers without a formal structure as obvious as that of the research paper are more likely to show defects in sequence. If you are writing a case report, review article, editorial, or book review, you may wish to reread the appropriate chapters from among Chapters 5 to 8 before you look at your first draft for possible problems in sequence.

Is all of the text really needed or can some be discarded? Does any of the text repeat information found elsewhere in the paper? Most first drafts, and even many finished papers, are overwritten. Introductions explain more than most readers attracted by a paper's title need to know. Results sections present data that have little or nothing to do with the main message of the paper. Discussions open with a restatement of points made in the Introduction. Or they run on with speculations about the study's findings that go far beyond hypotheses that can be tested in the near future. In shorter papers like editorials and book reviews, authors may succumb to airing pet peeves that break the line of argument.

Does your first draft have paragraphs that can be dropped? You may be reluctant to leave out any text when you have sweated so hard in getting through the first draft, but remember that the reader will not thank you for unneeded text. The reader will thank you for a paper that gets to the point, sticks to it, and presents only content directly relevant to that point.

Is any needed content missing? Although many papers are overwritten, at least in early drafts, some needed content may be forgotten in writing the first draft. The outline was defective, or your writing was interrupted and then resumed without your looking at the preceding text. Such gaps will probably jump to your attention when you read the first draft through.

Do data in the text agree with data in the tables? If you wrote the first draft with the tables before you, data in the text and the tables should agree. Your coauthors are likely to pick up discrepancies and know which figures are correct, but other reviewers may not know which of a pair of discrepant figures is correct.

Have you cited unnecessary references? Have you omitted needed references? Careful reviewers of your second draft may note redundant or unneeded references. Cite only the references needed to support key statements in the text. If you must refer to a textbook description of a disease so that you do not have to describe the disease, refer to 1 or 2 complete and reliable sources; do not give an additional 4 or 5 to show that you are familiar with all of the related literature. Be sure, too, that all statements needing support with references cite them. The Materials and Methods section of a research paper, for example, should include enough detail to enable another investigator to repeat your study, but methods previously described need be represented only by cited references.

Can you omit any of the tables or illustrations? As you read the first draft, you may see that some of the data you collected have little to do with the point of the paper. Be no less willing to drop unneeded tables than unneeded text. Illustrations should be limited to those that will show what cannot be conveyed in text. If a case report, for example, mentions an electrocardiographic tracing that confirms a diagnosis of acute myocardial infarction, do not illustrate the tracing. The reader should be willing to take your word that the tracing was diagnostic.

THE MECHANICS OF REVISION

You have read your first draft with these questions in mind. You have written notes in the margin on what to do in the second draft, notes such as "delete", "move to discussion", "cut 2 references", "combine Tables 1 and 2". You are ready to prepare the second draft. This is the time to consider some practical steps that may simplify preparing the second and subsequent drafts.

Additional Copies

If your drafts are being typed on a typewriter, make 2 or 3 copies of your first draft. You will probably need one copy to cut up for pasting of some paragraphs or parts of paragraphs in new locations for better sequence. Revising does not always call for complete rewriting of text, and each paragraph that can be moved intact is less writing for you and clearer copy for the typist. You should retain one copy of the first draft as a safeguard against accidentally losing 1 or more paragraphs in your cut-and-paste work. And sometimes parts of your first draft may prove to be better than their counterparts in the fourth draft.

With a word processor you may not have to make additional paper copies at this stage because paragraphs and other segments of text are readily moved with the block-move function. Be careful, however, to keep backup files of each draft.

Draft Numbers and Dates

Unless you dated each page and identified the number of the draft as it was completed, you may subsequently mix up similar pages of different drafts. See "Identifying Drafts" near the end of Chapter 9. With word-processing programs such notations can be made as headers or footers that will clearly identify on every page of a draft its sequence among drafts and its date.

Revision by Coauthors

If your coauthors believe entire paragraphs or pages need to be revised for content or sequence, they should prepare new drafts of those pages so that they leave no question as to the changes they recommend. Their new pages should carry their initials and dates of revision to distinguish them clearly from your drafts.

CONCLUSION

The first task in revision is reworking the first and subsequent drafts to be sure that the paper says no more than it must say, that it says all that it should say, and that all of its content is in the right sequence. Revision along these lines should continue until every coauthor or other reviewer agrees that the content and its sequence cannot be improved. Probably at least 3 drafts will be needed; a long and complex paper may have to go through many more drafts. Once you and your coauthors or colleague-reviewers are satisfied with the content of the paper, you can begin to revise it in details of prose structure and style.

11

Revising Prose Structure and Style

Whether a paper gets published depends far more on what it has to say than on the quality of its prose. If the editor sees the paper as important for the journal's audience, minor defects in style are not likely to block its getting into print. But the paper with a less important message may sit in the editor's mind between acceptance and rejection; if the paper is cast in turgid and unclear prose, these qualities may tilt the balance to rejection. So as you bring your paper up to the final version, you must look closely at how it says what it has to say. You must revise for the inevitable faults in the structure and style of your prose.

Revising prose is hard work. Few of us can write first drafts in fluent, clear, and flawless prose. The problems in content and its sequence get worked over in early drafts. The time comes when you must make sure that what you have to say is said with the 5 qualities of good scientific prose: fluency, clarity, accuracy, economy, and grace.

FLUENCY

Fluent prose runs along as the reader expects it to run; the reader is not jarred by defects that interrupt the line of thought. Fluency depends in part on sentence structures and other details in style. It depends more on the connections between paragraphs and the sequence of thought within paragraphs (Table 11.1).

CLARITY

Clarity is the second quality of good scientific prose. The devices that produce fluency can also foster clarity (see Table 11.1). But other details in prose style affect clarity. The English essayist George Orwell made the point in a memorable epigram (1): "Good prose is like a window pane". What you have to say should not be obscured by how

Table 11.1. The five qualities of good scientific prose

Fluency
> Forward-moving sequence of thought
>> Elements of critical argument in the right sequence (see Chapters 4 to 8)
>> Narrative sequence in the right order (see Chapters 4 and 5)
> Paragraphs connected
> Forward-moving line of thought in each paragraph
> No slowing or interruptions from obvious devices of style; from unclear, sluggish, excessively long sentences; or from graceless terms

Clarity
> Clear structure and movement of content; see "Forward-moving sequence of thought" under "Fluency" above
> Clear connections of paragraphs
> Intent of each paragraph clear at its outset; each paragraph limited to that intent; no paragraph unclear because it includes more than needed for that intent
> Clear use of modifiers
> Unambiguous antecedents for pronouns
> Right choices of verb tenses for the sequences of actions

Accuracy
> Correct choice of words and terms
> No misspelled words
> Right verb tenses for discontinuity or continuity of action

Economy
> No unneeded words or phrases
> Verbs rather than abstract nouns
> No unneeded clauses

Grace
> The qualities of fluency, clarity, accuracy, and economy
> Correct sex references
> Humane terms and phrases
> Standard formal usage

you say it. Another Englishman, T E Lawrence (2), put it this way: "Prose is bad when people stop to look at it". Errors or crudities in your prose are like blobs of mud on Orwell's window pane; they come between the reader and the message. Obvious devices in prose style have the same effect; the reader pauses, eye caught by the device and mind diverted from the message.

ACCURACY

Accuracy is the third and perhaps most valuable quality of good scientific prose. Accuracy depends in part on clarity but needs more. Fastidious attention to accuracy extends beyond verifying calculations and the other steps taken to validate evidence. You must be sure that the words you choose are the right and best words for the intended meaning. You must be sure that you do not convey a wrong meaning through misspelled words.

ECONOMY

Economy is the fourth quality of good scientific prose. Journal publication is expensive; editors have to make efficient use of their pages. The hard-working professional has little time to read; economical prose is usually much clearer than wordy prose. Cast out words not needed, words that slow the reader.

GRACE

What is graceful prose? The man or woman you call "graceful" goes beyond politeness to act with an eye to the needs and comfort of others, striving to make easier and more pleasant even the minor contacts of daily life. The qualities of graceful prose include fluency, clarity, accuracy, and economy; graceful prose does not irritate or bore readers and thus distract them from the message. Graceful prose guides readers along a line of thought; paragraphs are linked so that the reader does not start a new paragraph wondering how it relates to the one just finished. Graceful prose does not try to impress the reader with erudition, status, or clever stunts in style. Graceful prose does not offend sensitive readers with inhumane statement. All that the writer of graceful prose strives to do is done to serve the reader.

YOUR ATTITUDE TOWARD REVISING PROSE STYLE

The task of revising may bring back painful memories, those restless hours with the burdens imposed by fussy English teachers. What was the need for that nitpicking about dangling participles and ambiguous antecedents? We were not convincingly told then that we are judged not only by what we say but how we say it. Samuel Wesley (3) knew it: "Style is the dress of thought." You would not go out in dirty clothes to look for a job. Nor should you write a paper that must make its way on its message alone. If how you present that message offends the reader (the editor, the manuscript reviewer), the message may not get into print.

Revising your prose will be hard work if you have not been in the habit of thinking about the countless details that make up style. But the more you revise your writing, the more quickly you come to see faults. Possibilities for revision are endless. Many papers that editors would regard as well written can be tightened up further when worked over by a copy editor, shortened by at least 5 to 10%. I shall never forget having struggled to condense a letter-to-the-editor for *The Lancet* from 500 words to 250 words only to find that the copy editor cut it down to 225 without dropping any of its message. Training yourself in how to revise calls for becoming aware of what defects to expect to find, looking for them, and learning how to correct them.

A SCHEME FOR REVISING PROSE STYLE

In revising early drafts for better content and its sequence, you first worked on the big defects: missing content, unneeded content, wrong sequence. In later stages of revision you take care of smaller problems such as unneeded citations and errors in numerical data.

Revising your paper to improve its prose structure and style should also start with the larger elements of prose (paragraphs) and then move to dealing with the smaller elements (sentences, phrases, words). Improving paragraph divisions and linkages may call for rewriting entire sentences or for new sentences; these sentences themselves could turn out to have defects in some of their details.

1. Look at your paragraphs for length in relation to their content. Divide excessively long paragraphs at logical points for new divisions.
2. Look at how the paragraphs are connected. Consider how the closing sentence of a paragraph and the first sentence of the next might link them for clearer sequence. Revise the sentences to make the linkage clear.
3. Check each paragraph to see whether its internal sequence moves along a clear line of thought.
4. Look at the lengths and structures of sentences in each paragraph. Do too many have the same length and structure? Should you divide some sentences, or join some? Should some structures be inverted for variety in rhythm and for different emphasis?
5. Within each sentence are modifiers placed properly? Are any modifiers not needed? Are the antecedents of pronouns unambiguous? Does each verb have the right tense to make clear the sequence of actions?
6. Have you chosen the right word at each point for what you mean to say? Does each verb have the right tense to state accurately discontinuity or continuity of action? Are any words misspelled?

Table 11.2. A sequence for revising prose structure and style

Review and revise large elements first
  Paragraph lengths
  Connections of paragraphs
  Internal sequence of each paragraph
Move to sentences, the elements of paragraphs
  Sentence lengths
  Sentence varieties
Move to elements of sentences
  Clauses and phrases
  Modifiers
  Word choices
Read the revised text aloud to catch defects you overlooked in the steps above

7. Prune out all unneeded words. Can you tighten up your text by converting some abstract nouns to verbs? Can you replace any clauses by phrases?

8. Make sure that all sex references are accurate. Prune out slang, dehumanizing terms, and other details that make for graceless prose.

9. For the last step, read the paper aloud. You may become aware of defects such as weak paragraph links that interrupt the paper's flow. If you find yourself breathless or stumbling, you may not have gone far enough with shortening sentences or rebuilding their structure. You may find overlooked slang or unintended rhymes. Your fifth draft may have to go into a sixth.

Table 11.2 summarizes this sequence.

REVISING FOR FLUENCY

Paragraph Length, Connections, and Structure

What is a paragraph? Not only a unit of thought. A word is a unit of thought; a sentence is a unit of thought. Perhaps I can define a paragraph by describing what it does for the reader. Imagine how a paper would strike you if it had no paragraphs or text headings; it would be a massive, intimidating block of words broken only into columns. Would you have the courage to start reading it? The paper has the same content whether it is cut into paragraphs or not. Why is it less intimidating when paragraphed?

Reading a paragraphed paper is like being taken on a tour of the author's garden. We come to the gate and pause while we are told what kind of garden we are about to visit—the introduction. Then we step through the gate and pause by the tool shed to look at a map of the garden—a paragraph on study design. We step inside and pause while the author describes the tools—a paragraph on methods. At each paragraph the reader pauses while the author makes a point out of the details represented by the sentences. The end of the paragraph means that the author is now moving the reader to the next paragraph to see a new point or set of closely related points developed. The paragraph indentations are polite signals for pauses and progress along the author's argument. An English student of prose style, Herbert Read (4), sums up this function of the paragraph thus: "The paragraph is a device of punctuation".

Paragraph Length

An Alice-in-Wonderland rule for paragraph length might be "Just long enough and not too long". A paragraph should come to its close when what it promised at or near its beginning has been delivered. The length of a paragraph may have been determined when its topic was laid down in the first-draft outline. But when you finish the paragraph, it runs to 2 pages typed double-spaced. Is this too long? Probably. No authority can give you a firm rule on paragraph length, but paragraphs of more than 25 typed lines are likely to be too long. Paragraphs of fewer than 5 or 6 lines tend to have too little development of a topic or represent what is really a fragment of either adjacent paragraph.

An excessively long paragraph often can be broken into 2 shorter paragraphs by finding a logical way to divide its topic into 2 related subtopics. A review of adverse effects of a drug includes a paragraph on cardiovascular effects; the paragraph runs on for 30 typewritten lines. Perhaps the topic "cardiovascular effects" can be divided into the subtopics "effects on the heart" and "effects on peripheral circulation". If so, break this long paragraph into 2 paragraphs, each carrying 1 of the 2 subtopics. Breaking a long paragraph into 2 will probably call for more than simple division; you may have to write new opening and closing sentences to provide the right connections.

Paragraph Connections

Steady movement, a quality of fluent and graceful prose, should run through an entire paper. The stopping points at ends of paragraphs and ends of sections should not really be stops but pauses that close out units of thought and signal to the reader that a new start is about to be made. The signal comes in part from the format itself. A new section in a paper is signaled by a heading such as Materials and Methods. The start of a new paragraph is signaled by the paragraph indentation. But if you are to maintain that graceful quality of motion at the paragraph pauses, each new paragraph must seem to be linked to that preceding it.

One succinct definition (2) of the right structure for a paragraph advises that it ". . . should . . . have a start, a climax, couplings fore and aft, a finish." "Couplings fore and aft" means that the sentence closing a paragraph (the "coupling aft") should set up the basis for the starting sentence (the "coupling fore") of the following paragraph. One device for this linkage is stating in the last sentence of a paragraph a word or phrase that is central to the line of thought and can be stated again in the same or a similar form in the first sentence of the following paragraph. Note that I have linked the paragraph you are reading to the one above by this device. The paragraph above concluded that a ". . . new paragraph must seem to be linked to that preceding it". The paragraph you are reading opens with a sentence that includes the phrase "couplings fore and aft", a variation on "links" and "linkage". This device should not be so clumsy that you force the reader to see it, but it should be effective enough to show that a new paragraph is about to carry you from a point just developed in the preceding paragraph into a new but logically related point.

The "coupling fore" should not be so far down in the top half of the paragraph that the reader proceeds without a sense of linkage. Consider the sequence of paragraphs in a review on adverse effects of a drug. In your outline you arranged the sequence so that it runs from the most important adverse effects to the least important. The paragraph on the important cardiovascular adverse effects ends as shown below and is followed by a new paragraph.

> . . . and these cardiovascular effects are severe enough in some patients to make pleomycin an antibiotic not to be used in cases complicated by ischemic heart disease.
>
> Brown and Black (13) found two cases of occult gastrointestinal bleeding among 79 patients treated for mixed-flora bacterial pneumonias. A similar rate has been reported by White and Gray (14). A much lower rate was found in a review of 153 cases (15) at the Cheselden Hospital . . ."

The reader goes 3 sentences into the second paragraph without finding out that it is concerned with hematologic adverse effects. The opening sentence, "Brown and Black . . ." might be taken to imply a shift from cardiovascular effects to another topic, but "occult . . . bleeding" might also be read as a link into discussion of vascular effects in more detail. Why not provide a clear link?

> . . . cardiovascular effects are severe enough in some patients to make pleomycin an antibiotic not to be used in cases complicated by ischemic heart disease.
>   Hematologic effects can be serious enough in patients with peptic ulcer to justify . . .

Opening the new paragraph with "Hematologic effects" (a parallel to "cardiovascular effects") provides a linkage that tells the reader that you have finished discussing cardiovascular effects. After the brief mental pause signaled by the paragraph indentation, the reader knows without doubt that the author has moved into hematologic effects. The reader is not left uncertain as to where the line of the paper is moving.

Paragraph Structure

Sentences have structure and papers have structure; they need structure if readers are to grasp without too much work what they have to say. Paragraphs need structure too. The start of a paragraph should seem to be aimed toward a point; through the middle the reader should sense that the paragraph is moving to that point; at its close the point should have been reached. How you give the reader this sense of movement from a start through mid-ground to a finish depends on the subject of the paragraph.

Paragraph as Narrative.   Some paragraphs need the structure of narrative. A paragraph that serves as the introduction to a research paper is like a little story. It starts at a point in the past when some question emerged and suggested need for the research. We are moved along in time with a brief review of the answers to the question that came from the research efforts of others. The paragraph then brings us up close to the present by pointing out that these answers have not adequately answered the question. It concludes at the present by briefly announcing the authors' just-completed research that is the topic in detail of the rest of the paper. This paragraph is a narrative; it tells a story that moves forward through time.

Paragraphs in the case history that makes up the central part of a case report invariably have to describe details in a narrative sequence: the complaint, the hospital stay, death or discharge. One paragraph might suffice to carry the elements of this narrative if the case history is short. More often the successive parts of the story are told in separate paragraphs. Paragraph 1 gives the initial complaint, the admission history, and examination findings; paragraph 2 summarizes the initial laboratory data; paragraph 3 summarizes the clinical course in the hospital; and paragraph 4 describes the autopsy findings, first the gross findings at the autopsy and then the histologic findings issued later. The case history carries the story in 4 paragraphs but each has its own narrative sequence.

Paragraph as Argument. The narrative sequence may be inappropriate when a paragraph needs the structure of argument (see Chapter 4). A paragraph in a review of adverse effects of alcohol in various organ systems discusses effects on the heart. The paragraph starts at the present, making clear that the heart and the question of adverse effects are the subject, and then moves to consider studies that have shown adverse effects. These studies are not presented in chronologic sequence but in a sequence of increasingly convincing evidence. Next the paragraph assesses studies that have not shown adverse effects, again in a sequence of increasing strength of evidence, and moves on to weigh finally the conflicting evidence. The paragraph closes, as argument should, with the answer that emerges from the evidence weighed.

In reviewing your paragraphs for possible revision, pay heed to whether each paragraph has internal sequence and whether this sequence gives a sense of movement. Each paragraph should start, move along a line, and stop. The very short paragraph does not seem to start, move, and then stop. The very long paragraph may have a start, but then gets into interminable movement that gives the reader the feeling it will never come to a stop.

REVISING SENTENCE STRUCTURE AND LENGTH

Sentence structure can be rearranged into many kinds of sequences, with differing effects on meaning or emphasis. Some of the books described in Appendix 4 under "Prose Style and Structure" discuss possible variations and their effects. But even the novice author should be able to see and correct what may be the 2 most frequent defects of sentences in medical papers: unvaried structure and unvaried length.

You have probably read papers that run on like this passage.

Failure in early detection of breast cancer in women has been a major clinical problem for many years. Smith and Jones (15) found that 15% of physicians do not examine the breast in routine examinations. Brown and White (16) found a similar figure in their most recent study in Canada. Roe and Doe (17) found a lower figure only for physicians having wives with a history of breast cancer. Thomas and Stephens (18) have called attention to these figures. The last authors have concluded that failure in early detection of breast cancer is mostly due to failure to examine the breast routinely.

Every sentence in this passage is a declarative sentence. Each sentence has the same sequence of subject, predicate, and object. The same or similar phrases appear in several sentences. All the sentences have almost the same length. What about this variation?

Why has failure to detect breast cancer early in women been a major clinical problem for many years? A study in the United States (15) and one in Canada (16) found that about 15% of physicians did not examine the breast in routine examinations. Only physicians whose wives had a history of breast cancer showed a lower rate (17) of failure to examine. From these findings, Thomas and Stephens (18) drew the right conclusion: To detect breast cancer early, examine the breast routinely.

This version flows more easily. The irritating and hence arresting monotony of the first version has been erased. Sentence lengths and structures differ. A question is included. Instead of a catalog of points we get a line of thought.

REVISING FOR CLARITY

Accuracy is the most valuable quality of good scientific prose. But your prose can be accurate without being entirely clear: all of its elements can be correct, but their message may not be readily understood. Most defects in clarity arise from words correct in themselves but confusingly related to each other.

Piled-up Modifiers

Medicine and related fields use many compound terms made up of a noun and 1 or more modifiers that may themselves be nouns. The meaning of many compound terms is clear because they are used widely and frequently. But other compound terms may need rewording or the adding of hyphens for clarity. The term *liver function* test could mean either a "function test" applied to testing of "liver" or a "test" applied to "liver function". The second reading is the usual one even without the help of a hyphen to tie "liver" and "function" together, as in "liver-function test". The hyphen is not needed because we understand that the single term can also be read as a combination of "liver test" and "function test", the 2 modifiers "liver" and "function" each applying equally to "test". A similar compound term is *toxic shock syndrome*. We do not pause to ask whether this is a "syndrome" of "toxic shock" or a "shock syndrome" that also is a "toxic syndrome". Compound terms that contain no more than 2 modifiers usually are clear once established.

Compound terms with more than 2 modifiers may be unclear to readers save those familiar with the field in which the terms developed. A fictional example (derived from a real example) is "normal Fc receptor mediated marrow mononuclear phagocyte system function". Does this term mean "normal function" of "marrow mononuclear" cells serving as a "phagocyte system" through "Fc receptor" mediation? Or does it mean "function" of the "marrow mononuclear" cells as a "phagocyte system" "mediated" by "normal Fc receptor"? Another example is "hospital nurse physician staff interaction". Does this term refer to "interaction" of "hospital nurse" with "physician staff"? Or to "hospital nurses" and "hospital physicians" interacting in the "staff"? It probably refers to "interaction" of nurses and physicians in a "hospital staff" but who except the author can be sure?

If you must use a term with more than 2 modifiers, consider connecting by hyphens those related in function, or dividing the term into 2 terms, or taking both steps. The first example in the paragraph above might be made clearer by hyphenating and rearranging some of its elements: "normal function of the Fc receptor-mediated mononuclear phagocyte system in marrow" (if I interpret the term correctly to mean that the "mononuclear phagocyte" system is in the "marrow" and its function mediated through Fc receptors is normal). Semantic tangles of this kind can be avoided by not coining terms with more than 2 modifiers.

Unconnected ("Dangling") Modifying Phrases

The reader's eye sees what it expects to see, even if what it sees does not exist. This is why a common defect is often overlooked by authors and fast readers: the modifying phrase unconnected to a word that should be, or could be, modified. A frequent flaw of this kind is in sentences that begin with the modifying phrase "Based on . . .".

Based on our failure to find bacteria in the blood cultures, we concluded that the patient had fungal endocarditis.

Test for a dangling phrase by placing the modifying phrase right after the noun or pronoun it might be supposed to modify. What is "based on our failure"? Does this sentence mean "We, based on our failure to find . . ., concluded that . . ."? Or was the patient "based on": "We concluded that the patient, based on our failure . . . , had fungal endocarditis"? Surely the endocarditis was not "based on our failure to find . . .". The modifying phrase appears to be related logically to "Concluded" but the sentence cannot be read "we concluded, based on . . . , that . . .". The error in the sentence is failure to provide the truly modified but only implied word, "conclusion," the conclusion being logically derived from, and hence "based on," the "failure". A corrected version reads thus.

> Our conclusion, based on failure to find bacteria in the blood cultures, was that the patient had fungal endocarditis.

Based" is the past participle of the infinitive *to base*. Other frequently seen variants of this defect are unconnected modifying phrases that begin with a present participle (the verb form ending in *-ing*).

> Interpreting failure to find bacteria in the blood cultures as evidence of fungal endocarditis, the plan of treatment was changed.

Who or what was "interpreting"? Surely not "the plan of treatment": "The plan of treatment, interpreting failure . . . , was changed."? The action "interpreting" can be carried out only by a person. In the example above, "interpreting" presumably modifies some unstated person or persons.

> The attending physician, interpreting failure . . . , changed the plan of treatment.

There is a general rule for detecting an unconnected, or "dangling", participial modifier. Test the clarity of a sentence that begins with a modifying phrase headed by a verb form (present or past participle) by reading the sentence with the phrase or clause placed right after the word it seems to modify. Sometimes that word cannot be found, as in the "interpreting" example above, and must be added, or the sentence must be rewritten entirely.

Misplaced Modifiers

A closely related defect is the modifier so far from the word it modifies that the connection is lost.

At the nadir, with the highest doses thrombocyte counts were decreased in these patients to an average of 10% of initial values.

What does "at the nadir" modify? What thing was, or action occurred, "at the nadir"? Not "doses"; the content of the sentence indicates that the drug effect followed initiation of "the highest doses". Not "thrombocyte counts": the thrombocytes were being counted throughout the course of treatment. "At the nadir" seems to tell us when "counts were decreased" to the stated level.

With the highest doses, thrombocyte counts in these patients were decreased at their nadir to an average of 10% of initial values.

The sentence may still be unclear because of the unfamiliar term "nadir" (lowest point). A simpler version would be clearer.

With the highest doses, the lowest thrombocyte counts in these patients were an average of 10% of initial values.

Modifiers should be kept close to what they modify.

Ambiguous Antecedents

Your meaning may be confused if you do not make clear the word to which a pronoun refers, its antecedent.

Failure of treatment with penicillin could not have been unpredicted because of the defective assay method used. Unfortunately, this occurs in many hospitals.

What is the "this" that occurs in many hospitals—being unable to predict, use of a defective assay method, or failure of treatment? Similar confusion arises from using *it* as an indefinite subject and *it* as the third-person neuter pronoun in the same sentence.

Cimetidine is highly effective in suppressing gastric acid secretion in such cases. It is unfortunate that it is not prescribed more frequently.

The indefinite subject *it* at the beginning of the second sentence and the neuter pronoun *it* referring to "cimetidine" momentarily seem to refer to the same antecedent, but they do not. Revising to drop the indefinite *it* improves clarity.

> Cimetidine is highly effective in suppressing gastric acid secretion in such cases. Unfortunately it is not prescribed often enough.

Another type of ambiguous antecedent results from the false modesty that leads authors to refer to themselves as "the authors" rather than "we".

> Smith and Jones(16) found statistically significant lowering of diastolic blood pressure by hypopressol and only minor adverse effects, whereas Brown and White (17) report that its use is frequently accompanied by episodes of cerebral ischemia. The authors conclude that the drug should be used only in carefully selected cases.

At the beginning of the second sentence, who are "the authors", Smith and Jones, or Brown and White, or the authors of the passage? The lack of citation numbers after "the authors" implies the authors of the passage. Dispel ambiguity and write, "We conclude that . . .".

Unclear Sequences Due to Wrong Choice of Verb Tenses

Sequences of events may be unclear when verb tenses are not chosen carefully. This fault often appears in case reports. A case description, for example, starts with the statement, "The patient was admitted to Erewhon General Hospital on 1 November 1978 with a bleeding duodenal ulcer". After a description of clinical events during that admission comes a paragraph about preceding events with the opening statement, "In June 1976 the patient was admitted to Utopian County Hospital with hematemesis not diagnosed during that hospital stay". The earlier date in the second statement should show that the event at Utopian County Hospital occurred before the event of November 1978 at Erewhon General Hospital. But the sequence of the two descriptions tends to confuse the reader; perhaps the "1976" is wrong. This confusion could have been avoided by using the past perfect tense in the second description, "had been admitted," to make clear it refers to an event antedating that described in the first sentence: "The patient had been admitted to Utopian County Hospital in June 1976 with hematemesis . . .".

REVISING FOR ACCURACY

Accuracy is the most valuable quality of good scientific prose. Correct use of scientific nomenclature (see "Nomenclature" in Chapter 12) is the main ingredient of accurate scientific prose, but accuracy also depends on carefully choosing other words.

Confused and Misused Word Pairs

Some pairs of words with closely related, but not identical, meanings are frequently misused in the medical literature. The words defined below are some of the most frequently misused pairs.

accuracy: the degree to which a measurement or statement is correct
precision: the degree of refinement to which some thing is measured, or to which a measurement is reported; *precision* applied to statements implies qualities of definitiveness, terseness, and specificity

case: an episode or example of illness, injury, or asymptomatic disease; not a patient (see comments below under "Dehumanizing Words" in "Revising for Grace")
patient: the person cared for by the physician, nurse, or other professional person

dosage: the amount of medicine to be taken or given in a period, or the total amount; not the amount taken at one time
dose: the amount of medicine taken or given at one time; the sum of doses may be *dosage* or *total dose*

effect: as a noun, the result of an action; as a verb, to bring about or cause to come into being
affect: as a noun in psychiatry, the sum of feelings accompanying a mental state, or the appearance of emotion or mood; as a verb, to modify or to elicit an effect

etiology: the study or description of the causes of a disease
cause: the agent, single or multifactorial, bringing about an effect, such as inducing a disease
incidence: the number of cases developing in a specified unit of population per specified period
prevalence: the number of cases existing in a specified unit of population at a specified time

infer: to conclude or deduce from an observation or premises
imply: to suggest a conclusion to be drawn from allusion or reference

pathology: the study or description of disease; do not use for *disease, lesion, abnormality*
disease: lesion, abnormality; terms not synonymous with *pathology*

people: a group of persons, either a large group such as the inhabitants of a nation or a small not-enumerated group with characteristics held in common persons: individual human beings, even in references to a group, as in *10 persons injured in a train wreck*

theory: working hypothesis suggested by experimental observations; do not use loosely for *idea, concept, hypothesis*
hypothesis: a proposition for experimental or logical testing

varying: as an adjective, *changing*; as a verb, causing a change
various: having dissimilar characteristics; synonymous with *differing*

which: relative pronoun used to introduce a nonrestrictive (nonessential) clause ("These diseases, which cause most of the deaths each year in the United States, are the main subject of this textbook".)
that: relative pronoun used to introduce a restrictive (essential) clause ("This is the one lesion that is usually fatal".)

Additional examples of frequently confused and misused pairs of words can be found in style manuals (5, 6).

Spelling Errors

You will probably spot misspellings that result from typing errors; it is the words of whose spelling you are not sure that will slip by uncorrected. Unfamiliar scientific terms, such as chemical names for drugs more widely known by their generic names, must be checked in a scientific dictionary or other references such as those described in Appendix 4. Nonscientific words that sound right but look vaguely incorrect need to be checked in a standard dictionary: *fluorescent* is not "flourescent"; *principle* is not *principal* (and vice versa); *consensus* is not "concensus"; *prevalent* is not "prevalent". Use the same caution with singular and plural forms of Latin terms such as *medium* (singular) and *media* (plural).

The spelling-checker utility available in many word-processing programs can be applied at this point in revision to catch misspelled words. The checker will not, however, catch correctly spelled words that sound alike but have different meanings, such as *principle* and *principal*.

Wrong Choice of Verb Tense for Completed or Continuing Actions

If the reader is to know whether an action was completed at one time or continued, you must use the right tense of verbs. Defects in tense occur frequently in referring to published papers. If a paper published years ago now has mainly historical value, an accurate statement would be, "In 1963 Smith and Jones reported that . . .". The use of the simple past tense "reported" indicates that the event was completed; this meaning is backed up by the date. The use of the simple past tense without a date ("Smith and Jones reported that . . .") implies that the intellectual content of the report may have come to the end of its useful life, even though the report probably still exists in published form. If the statement is "Smith and Jones have reported . . .", which uses the present perfect tense, it implies that although the report was published in the past it was probably published in the recent past and continues to have intellectual importance. The present perfect tense cannot be used with a date; "In 1963 Smith and Jones have reported . . ." is a contradiction because the present perfect tense indicates continuing action, in this case the continued existence of the reporting as a published paper. In referring to papers just published with messages of current importance, the present tense is appropriate: "On the other hand, Smith and Jones report that . . .".

Such nuances may sound like an editor's nitpicking, but the right tense, a simple tense or a "perfect" tense, establishes accurately that an event was an occurrence not continued or a continuing action or state. Authors well educated in English idiom usually have no uncertainties as to the right tense. If you do not trust your ear for the right choice, turn to one of the books cited in Appendix 4 as a reference on English grammar or ask the advice of a colleague or other friend with a firm grasp on good idiom.

REVISING FOR ECONOMY

A tightly written paper is clearer and easier to read than a wordy paper. After you have dealt with the defects discussed above, go through your text and replace long words with shorter equivalents. Strike out unneeded words and phrases

Which of these sentences do you prefer?

We conclude that penicillin is the best antibiotic for treatment of streptococcal infections.
After careful consideration of all the foregoing lines of evidence, it is apparent to us that among all the antibiotics discussed penicillin is the one that should be chosen for the treatment of infections caused by the streptococcus.

The message in the second sentence is clear enough, but most readers will prefer the shorter version. The point made by these examples could be made in other ways.

> We conclude that streptococcal infections are best treated with penicillin.
> Clearly, streptococcal infections are best treated with penicillin.
> We conclude: treat streptococcal infections with penicillin.

Each version has its virtues and faults. The best choice could depend on the place of the passage in the text, the degree of economy in the rest of the text, the tone the paper should carry. The briefest possible statement is rarely the best. Brevity carried too far can lead to unidiomatic sentences, cryptic statements, or lost meaning.

> Penicillin is best for streptococcal infections.
> Streptococcal infections? Penicillin!

Do not push to recast sentences in shorter versions and rid your prose of unneeded words and phrases at the risk of writing prose that strains for economy. Remember T E Lawrence's point (2) that prose is bad when the reader stops to look at it.

Prose carefully revised for economy but still idiomatic has advantages in papers competing for publication. The text speaks forthrightly, carries a clear message, and suggests that the author knows the subject. Many a paper gets a low priority for publication from reviewers because it lacks the tone of authority. Prose style is not all that determines a paper's tone of authority, but it can support that tone.

Verbal economy in your paper also raises the odds that it will be accepted. Journal publishing is expensive; editors need to make the best use of the space they have. Of 2 papers with equal importance, the shorter is more likely to be accepted. Many journals specify short formats ("brief communications", "short reports", "clinical notes") to indicate to authors that their messages should be presented as economically as possible. Lean and forceful prose is a main ingredient for a concise paper.

Revising to Correct Excessive Use of Weak Verbs and Connectives

In his sharp analysis of medical prose style, Lester King (7) points out the characteristic structure of the excessively long and dull sentence: Too many words (nouns and other non-verbs) are strung together by forms of the verb *to be* or *to have* and connective words such as *and, of, with*. *To be* and *to have* are weak verbs, one expressing a state, not action, and the other describing only static possession. To revise sentences with this fault, reduce the number of non-verbs and increase the number of active verbs, converting, when possible, abstract nouns to verbs or verb equivalents. Consider this example.

> It is especially important that health-science schools have policies and guidelines for the education of undergraduate professional students, nurses, and house officers so that there is thoughtful consideration and discussion of the ethical, legal, and emotional aspects of abortion.

This sentence has 37 non-verbs, including 11 connectives and only 3 verbs, of which 2 are the weak verb *is* and 1 is the barely stronger *have*. Consider this version.

> In educating undergraduate professional students, nurses, and house officers, health-science schools need policies and guidelines to ensure that ethical, legal, and emotional aspects of abortion are thoughtfully considered and discussed.

This version has only 24 non-verbs, including only 7 connectives. The verb *need*, which by itself implies importance, replaces "It is especially important that" (which contains the weak indefinite pronoun *it* and the weak verb *is*). The verb forms *educating, are considered*, and *are discussed* replace the abstract nouns "education", "consideration", and "discussion." The number of verbs and verb equivalents has been raised to 5; "are discussed" and "are considered" are passive but are stronger than their noun equivalents.

Replacing Abstract Nouns

I have just pointed out that replacing abstract nouns with equivalent verb forms both shortens and strengthens a sentence. Abstract nouns ending in *-ion* should alert you to a possible need to revise. Many stuffy, long-winded passages can be cleaned up by replacing abstract nouns with verbs or verb equivalents. Consider this example.

> The identification and classification of the various histologic types of lymphomas are vital steps toward the introduction of new therapies and the reduction of mortality.

Here are 4 abstract nouns ending in *-ion* and 24 words linked by 1 verb, *are*. Here is one possible variant.

Identifying and classifying the histologic types of lymphomas are vital steps toward introducing new therapies and reducing mortality.

The 4 abstract nouns have been replaced by their verb equivalents ending in *-ing*. The 2 halves of the sentence are still connected by the weak verb *are*, but the total number of words has been cut by 7.

Cutting Out Clauses

Clauses beginning with *which* often add subordinate detail to sentences that takes up too much length for its value in meaning.

Cancer of the breast, which is known to be a leading cause of death in women in the United States, too often escapes detection in an early stage.

The relative, nonrestrictive clause that begins "which is known ..." could be omitted without distorting the main point. The detail provided does support the idea that early detection is needed, but dropping "which is..." and converting the clause to a phrase clearly subordinates this detail to the main point and cuts out 8 words.

Cancer of the breast, still a leading cause of death in women, too often escapes detection in an early stage.

The statement "known to be" is not needed; stating the fact, "still a leading cause of death", indicates that it is known. The paper is about practice in the United States and is written for an American audience; "in the United States" can be assumed. These changes shorten the sentence by almost 30%, the equivalent of shortening a 10-page manuscript by 3 pages.

Deleting Empty Phrases and Words

In lectures and conversations we often fill spaces between the true units of thought with words and phrases not really needed for meaning. These fillers gain for us time in which our brains can select and process the words truly needed to carry what we have to say. In revising prose these fillers should become throwaways. Consider this example.

In order to get a complete history from the patient, it would appear that the inexperienced clinician needs a systematic line of inquiry.

Two empty phrases can be dropped.

To get a complete history from the patient, the inexperienced clinician needs a systematic line of inquiry.

"In order . . ." and "it would appear that . . ." are two fillers of the con-
versational kind. They also serve as verbal flourishes that imply a deliberate and judicious concern with coming to the right judgment, but
these flourishes added to the statement only a pose. They call for notice by the reader and draw attention away from the message. They
are smudges on Orwell's window pane of thought.

Below are examples of empty phrases; shifting to shorter
equivalents or deleting such phrases saves the reader time and effort.
A longer list can be found in "Prose Style", Chapter 17 of *Medical Style
and Format* (5).

Empty Phrase	Equivalent
a majority of	most
a number of	many
accounted for by the fact that	because
are of the same opinion	agree
as a consequence of	because
at the present moment, at this point in time	now
by means of	by, with
despite the fact that	although
due to the fact that	because
during the course of	during, while
during the time that	while
fewer in number	fewer
for the purpose of	for
the reason that	because
give rise to	cause
has the capability of	can
if conditions are such that	if
in all cases	always, invariably
in a position to	can, may
in a satisfactory manner	satisfactorily
in an adequate manner	adequately
in close proximity to	near
in connection with	about, concerning
in (my, our) opinion it is not an unjustifiable assumption that	(I, we) think

in order to	to
in the event that	if
in view of the fact that	because
it has been reported by Jones	Jones has reported
it is clear that	clearly
it is often the case that	often
it is possible that the cause is	the cause may be
it is worth pointing out that	note that
it may, however, be noted that	but
it would appear that	apparently
lacked the ability to	could not
numbers of	many
on account of	because
on behalf of	for
on the basis of	because, by, from
on the grounds that	because
owing to the fact that	because
prior to (in time)	before
referred to as	called
subsequent to	after
take into consideration	consider
the question as to whether	whether
through the use of	by, with
was of the opinion that	believed
with a view to	to
with reference to	about (*or omit*)
with regard to	about, concerning (or omit)

Deleting Unneeded Adjectives and Adverbs

Close cousins to these empty phrases are single words that are not needed or that should be replaced by stronger and clearer words. In the sentence, "The usual metastatic lesions in bone are very painful", what does "usual" tell us unless the author is also discussing unusual metastatic lesions? Does "very" add enough to "painful" to keep it? Either "Metastatic lesions in bone are painful" tells us enough or we need a more exact statement, "Metastatic lesions in bone cause severe pain". Unmodified "metastatic lesions" implies "usual" or "typical" metastatic lesions. If a word serves no real need for the meaning, delete it; if another word would be more effective, substitute the better choice. The general rule has been stated neatly by Herbert Read (8):

". . . omit all epithets that may be assumed and . . . admit only those which definitely further action, interest, or meaning".

REVISING FOR GRACE

Graceful prose does not offend readers or divert their minds from the message. Graceful prose moves smoothly along a clear line of thought. In revising your text, think of serving your readers as you would serve your closest friends.

Some of the defects discussed below that lead to graceless prose are defects in accuracy or clarity. They are better seen as defects in grace because they show the author to be an insensitive scribbler or a poser.

Defects in Sex Reference

Not all nurses are women; not all physicians are men. Some patients other than those seen by gynecologists are women. Keep these points in mind as you review your text and find sentences with references to sex.

The noncompliant patient may not intend to disregard your instructions; he may simply forget them.

Why assume that patients in general are men? Such assumptions about the sex of unidentified patients often can be dealt with by switching to plural forms.

Noncompliant patients may not intend to disregard your instructions; they may simply forget them.

In some sentences the pronoun can be eliminated.

The patient should choose the treatment he wants.
Patients should choose the treatment.

Such changes should, however, be consistent in number (plural or singular) throughout the text; there should not be shifts back and forth between *they* and *he* or *she*.

Some devices that get around inaccurate references to sex strike some of us who do believe in accurate statements as offensive to the ear or damaging to established meaning. "Chairperson" and "chair" are avoidances of "man" in *chairman*. To my ear "chairperson" is as ugly as "utilization", now so often a pompous substitute for *use*. And "chair" for *chairman* adds a radically different meaning to a long-established noun of simple meaning. Better substitutes are sometimes available. The term *convenor* can substitute for *chairman*; *convenor* graciously suggests the person who brings a group together but it does not connote a sex.

Dehumanizing Words

I pointed out under "Revising For Accuracy" the difference in meaning between *case* and *patient*. *Case* is the instance or episode of disease; *patient* is the person needing care. Ignoring this distinction turns persons into "cases".

> Recurrent urinary tract stone was shown to be a manifestation of primary hyperparathyroidism in 2 cases who were subsequently admitted for parathyroidectomy.

"Cases" are not admitted; patients are. In writing papers, forget that you hear physicians and nurses talk about the "unusual case who came in yesterday for the 10th time" or "the noisy case in Room 315". Such slang may pass in the surgical locker room, dining room, or elevator, but it is not graceful in print.

A close cousin to the misuse of *case* for *patient* is the widespread and insensitive use of *individual* for *person*. One definition of *individual* is a single human being, but the word is most accurately used under this definition to contrast single persons with persons considered as a group.

> The need of some individuals for full-coverage medical insurance comes into political conflict with the demands of the working class for lower taxes.

With its origin in the Latin *persona,* the English term *person* connotes, beyond its definition as a single human being, the view of a single being with his or her to-be-respected uniqueness. This connotation is closely related to that of *patient*, which, linked to *patience*, suggests the picture of a person with disease or suffering waiting for care.

Some terms applied to patients seem more appropriate for animals. The best examples are "male" and "female" applied to men and women. *Females* may economically substitute as a collective term for "women and girls", but describing a patient as "a 38-year-old female" is graceless prose.

No less dehumanizing are the syndromic tags, terms for patients such as "diabetics" and "schizophrenics". These terms may pass as acceptable for chatter in hospitals, but in print they brutally reduce persons to instances of disease instead of ill persons who need care. It is a simple task to revise your prose to refer to the "diabetic patient" or the "schizophrenic patient".

Pomposity

Some authors write papers to try to reach a higher level of distinction than their associates. This motive all too often leads authors to believe that prose filled with polysyllabic and abstract words, qualifying clauses and phrases, and long sentences reflects erudition. Authors must not forget that pompous prose can also be seen as coming from an inconsiderate windbag arrogantly wasting a reader's time.

If you must write pompous prose, here are some rules to follow.

1. Write long sentences with many nouns and connectives and a small number of weak verbs.
2. Make all of your sentences long; avoid mixing long and short sentences.
3. Use abstract nouns instead of their verb equivalents: you do not "investigate" but "carry out an investigation of."
4. Use empty phrases: Do not write "to make the diagnosis in most cases", but "in order to make the diagnosis in a large fraction of cases".
5. Imply that your views are those of a remote, lofty authority by avoiding first-person statements: Write "it is an inescapable conclusion that," not "I conclude that".
6. Use polysyllabic, vague, and voguish words: "utilize" rather than use; "etiology" rather than cause; "symptomatology" rather than signs and symptoms; "parameter" rather than index, indicator, or variable; "impact" rather than effect.

Slang and Jargon

The clinical sciences have their own idioms, their ways of making concise statements. An example is a report by a surgeon.

The patient left the operating room in good condition.

A reader not familiar with surgical idiom—like your high-school English teacher—might see a picture of a patient climbing down from the operating table, mopping up the floor, and walking out from the now-tidy operating room. But the surgeon's way of speaking is the accepted, formal, and accurate idiom in surgery. These idioms (or jargons, because they are often not readily understood by outsiders) are efficient and normal ways (9) of speaking and writing for professionals. But informal idioms, or slang, in clinical fields are not acceptable in formal writing. You can complain at the lunch table in the hospital about having a hard time "intracathing the case in Room 169", but keep such slang out of papers for publication. The list of slang terms is long: "prepped", "lab", and "temp" are examples. Avoid using slang in formal papers; its meaning may be obscure to readers not familiar with your local slang (such as readers abroad) and it breaks the otherwise formal and accustomed tone of a paper, moving the reader's attention away from the line of thought.

Some terms and phrases gradually slip from slang into acceptable jargon. "Biopsy", accepted in formal writing only as a noun meaning the process of obtaining a sample of tissue from a living patient, has come to be used in jargon as a verb: "The large thyroid nodule was biopsied 3 times". Be careful about what you accept as jargon: "nodule was biopsied" will probably pass the editor's eye, but "the patient was operated" will not. Medical dictionaries offer little help on what is slang and what is acceptable jargon, but if a term or word you are accustomed to hearing used by your colleagues is not in a medical dictionary, it is likely to be slang.

Other Details of Graceless Prose

Any detail in prose that catches the reader's eye or ear is a defect to be corrected. Defects like slang in a formal paper are deviations from euphony, an agreeable sound. You may be able to catch other defects by reading the text of your paper aloud after you think you have revised it adequately. You may find unintended alliteration: "The professional paper put together in haste may prove pompous when perused by your partner". You may find jingles: "The patient suffered unintended strain from unremitting pain". Such defects are often more easily heard than seen.

Eliminate modish details of style that too easily creep into one's writing from unfastidious writing and speech in other fields. The examples are myriad. One kind of modish trend is the substituting of "more forceful" words that in fact represent new imprecisions: an example is the use of "impact" for *effect*. Another trend is the corrupting of punctuation, usually with its origin in another field: an example is the use of the slant line where the hyphen is standard; instead of *Section of Hematology and Oncology* or *Hematology-Oncology Section*, we are served up "Hematology/Oncology Section", a legalism that corrupts the standard use in scientific writing of the slant line for fractions and "per" constructions.

USING COMPUTER PROGRAMS TO REVISE

Clues to passages that may need revising have been pointed out above. Some examples are abstract nouns ending in *-ion*; noun phrases with *of*; and modifiers like *very* that add little or no meaning. The search utility of a word-processing program can let you run through your text to find each passage with such clues. As you find each clue you can decide whether you need to revise that passage. The abstract nouns ending in *-ion* and their plural forms ending in *-ions* can be found, for example, by searching for the character strings "ion" (the letters i, o, n; a space) and "ions" (the letters i, o, n, s; a space). Searching for "of" will often turn up phrases with an abstract noun that can be converted to a verb.

His interpretation of the data was wrong.
(*converts to*)
He interpreted the data wrongly.

Some special programs can provide additional help, such as calculating average length of sentences, pointing out passive verbs, spotting some grammatical errors. Among the best known of these are *Grammatik III* and *RightWriter*. These programs do not help with the bigger problems in prose structure and with nuances in prose style, but they can help the novice writer learn how to spot many small defects.

════════════════════ CONCLUSION ════════════════════

The content of a paper is more likely to determine whether it is accepted than its prose style, but style with the qualities of fluency, clarity, accuracy, economy, and grace can give readers of your paper a sense that you know what you are writing about. The first of those readers will be an editor and the manuscript consultants; how your paper impresses them will probably decide its fate. Use all the skills you can muster in revising your paper for paragraph length and structure, paragraph linkage, sentence variety, and the myriad details of word choice and use. Go through the work of revising with an efficient, thorough, and organized sequence.

REFERENCES

1. Orwell G. Why I write. In: An age like this 1920-1940; vol 1. Orwell S, Ian A, eds. The collected essays, journalism and letters of George Orwell. New York: Harcourt, Brace and World; 1968:7.
2. Lawrence TE. Men in print: essays in literary criticism. [London]: Golden Cockerel Press; [1940]:44.
3. Wesley S. An epistle to a friend concerning poetry. 1700. Quoted in: The Oxford dictionary of quotations. 2nd ed. London: Oxford University Press; 1953:565.
4. Read H. English prose style. New York: Pantheon Books; 1952:52.
5. Huth EJ. Medical style and format: an international manual for authors, editors, and publishers. Philadelphia: ISI Press; 1987:262-275. Now available from Williams & Wilkins, Baltimore.
6. CBE Style Manual Committee. CBE style manual: a guide for authors, editors, and publishers in the biological sciences. 5th ed. Bethesda, Maryland: Council of Biology Editors; 1983.
7. King LS. Why not say it clearly: a guide to scientific writing. Boston: Little, Brown; 1978.
8. Read H. English prose style. New York: Pantheon Books; 1952:16.
9. Bross IDJ, Shapiro PA, Anderson BB. How information is carried in scientific sub-languages. Science. 1972;176:1303-7.

12

Scientific Style

All who write for formal publication—novelists, poets, compilers of catalogs, scientists—are expected to spell words in standard forms established by dictionaries. All who write in the medical sciences are also expected to use generally accepted styles for units of measure, drug names, names of microorganisms, and other kinds of scientific terms. The journal for which you are preparing your paper may specify in its information-for-authors page the conventions of scientific style it prefers. Be sure that you apply these in the text, tables, and illustrations of your paper.

This chapter describes briefly the main conventions of scientific style in clinical journals. You can find much more detailed guidance on scientific style in *Medical Style and Format: An International Manual for Authors, Editors, and Publishers* (1) and the other style manuals also described in Appendix 4.

ABBREVIATIONS AND SYMBOLS

Guides to scientific writing do not always make clear the difference between *abbreviation* and *symbol*. The 2 terms do not have the same meaning. Some symbols are not abbreviations, and most abbreviations are not used as symbols.

An abbreviation is a short representation of a word or phrase formed from one or more of its letters: g is a short form of, and hence an abbreviation for, *gram*; Cl is an abbreviation of *chlorine*; HIV is an abbreviation for *human immunodeficiency virus*. DHHS is an abbreviation for *Department of Health and Human Services*.

A symbol is a conventional representation of, or sign for, a quantity, a unit, an element, a unit structure, an operation, or a relation. A symbol may be an abbreviation (Cl for *chlorine*) or may not be an abbreviation (pH for *negative logarithm of hydrogen ion concentration*).

The important difference between abbreviations and symbols is in their uses. Symbols are frequently joined to other symbols to form a representation with new meaning; for example, H for *hydrogen*

137

and Cl for *chlorine* are joined as HCl to represent *hydrochloric acid*. Symbols may be used in equations that indicate the relations among the quantities they represent; for example, F for *force*, m for *mass*, and a for *acceleration* are combined in Newton's Second Law of Motion, $F = ma$, to indicate how they relate to each other. Authors must know this distinction between *abbreviation* and *symbol* because of what it implies for correct usage. Symbols in scientific publication generally are well established by a formal agreement within a professional society or among experts, or through long use. Authors must use established symbols lest what they write be misunderstood. To be sure that any symbols in your paper are standard symbols, check them against a standard source such as a style manual (1, 2) or the information-for-authors page of the journal for which you are writing. If you must use nonstandard symbols, explain their meaning in your text.

Text

Journals differ greatly in what abbreviations they will accept. Authors can often decide on acceptable usage by consulting the journal's information-for-authors page and scanning recent issues. The more specialized the content of a journal, the more likely it will accept abbreviations widely used in its field even if they are informal ones unfamiliar to clinicians in other fields. If you can not find out whether an abbreviation is acceptable to a journal, write out the term. Editors rarely ask that terms be converted to abbreviations, but their requirements for revision are likely to stipulate that you not use certain abbreviations. Any nonstandard abbreviations in your paper must be explained at its first mention in the text by giving the full term followed by the abbreviation within parenthesis marks: "the acquired immunodeficiency syndrome (AIDS)". You may then use only the abbreviation in the rest of the text; if it appears in a table or figure, it must be explained there.

Some authors use abbreviations freely (and coin new abbreviations) because they are too lazy to write out full terms or to pause to decide whether an abbreviation is truly needed in a particular sentence. Consider the example of SLE, widely used for *systemic lupus erythematosus*. In a paper solely about patients with systemic lupus erythematosus, a sentence about prognosis in its Discussion section might be "SLE patients without proteinuria at the first visit to a physician are likely to live longer than those with proteinuria". If no other kinds of patients are considered in the paper, why not simply write, "Patients without proteinuria at the first visit . . ."?

The author who wants to hold down the use of abbreviations in a paper should read a near-final draft and pause at each abbreviation to ask 2 questions.

- If the abbreviation is used alone as the equivalent of a noun or a noun phrase, can it be dropped completely? Can "the prognosis with SLE" be replaced with "the prognosis" without loss of meaning in the context?
- If the abbreviation cannot be dropped without leading to confusion, can it be replaced with a short substitute noun? In a paragraph that describes specifically 2 transaminases, "The serum levels of ALT and AST were within the normal range" can be replaced with "The serum transaminase levels were ..." without loss of meaning because no other transaminases are discussed in that paragraph.

Neither of these examples would be clear without the abbreviation if the sentence had to stand alone, but the altered form is likely to be clear in its place within a paragraph or longer section of the paper.

A third test to apply in eliminating abbreviations is the number of times each abbreviation is used after its first mention. The abbreviation SIADH for *the syndrome of inappropriate secretion of antidiuretic hormone* may conveniently substitute for the full term in a long review article about the syndrome written for nephrologists. But what if the abbreviation occurs only twice in a review of recently described paraneoplastic endocrine syndromes written for physicians in primary-care medicine? Is it asking too much of the author that he or she write out the full term at each of the 2 mentions?

Symbols generally should not be used alone in text. A case description can correctly note that a patient "was 1.82 m tall and weighed 68.2 kg" but a description of hospital-admission procedure should say "Patients' heights are measured in meters and their weights in kilograms", not "... measured in m and weights in kg". But symbols representing long phrases are often acceptable: "Measurement of fluid pH is not useful in the differential diagnosis of pleural effusion", rather than "Measurement of fluid acidity expressed as the negative logarithm of hydrogen ion concentration is not useful ..." or even the shorter equivalent, "Measurement of the fluid's hydrogen ion concentration ...".

Titles

Avoid using abbreviations in titles. It may be necessary, however, to use abbreviations for very long terms. Consider an oncologic paper with a title that begins, "A Modified-MOPP Regimen for Treatment of ...". MOPP stands for *nitrogen mustard, oncovin, procarbazine, and prednisone*. A version of the title with MOPP written out would probably be rejected by the editor. The symbol pH would also be acceptable in a title ("Measurement of Pleural Fluid pH") because of the length of its full equivalent, but the title, "The Influence of Gravity on the Heart," on a paper for a journal in cardiology could not be written as "The Influence of g on the Heart."

The prohibition of abbreviations in titles may be increasingly relaxed with more searching of online bibliographic databases. Some searchers will expect to find papers about AIDS or HIV through searching for titles carrying those abbreviations. For this reason editors may become willing to let such abbreviations accompany their full terms in titles: "Central Nervous System Infections with the Human Immunodeficiency Virus (HIV)".

Abstracts

Abstracts written by authors to accompany the published version of their papers often are published separately as well, in another section of the journal or in a publication that reproduces abstracts from many journals. No matter where an abstract is to appear, it should be governed by the same rules for abbreviations and symbols that govern the rest of the paper. An abstract should be readable by itself, as an entity separate from the paper. Within its short format, terms are seldom used many times, and as noted above, it is not necessary to use abbreviations for terms occurring only once or twice within text. If an abbreviation is needed for a term frequently used in an abstract, that abbreviation must also be explained when first used in the body of the paper.

Tables and Illustrations

Just as in the text, widely accepted symbols for units of measure and statistical terms (such as p for *probability*) can be used in tables and figures without explanation. Nonstandard symbols and abbreviations must be explained in footnotes or in the legend. A reader should be able to understand the content of a table or illustration without having to refer to the text for explanations of abbreviations. Because of the space limits in tables and illustrations, editors may allow use of abbreviations in them that they would not accept in the text if the abbreviations are explained in a footnote or the legend.

NUMBERS

Rules for numbers, numerals, and numeric terms differ among journals and are too complex for a complete summary here. Some rules are widely accepted.

1. Use numerals with standard units of measure: "The diameter of the cyst was 15 mm".
2. Numbers in the text of scientific papers that are accompanied by a unit should be in numerals: "The patient had been bitten by 1 of her 10 cats".
3. Numbers 10 and smaller in a nonscientific paper or a nonscientific context in a scientific paper can be written as numeric terms: "Social upheavals of this kind developed in ten countries immediately after the end of the war".
4. Do not begin sentences with numerals; substitute numeric terms: "Thirty-five of the 120 patients were given the drug".
5. Because the comma is used as the decimal point in some countries, do not use the comma to separate 3-numeral groups in large numbers; space the groups. But when 4-digit numbers appear only with numbers of the same, or a smaller, class, do not separate the numerals.

> Not   37,546,321   But   37 546 321
>   6,732   6 732

If 4-digit numbers appear with 5-digit, or larger, numbers, use the spaced style for all numbers.

> . . . in 15 678 men and 4 632 women

6. Use a zero before the decimal point for numbers between 1.0 and − 1.0: For example, 0.75 m.

A detailed discussion of the use of numbers in medical writing can be found in the chapter "Numbers, Units of Measurement, and Time" in *Medical Style and Format: An International Manual for Authors, Editors, and Publishers* (1).

UNITS OF MEASUREMENT: METRIC USAGE

Virtually all journals publishing instructions for authors indicate their requirements for units of measurement. Most clinical journals now use metric units almost exclusively, with some allowing exceptions for body measurements like weight in pounds, height in feet and inches, and temperatures in degrees Fahrenheit.

Metric usage is not as simple for authors today as it was 20 or 30 years ago. Many journals have shifted to the new system of metric units, SI (from *Système International d'Unités*: in English, International System of Units). The SI units include many of the older metric units, but emphasis is shifting to reporting in newer compound units in such fields as respiratory physiology and clinical chemistry (for example, millimoles per litre for concentrations rather than grams per 100 millilitres). Many clinical journals in the United States now require SI units for clinical chemistry and hematology, and others are shifting to this requirement. Some journals are accepting manuscripts with non-SI metric units but are requiring authors to convert when the paper is accepted. Helpful summaries of the metric system, including the SI units, can be found in the 2 style manuals (1, 2) referred to above. One of them includes a detailed description (3) of SI units, their style requirements, and detailed tables giving non-SI and SI units for clinical chemistry and hematology, with conversion factors and specifications for "significant digits".

Although hecto-, deka-, deci-, and centi- are SI prefixes, they should generally not be used except for the SI unit-multiples for area and volume and for the nontechnical use of centimetre. For measurements of length (and height) in the medical sciences, the metre and the millimetre should be used in preference to the centimetre. The diameter of a cyst, for example, should be given as 37 mm rather than as 3.7 cm; a patient's height should be given as 1.54 m rather than as 154 cm. The style rules for metric units and symbols are well-established. Incorrect usage in your manuscript will be corrected by the copy editor for the journal if your paper is published. Nevertheless, use of proper style in your manuscript will be evidence to the editor and manuscript consultants that you know what you are doing.

The rules for metric style are worth knowing.

1. Names for metric units are capitalized only at the beginning of sentences and in other locations, such as titles, where capitalization is the rule for main words. Symbols for units named after persons are capitalized, but not the names of the units: the unit for pressure is the pascal; its symbol is Pa.
2. Use upright letters for unit symbols, such as m for metre; quantity symbols, such as m for mass, are italicized (underlined in typewritten manuscript).
3. Do not use periods after symbols except at the end of a sentence: "He was 1.71 m tall." and "His height was 1.71 m.".

4. Use plural names for units with numeric values greater than 1, less than -1, or equal to 0: 1.1 metres, 0 degrees Celsius, -1.2 degrees Celsius; 0.95 metre, -1 degree Celsius.
5. Symbols for units are singular whether the units would be read as singular or plural: 1 m; 100 m.
6. Do not leave space between the degree symbol and Celsius: 37.1 °C, not 37.1° C; note that the paired symbols " ° " and "C" are combined unspaced as a single symbol for degree Celsius.
7. Squared or cubed units are designated by superscript powers, not words: 1.7 m^2 body surface area; not 1.7 square m body surface area.
8. In a symbol for a compound unit that is a product, use the "product dot" between the individual symbols: N·m.
9. Compound units with a denominator are written with "per" for the term but with a slant line ("slash") for the symbol: moles per litre; mol/L.
10. Compound units incorporating more than 1 unit in the denominator should not be written with more than 1 slant line. For example, 1.4 $mmol/cm^2/s$ should be written in one of these styles, in decreasing order of preference.

   1.4 mmol·cm $-^2$·s $- 1$
   1.4 mmol/cm^2·s
   1.4 mmol/(cm^2·s)

STATISTICS

All mentions of quantitative differences thought not to be due to chance should be supported by statistical statements, which presumably are available as the result of appropriate statistical tests described in the Methods section. These statements, accompanied by a brief statement of the statistical method by which they were derived, should appear wherever in the paper quantitative differences are reported: abstracts, text, tables, and illustrations (or their legends).

Statistical statements of the form nn.n $\pm$ n.n must specify whether the $\pm$ n.n part represents a standard deviation or a standard error; a preferable form is nn, SD nn or nn, SE nn.

Not   12.0 $\pm$ 0.4   *but*   12.0, SE 0.4

Statements of confidence intervals must specify the percentage span of the interval, as in "95%CI, -1.2 to 5.2". The 2 components that define the limits of the interval (in the example just given, -1.2 and 5.2) must be separated by the preposition *to*; a dash can be misread as a minus sign.

The symbols for the most frequently reported statistical variables are preferably italicized, in accord with the recommendations of the International Standards Organization.

sample size   *n*
arithmetic mean of a sample $\bar{x}$
standard deviation of a sample   *s*
standard error of the mean $s_{\bar{x}}$
probability   *P*

Additional detail on statistical reporting can be found in the chapter "Mathematics and Statistics" of *Medical Style and Format: An International Manual for Authors, Editors, and Publishers* (1) and a paper by Bailar and Mosteller (4).

NOMENCLATURE

Chemistry and Biochemistry

Chemical compounds mentioned in clinical papers can be identified by either a formal chemical name or a shorter "trivial" (from the chemist's point of view) name. An example is hydrocortisone, an adrenocortical hormone; its formal chemical name is 11B,17,21-trihydroxy-pregn-4-ene-3,20-dione, which is rarely used outside of the biochemical and endocrinologic literature. Papers written for clinical journals should usually use the trivial, or common, name for an organic compound. An organic compound not widely known by a trivial name should be identified, however, by its formal chemical name, at least at its first mention in a paper (after which it may be conveniently identified by the trivial name or, in some cases, by an abbreviation). Inorganic compounds should usually be identified by their chemical names rather than by trivial names: *hydrochloric acid* rather than *muriatic acid*. An authoritative source for verification of full chemical names and trivial names is *The Merck Index* (5).

Drug Names

A drug should be identified by its generic (nonproprietary) name. If the drug's chemical structure is important for some aspect of the paper, such as discussion of its metabolites, its formal chemical name also may have to be given. If you need to identify the particular brand of drug (such as for acknowledgment of supply of the drug by a pharmaceutical firm, comparisons of several brands of the same generic drug, a report of an adverse effect that may be attributable to a particular brand), use the brand name of the drug to distinguish it from the drug's generic name. Brand names of drugs should, like other trademark names, have their initial letter capitalized; generic names of drugs start with a lowercase letter except where capitalization is needed for another style convention, as in a title.

Generic drug names can be verified in the most recent edition of *USAN and the USP Dictionary of Drug Names* (6); this source carries additional useful information, including formal chemical names of drugs, trade names, previously used generic names, and code numbers for investigational drugs. Trade names can be verified in *American Drug Index* (7), which also lists multi-ingredient proprietary drugs.

Disease Names and Eponyms

If a disease is known by several names, use that most familiar to your probable readers. If one of the synonyms for a disease is an eponym (name derived from a proper name, like *Addison disease*), use the noneponymic name unless the eponym is more widely known. Your decision may have to be arbitrary. For example, *Crohn disease* and *regional enteritis* are probably equally well-known; *regional enteritis* should be preferred because it concisely characterizes the disease as localized inflammation of the bowel. Osteitis deformans is probably more widely known by *Paget disease of bone*; hence the eponym may be preferred for a clinical audience, the descriptive, non-eponymic *osteitis deformans* for an audience of pathologists. If you choose the eponym, be sure that it refers to no more than one disease or is the complete eponymic name. *Paget disease*, for example, is used in *Paget disease of bone*, *Paget disease of the breast*, and *Paget disease of the vulva*; if you are writing about one of these diseases, you should use the full eponym, not simply "Paget disease". This last point also applies to compound terms. To avoid any ambiguity with *lupus vulgaris*, *lupus erythematosus* should not be amputated to the jargon form "lupus".

In some journals the preferred form for eponyms is the nonpossessive form: *Crohn disease*, not *Crohn's* disease; *the Cushing syndrome*, not *Cushing's syndrome*. Many journals still use some possessive forms. For these journals 2 rules can be easily applied to most eponyms: if the eponym is derived from the name of a single describer, use the possessive form: *Parkinson's disease, Hodgkin's disease*; if the eponym is derived from the names of 2 or more describers or from the name of a patient, family, or place, use the nonpossessive form: *Creutzfeldt-Jakob disease, Hippel-Lindau disease; Christmas disease, Byler disease; Minamata disease.*

Note that eponymic terms ending with *syndrome* open with the article *the: the acquired immunodeficiency syndrome, the CREST syndrome.*

Eponyms are capitalized but not adjectives or nouns derived from them. Thus, *addisonian* in *addisonian crisis* (from *Thomas Addison*) is not capitalized, nor is *parkinsonism* from *Parkinson disease.*

Disease names derived from capitalized names of microorganisms are not capitalized: *brucellosis* from *Brucella; salmonellosis* from *Salmonella.*

Names in Microbiology, Zoology, and Botany

Binomial taxonomic names for organisms (genus and species) should be italicized (indicated in manuscript by underlining): Staphylococcus aureus in manuscript, *Staphylococcus aureus* in published form. Formal names at a higher level (order, family, and tribe) are capitalized but generally not italicized, thus *Pseudomonas* for the genus but Pseudomonadales for the order.

A genus name may be abbreviated after its first mention only if it is followed by a specific epithet: *Staphylococcus aureus*, subsequently *S. aureus.* If you are referring to species in several genera whose names begin with the same letter, use several letters for the abbreviation of the generic name: *Staph.* for *Staphylococcus, Sh.* for *Shigella.* The best way to avoid confusion of similar abbreviations, however, is to write out the full generic name.

Common names for bacterial species, like *the gonococcus* for *Neisseria gonorrhoeae*, are acceptable in many contexts, but these should not be used as an equivalent to the formal taxonomic name. Because the common names for the same organism may differ in some countries, the first use of a common name in a paper should be followed by the formal name within parenthesis marks.

Adjectival forms like "streptococcal" and "staphylococcal" are well known and acceptable. If a genus name has to be used adjectivally because a specifically adjectival form (8) is not well established, italic type and initial capitalization are not used: pseudomonas meningitis, not "*Pseudomonas* meningitis".

Taxonomic names in zoology and botany call for similar styles: *Drosophila melanogaster* for the fruit fly; *Rhus toxicodendron* for the poison oak.

=============== CONCLUSION ===============

This chapter has only touched on some of the main principles and rules that guide scientific style in clinical fields. Many fields of medical science such as biochemistry, genetics, immunology, pulmonary physiology, and radiology have well-developed and detailed conventions for nomenclature and symbolization; virtually all of these are summarized in the chapter "Scientific Style in the Medical Sciences" of *Medical Style and Format: An International Manual for Authors, Editors, and Publishers* (1). The journal for which you are writing your paper may specify the conventions most likely to be needed by its authors. If it does not, it may nevertheless have its own internal rules that will be applied when the manuscript of your paper is marked for the printer.

REFERENCES

1. Huth EJ. Medical style and format: an international manual for authors, editors, and publishers. Philadelphia: ISI Press; 1987.
2. CBE Style Manual Committee. CBE style manual: a guide for authors, editors, and publishers in the biological sciences. 5th ed. Bethesda, Maryland: Council of Biology Editors; 1983.
3. Young DS. Implementation of SI units for clinical laboratory data: style specifications and conversion tables. In: Huth EJ. Medical style and format: an international manual for authors, editors, and publishers. Philadelphia: ISI Press; 1987:288-320.
4. Bailar JC, Mosteller F. Guidelines for statistical reporting in articles for medical journals: amplifications and explanations. Ann Intern Med. 1988;108:266-73.
5. Windholz M, ed. The Merck index. 11th ed. Rahway, New Jersey: Merck; 1989.
6. Griffiths MC, ed. USAN and the USP dictionary of drug names. Rockville, Maryland: United States Pharmacopeial Convention. Published annually.
7. Billups NF, Billups SM. American drug index. Philadelphia: JB Lippincott. Published annually.
8. [Huth EJ.] Style notes: taxonomic names in microbiology and their adjectival derivatives. Ann Intern Med. 1989;110:419-20.

13

Tables

When you were preparing to write your paper, you probably had to decide whether some of your evidence should be in the form of tables. If the paper is to report clinical or laboratory research, an epidemiologic study, or a drug trial, you gathered numerical data in tables for analysis of your findings before you began to write. If your paper is a review article, you may have compiled tables to help you pull together concise summaries of what you had read. At some point between the first draft and the final version, you must decide which tables you really need, which tables you should replace by graphs, and which tables you discard in favor of summarizing the data in the text.

DECIDING ON USE OF TABLES

The journal for which you are preparing the paper may state in its information-for-authors page its limit on the number of allowed tables. If it does not, look at papers in some recent issues, estimate the number of text words (excluding references), count the tables and illustrations (single or multipart figures), and calculate the number of tables and illustrations per thousand words of text. Then estimate the length of your text and round the estimate down to the nearest thousand. Multiply the calculated limit of numbers of tables and illustrations per thousand by the estimate of your text length in thousands, and you have the maximum number of tables you can probably use, assuming you are using only tables and no illustrations.

If a typical paper in the journal has an estimated text length of 3300 words accompanied by 4 tables, the ratio of tables to text is 4/3.3 thousand or 1.2 tables per 1 thousand words of text. If your paper has a text of about 4800 words, round this figure down to 4000. Then $4 \times 1.2 = 4.8$ tables; in round numbers, 5 tables.

A useful general rule is no more than 1 table (or illustration) per 1000 words of text. Because the average page of text in a manuscript typed double-spaced with 1-inch (or 3-centimeter) margins usually runs to between 200 and 250 words, the rule can be stated as no more than 1 table (or illustration) per 4 pages of manuscript text. Thus the first step in deciding on use of tables is figuring the maximum number the journal will probably accept in relation to the length of the paper. If you estimate that 5 tables and illustrations would be acceptable, and you will need 1 illustration, you will be able to use no more than 4 tables. But do you really need the maximum number the journal might accommodate? Manuscript consultants and editors are likely to point out tables with so few data that they can be dropped in favor of giving the data in the text. Tables are more expensive to typeset than text, so editors are prone to ask authors to eliminate tables. What if you have too many tables for the length of your text? What if you wish to reduce the odds that you will have to delete tables in a last-minute revision asked for by the editor? Which tables, then, can you eliminate and which should you keep?

Tables of Numerical Data

If you have read a short version of your paper at a research meeting, you may have shown some slides with simplified structures that made them easy for an audience to read rapidly. That would have been good judgment; a simple table can economically summarize and emphasize data for the desired effect on an audience. Such a table is illustrated in Figure 13.1. Do not use this kind of table in your paper; its content can be easily summarized in the text.

Of the 3 patients with negative penicillin skin-tests, 1 was positive to noxicillin. Of the 7 patients positive for penicillin, 2 were positive for noxicillin. The difference in noxicillin positivity between the 2 penicillin groups is not statistically significant, Fisher's exact test ($P>0.05$).

If you persist in using a large number of such simple tables in your paper, you give the editor the impression that you have spent little time in thinking about how to translate your meeting talk into a journal paper.

Some tables should be dropped, not to be replaced by text statements but by illustrations. These are tables of data important for their known or potential relationships.

Table 1. Skin Reactions to Noxicillin		
Patient	Penicillin	Noxicillin
1	0	0
2	+	0
3	+	0
4	+	+
5	0	0
6	+	0
7	+	+
8	+	0
9	0	+
10	+	0

Figure 13.1. A table put together to summarize data for the authors before they began to write their paper; the table was also used as a slide for a talk. The findings are readily summarized in words in the text; the table should not be used in the paper.

- *Data on two related variables*: a dependent variable whose values are determined by an independent variable, such as maximum systolic blood pressure after different doses of epinephrine, maximum blood levels of alcohol after different doses of whiskey.
- *Data on one or more variables changing through time*, such as clinical data like temperature, blood pressure, blood counts for a patient during a hospital stay.
- *Data important to the reader for the extent of their differences and how these differences might be related to unknown factors*, such as differences in mortality rates for stomach cancer in the individual states of the United States.

Data of these kinds can usually be presented more effectively in one or more types of illustrations: graphs, charts of patients' clinical courses; epidemiologic maps; and other types.

Use tables when the reader will want exact values for numerical data. In a study of serum electrolytes (sodium, potassium, chloride, calcium, phosphate, magnesium) and acid-base variables (pH, CO_2, bicarbonate), some readers may be interested in carrying out their own calculations of relations among the data. You could not meet these possible needs in the text without providing a long stretch of text crowded with numbers and hard to read.

The rules for use of tables with numerical data can be summarized thus.

- Do not use tables when the data can be summarized in the text with a few sentences, or when the relations of data to each other or to a time sequence can be made more clearly in a graph.
- Use tables when the readers will want the exact values of more data than can be summarized in a few sentences of text.

Tables Instead of Text

In some papers descriptive information may be more efficiently presented in a table than in text. The most frequent use of a table in place of text is to summarize cases in a review article or a case-series analysis. Full description of 5, 10, or more cases in the usual format of case reports can take up many pages of text. Even though each case may have its own nuances of clinical variation, the cases are likely to have many features in common, and each case description reads a good bit like the next. An efficient solution may be a large table that gives for each case only the essential numerical data (age, weight, temperature, and laboratory-test values) and brief descriptive phrases for symptoms, physical findings, roentgenographic findings, and so on. You might retain a full case report or 2 in the text to give the clinical "flavor" of the disease or syndrome. In constructing large case-summary tables, you will have to be very careful to find out what size tables may be acceptable to the journal.

If your paper is to be synoptic (a "teaching" article, a review), you can emphasize important points by listing in small tables the main features of a disease or syndrome, symptoms and signs of adverse effects, and differential diagnoses. Such "list" tables often include the frequency or percentage of occurrence for each item; these additional data help to make clear the relative importance of the listed items. The sequence in such tables should have a readily grasped logic: descending order of frequency; grouping by body systems; chronologic order.

Relations of Tables

When you have decided which tables are needed and which can be discarded, check the relation of the remaining tables to the text to be sure that their sequence is correctly tied into the text sequence; then number the tables accordingly. Next consider the tables as a sequence, with appropriate relations to one another. In many clinical papers the title of the first table may adequately identify the main subject of the paper, with shorter titles for the following tables. The

Title → Table 1. Tired-Author Syndrome: Case Features at Admission							

Patient*	Age (yr)	Sex	Weight (kg)	Height (m)	Temperature† (°C)	Chief Complaint
1	27	F	50.2	1.73	37.0	Double vision
2	31	M	65.7	2.01	36.4	Poor memory
3	42	M	75.3	1.94	37.2	Cramp in right hand
4	57	M	68.8	1.92	36.4	Loss of appetite
5	61	F	63.5	1.81	37.1	Restlessness

Column Headings — Row Headings — Row — Column — Field

* Patient 1 was seen at the University Hospital; Patients 2-5 were seen at the General Hospital.

† Temperature of Patient 1 was measured rectally; the other temperatures were measured orally.

(Footnote)

Figure 13.2. A case-summary table illustrating the usual parts of a table and their names.

first table, for example, in a review of 25 cases of puncture wound of the heart, might be titled "Puncture Wound of the Heart: Clinical Features". The second table might then be simply "Operative Findings and Postoperative Course". A look at the tables by themselves in the proposed sequence will help you judge whether the tables are understandable on their own (and they should be) and how well their titles are related to one another.

PARTS OF A TABLE

Editors and printers identify the parts of a table by terms that should be known by authors. These terms often turn up in correspondence or phone calls (especially from manuscript editors) about revision of papers (Figure 13.2).

- The *title* briefly describes the content of the table and includes the table number.
- The *field* is the space carrying numerical data and descriptive terms or phrases that together carry the table's message; the content of the field is arranged in horizontal *rows* and vertical *columns*.

- Each *column heading* identifies the kind of data and descriptions lined up vertically in the column beneath it.
- Each *row heading* identifies the kind of data and descriptions aligned in the horizontal row to its right.
- The *footnotes* explain details of content of the table.
- The column headings for the field are also known collectively as the *box heading;* the column heading for the row headings beneath it is called the *box heading for the stub (stub is a term for the group of row headings).*

Journal Style and Specifications for Tables

Journals rarely describe the details of style to be used in their tables, but these details can usually be quickly deduced from tables in recent issues. The size of acceptable tables is likewise rarely specified, so you will probably have to scan tables in a recent issue to work out estimates.

A useful rule for the width of a single-column table in a journal with a double-column page is that the width should not exceed more than 60 characters (and equivalent spaces) in a row (with its row heading). The width of a table running the full width of a page should not exceed 120 characters and spaces, including row headings. If you must use an even wider table, the journal may be willing to accommodate it on facing pages, but before you prepare and submit such a table, consider whether its data could be divided between 2 tables. For example, a very large table summarizing cases might be divided into 1 table for clinical features and a second table for laboratory-test data. If you must use a wide table that will span 2 facing pages, the reader may have trouble following each row across from the left-hand page to the right-hand page. Each row will be scanned more readily if the row headings at the left-hand end of the rows are repeated at the right-hand end of the rows (the right-hand edge of the field).

Another solution for a wide table is reorienting the table so that columns and their headings become rows with row headings and the rows become columns. Such a change could be made, for example, with a table of data on 20 different laboratory tests for 2 patients. The data would usually be arranged so that the data on the tests for each patient form a 20-item row and the data for each test form a 2-item column. This arrangement would produce a very wide but very flat table; it would probably not fit on a single page. If the data are rearranged so that they form 2 columns, 1 for each patient, and 20 rows (each row giving the data on a test for the 2 patients), then the wide table becomes a tall, narrow table that will fit into a single column of a double-column page. A good test to apply to your table's format is to compare the number of column headings to the number of row headings. If the ratio is greater than 2:1, consider reorienting your table.

Logical Structure for Tables

Each of your tables should be readily understood without referring to the text; an adequate title will help to ensure that understanding. Needed even more is a logical structure for the data in the field that can be deduced from the column headings and row headings. Consider a table summarizing data from several cases. Most readers will expect to find the data arranged in a sequence of columns read from left to right that corresponds to how the data were collected in the clinical course. In such a table the rows might be logically arranged so that "Patient 1" (the first row) is the youngest patient and "Patient 6" (the sixth row) is the oldest. Another sequence of rows might progress from the "mildest cases" at the top to the "severest cases" at the bottom. In a table reporting data from a drug trial, the left-hand column might include pretreatment data and the right-hand column, post-treatment data. The rows would probably be arranged so that the top part of the table carries data from the "placebo group" and the bottom part data from the "drug group."

BUILDING AND TYPING A TABLE

Title

Although the title of a table should be specific enough to enable the reader to understand the table with referring to the text, the title should avoid stating the information carried by the column and row headings. Consider a table summarizing in three groups of columns the admission diagnosis and roentgenographic and autopsy findings in 20 fatal cases of pulmonary embolism. Its column headings identify the nature of the findings as "admission diagnosis", "chest film", and "autopsy", and its row headings run down from "Patient 1" to "Patient 20". The table title can be simply "Cases of Fatal Pulmonary Embolism" rather than "Twenty Cases of Fatal Pulmonary Embolism: Admission Diagnosis, Chest Film, and Autopsy Findings". If the reader needs details that the title cannot carry without being too long and that are not in column or row headings, these details can be carried in footnotes. Footnotes may specify, for example, drugs, dosage, and administrative procedure in a table with data from a drug trial.

Column Headings

Each column heading for numerical data should include the unit of measure for the data. That unit should apply to all data under the heading. Another unit of measure (and corresponding data) should not be used farther down in the column. Rather than forcing the reader to take note of a second kind of unit in a single column, restructure the table to accommodate the second kind of unit and its accompanying data in another column.

If groups of columns logically belong together, label them with a grouped-column heading and place a heading straddle rule over the column headings to which it applies.

Patient	Admission laboratory data		
	Hemoglobin g/L	Serum glucose mmol/L	Serum albumin g/L

The straddle rule will eliminate any uncertainty about which column headings are included under the grouped-column heading.

Row Headings

If groups of rows are logically related, indicate such groupings and subgroupings with appropriate headings and indentations that will make clear their relations with each other.

Placebo groups
  Men
  Women
Drug treatment groups
  Men
  Women

If the row headings designate numerical data, give the unit of measurement immediately after headings (within parenthesis marks or after a comma, according to the journal's style).

Blood glucose, mmol/L
Blood glucose (mmol/L)

The Field

The columns should be centered under their headings, and numerical data should be centered on expressed or implied decimals.

	Patient 1	Patient 2
Serum glucose (mmol/L)	4.05	5.45
Serum creatinine (μmol/L)	105	97
Serum uric acid (mmol/L)	0.12	0.24

Intersections of columns and rows should not be left blank. If the appropriate datum at such an intersection is "none", indicate this fact with a zero.

Contraceptive	Healthy	Thrombophlebitis	Pulmonary embolism	Total cases
Oral	120	10	3	133
None	129	3	0	132

If an intersection does not have a datum, the absence should be indicated by 3 dots (. . .) or an abbreviated notation explained in a footnote, such as ND for "not done" or NA for "not available" or "not applicable".

Large numbers that need not be given with a high degree of accuracy can be expressed in smaller numbers with the appropriate multiplying column heading.

Tuberculosis cases (thousands)		Tuberculosis cases
20	rather	120 000
1.5	than	1 500

Do not use such headings as "× 10^3" for thousands or "× 10^6" for millions; these may be ambiguous as to whether the data given below should be multiplied by such a factor or already have been multiplied by the factor.

Do not mix units in a single column of data (see related comment above under "Column Headings"). If, for example, a column gives data on duration of an effect on symptoms and some of the data are in days and some in weeks, change the weeks to equivalent totals of days so that the single column-heading "days" can apply to all data in the column.

Avoid pseudo-precision in giving percentages. Journals differ in what denominators they will accept as an adequate basis for a percentage. One rule used by some clinical journals is to allow percentages only for fractions with denominators greater than 50. The field of a table following this rule might carry data expressing cases with particular findings as a fraction of total cases examined, with percentages being given for the reader's convenience only for fractions with denominators greater than 50.

100 (98%)	47/58 (81%)	31/76 (41%)
32/46	12/25	7/10

Percentages given for compared fractions with small denominators are likely to imply statistically significant differences; if such differences are assessed statistically, the assessment must be based, of course, on the absolute numbers, not on the percentages. If the presence of data with and without percentages seems confusing, omit the percentages. If percentages are given for small numbers, confidence intervals provided for the percentages will, obviously, indicate their low precision.

If data in the field have been assessed statistically, indicate by footnotes the exact meaning of indicated assessments. For example, "12.1 ± 0.3" could indicate a mean of 12.1 with a standard error of the mean of 0.3 or a standard deviation of 0.3 for the distribution of the values represented by the mean. Two means in a table assessed for statistical significance of difference between them should each be tagged with the same footnote sign referring to a footnote explaining the test used and the conclusion drawn from it.

Group	Cases n	Serum calcium* mmol/L
Group 1	27	2.42 ± 0.13
Group 2	33	2.91 ± 0.05

* Plus-minus values (±) are standard errors of the mean. Difference between means assessed by Student's t-test, $P < 0.05$.

Make sure that all data in a table agree completely and exactly with their presentation anywhere else in the paper (title, abstract, text, or another table). Make sure, too, that all the data in a table are internally consistent—for example, that percentages that should add to 100% do add up correctly. Check all addition, subtraction, and any other mathematical operations implied in the table.

To save space, editors often allow some abbreviations to be used in tables that they would not allow in text. All abbreviations in tables (but not standard symbols for units of measurement) must be explained in footnotes, even if they are abbreviations explained in the text.

Dates

Shorthand forms for dates such as 5/15/69 can be understood differently in different regions. In Europe 4/11/81 means 4 November 1981; in the United States it usually means 11 April 1981. Use the form, number of day [space] abbreviated month [space] abbreviated year, to avoid misunderstanding: 4 Nov 82.

Footnotes

As already discussed, footnotes can be used to explain abbreviations, define study conditions, state statistical assessments, acknowledge source of the table (if it has been adapted from a published table), and in other ways make a table entirely understandable by itself. Some journals prefer to have elements in the table that are explained in footnotes tagged with superscript numbers corresponding to numbers of the footnotes, but superscript numbers can be confused with powers (squared, cubed) and reference numbers. Other journals thus prefer either a conventional sequence of footnote signs (*, †, ‡, §, ||, ¶, #, **, ††) or superscript lowercase letters in alphabetic sequence ([a], [b], [c], and so on).

Typing

All parts of a table should be typed double-spaced, including column headings and footnotes. Double-spacing is needed to give the copy editor enough room for marks to indicate publication style to the printer and for the printer to insert typesetting codes.

Journals differ in use of horizontal lines (rules) and vertical lines in tables. In general, avoid rules and lines in the table except for a rule under the column headings to separate them clearly from the field (and straddle rules for grouped-column headings); the journal's manuscript editor can add rules and lines if they are needed for the journal's style.

Start each table on a separate page. If a table cannot be completed on a single sheet, it can be continued onto a second sheet, with the title-number designation repeated, followed by "continued". If the table is extended down onto the second sheet, column headings, too, should be repeated to avoid any uncertainties about column alignments; if the extension is to the right on a facing sheet of paper, repeat the row headings.

CONCLUSION

The number of tables that can be used in a paper may be limited by the journal. You may avoid having to revise the paper to remove tables before publication by consulting the journal's information-for-authors page for the limit or by examining papers in recent issues and estimating the ratio of tables per thousand words of text.

Tables should not be used for numerical data if the data can be summarized in the text or their relationship needs to be made clear in a graph. Tables can sometimes be used to summarize or emphasize descriptive content in the text.

The structure of each table should be carefully thought out for a logical internal sequence. Tables should relate to each other logically in sequence and title.

Great care should be taken with proper use of units and clear presentation of the data in the field of the table.

14

Illustrations

Before you began to write the first draft, you pulled together the materials you needed to start work on it. These may have included photographs, roentgenograms, scans, electrocardiographic tracings, and graphs of experimental data. Some time before you prepare the final draft for typing (see Chapter 15), you must decide which illustrations to use or whether to use any at all. This decision should be made as far in advance as possible before preparing the final manuscript. You will probably need the services of a professional graphic artist or photographer; the consulting time likely to be needed and the time needed for the work on illustrations are usually greater than anticipated.

DECIDING ON USE OF ILLUSTRATIONS

Illustrations should be used not just because they are available, but for 1 or more of 3 needs.

- Evidence - Efficiency - Emphasis

The editor of the journal may not agree that all of the illustrations serve these needs. If you can anticipate how the editor is likely to judge their usefulness, you may save some time, effort, and money by not having to discard illustrations and in revising the paper to rewrite the text related to them.

Evidence

Illustrations should be used in research papers only when they carry evidence needed to support a conclusion. If a paper is about a new species of *Legionella* as a pathogen in a case of pneumonia, a chest roentgenogram showing typical findings of pneumonia should not be used just because the film is available. The reader can be expected to take your word for a not-unusual roentgenographic diagnosis. But if the paper is about newly discovered structural details of a bacterium's flagellum, the electron micrograph is the main part of the paper's evidence.

Efficiency

An illustration may be far more efficient in presenting the evidence for a conclusion than a long statement in text. A family tree, for example, can quickly make clear that a newly identified syndrome appears in members of the family as a mendelian autosomal dominant trait; a written description of the same evidence would run on for many lines of text and not make the point as efficiently. Numerical data make the same point whether presented in a table or a graph, but if the point is the relation of 2 variables, the reader will see it more quickly in a graph.

Emphasis

Emphasis is the reason least likely to be accepted by the editor for use of illustrations. A simple bar graph comparing deaths from lung cancer in men and women between ages 50 and 70 might effectively emphasize a big difference in mortality, but the same point could be stated just as efficiently, or more efficiently, in the text. Unless the difference in mortality is the main conclusion of the paper and the editor agrees that this point merits emphasis, you will probably be asked to drop the bar graph. The emphasis needed in a lecture to make sure that a point is caught by the audience is less likely to be needed in a paper. A slide in a lecture can help to drive home a point that might be forgotten by the audience as you move on to other points. The lecture cannot be replayed in the head; the text of a paper can be scanned again if the reader has missed a point.

WHEN NOT TO USE ILLUSTRATIONS

After reviewing the illustrations you have planned to use, retaining those that seem justified by the needs of evidence, efficiency, or emphasis and discarding the rest, you may still have too many. You can not be sure that the editor will let you use your final selection if the paper is accepted. Editors must hold down numbers of tables and illustrations because of their high cost and potential difficulties in layout.

Check the journal's information-for-authors page again for limits on illustrations. If you cannot find a limit, you can estimate a probably safe limit by scanning recent issues of the journal or using the procedure given at the beginning of Chapter 13. A usually safe maximum for the total number of illustrations and tables (any combination of the 2) is 1 per 1000 words of text. If the total you are planning to use exceeds the journal's specified limit or your calculated limit, you have 2 possible solutions: Discard tables or illustrations in favor of equivalent statements in text; combine 2 or more illustrations into a single, multipart illustration (or do the same with 2 or more tables). The illustrations to be combined should be related in subject; if they are graphs, they should also be similar in proportion and scale of lines and lettering. Finally, do not use illustrations that duplicate data presented in tables.

When you are not sure about whether to use an illustration, consider applying the rule that can be usefully applied to all parts of a paper: "When in doubt, leave it out".

PREPARING ILLUSTRATIONS

Unless you are competent in illustration methods, in photography, or computer graphics, you are likely to need the services of professionals in these fields. They will be aware of the technical details needed for illustrations that will make their points and will be technically acceptable to the journal. Incompetently prepared illustrations may lead the editor and manuscript reviewers to wonder about the competence of the author and perhaps even about the soundness of the text. Professional illustrators and photographers do need guidance from authors about what points the illustrations must make. Obviously, authors also have to provide both the raw materials for the illustrations—for example, numerical data, tracings, roentgenograms—and the journal's specifications.

If you plan to prepare your own illustrations you will find helpful various principles discussed in the books on illustration described in Appendix 4. A notably valuable and comprehensive source is *Illustrating Science: Standards for Publication* (1).

Line Illustrations

A wide variety of illustrations can be prepared with black lines inked on white paper. The simplest are graphs showing the relations of 2 variables, for example, a graph showing diastolic blood pressure for a large number of persons plotted against their ages. Many types of graphs and diagrams can represent clearly even complex data and relations; the possibilities are illustrated in detailed guides to graphic illustration; see Appendix 4 for some recommendations. The most complex line illustrations are drawings used instead of photographs to depict subjects like surgical procedures and anatomic views. Such drawings take a lot of a professional illustrator's time and are much more expensive than photographic equivalents.

Graphs and Diagrams

The illustrator needs the actual values for the numerical data to be shown, not just a freehand sketch of the graph or diagram you envision. Just as for a table, the units in which the data are expressed will have to be given. An independent variable is usually shown on the horizontal (x) axis, the dependent variable on the vertical (y) axis. If a graph is to show a line fitted to the data points, you should calculate enough values of y for values of x to enable the illustrator to place the line precisely. Be sure to specify that the graph or diagram is to be used for publication. Slide illustrations for a paper to be presented orally usually have to be more simplified than may be desirable for illustration in a published paper. A copy of the journal and a copy of its information-for-authors page may help the illustrator in deciding how to proceed.

Computer graphics-methods can be used to produce a wide variety of graphs, but care must be taken to produce copy of adequate quality; see "Computer Graphics" below.

Electrocardiographic and Other Kinds of Tracings

Tracings recorded against a clean white background or an even-toned gray background may be copied photographically to yield the photographic equivalent of a line drawing (black lines against a white background). If some parts of the tracing lines are very thin, the photographer may not be able to reproduce the fine detail. Occasionally, tracings are better reproduced as a facsimile drawn on clean white paper that is then photographed. When this method is used, check closely on the drawn reproduction to be sure that it preserves exactly the characteristics of the original tracing.

Flow Charts

Diagrams can be used to illustrate relations of connected units—for example, a sequence of procedures such as in a diagnostic algorithm, or a "table" of organizational titles and responsibilities. For such diagrams the illustrator will probably want to have at least your rough sketch of what has to be shown and certainly will need exact terms and titles. You should type or print neatly any text to be used in the diagram to avoid misspellings by the illustrator.

Family Pedigrees

Diagrams showing relationships among family members and generations should use well-established conventions, which are illustrated in text books on human genetics and described in the *CBE Style Manual* (2). Generations are numbered with Roman numerals, the oldest generation represented being designated by roman numeral I. The symbols for members of a generation are usually arranged on a single line, with the symbol for the most senior placed at the left and numbered 1 (with the roman numeral for the generation, for example I-1) and the symbol for the most junior at the right (for example, I-5). Women and girls are represented by circles, men and boys by squares.

Computer Graphics

Text, tables, or graphs generated by a dot-matrix printer connected to a computer may be reproduced as line illustrations if the printer's impressions are dark enough; too often the photographs made from such copy contain too many lines, letters, numerals, or symbols that will not reproduce legibly. Your illustrator or photographer will be able to advise you on whether the copy will photograph well enough or should be prepared in a hand-lettered, drawn, or typed version before being photographed. Many of these problems can be avoided if copy is printed out with a high-density dot matrix printer using a program that yields high-resolution images. Graphics generated by a laser printer are usually adequate for journal reproduction.

Continuous-Tone Illustrations

Even if you are skilled enough to draw graphs and diagrams acceptable for publication you are likely to need a photographer to produce satisfactory prints of clinical views, roentgenograms, and photomicrographs that cannot be accurately or economically represented by line drawings.

Patients

Written permission to reproduce photographs of patients in which the patient might be identified should be acquired when the pictures are taken. Preferably, specific permission for use of a photograph in a journal paper should be sought again when you begin to plan the paper (as discussed in Chapter 3). Parts of photographs that would identify a patient should be blacked out or cropped, if possible. Keep in mind that although a close-up of a skin lesion, for example, may show what you wish to show, you (or the editor) may decide later that a longer view may also be needed to show the lesion's location.

Roentgenograms

If only a section of a roentgenogram is the subject of interest, the whole film need not be photographed, but be sure that the field of view is large enough to include structures that show the location of the lesion. Roentgenograms should not include labels that identify patients by name or case number. If successive films were taken on different dates, verify the dates and be sure the photographic copies are in the right sequence. Left and right orientations should be indicated if they are important.

Some roentgenographic abnormalities are difficult for readers to identify because of complex details in the view or subtleties apparent only to experts. The reader may be helped in seeing important details if the photograph of the roentgenogram is accompanied by a line drawing showing in simplified or outline form the shape of the abnormality.

Photomicrographs and Electron Micrographs

A professional photographer will use lighting and color filtration to ensure the best images but will need your guidance on what fields are to be shown and whether low-power views will be needed to orient the reader on the location of high-power views. The photographer should keep records on the powers of microscope objectives used and the relation of the photographic print to the image size. A scale applied to the illustration can show the dimensions of the subject regardless of the degree of reduction applied to the photograph for fitting it into the journal's page layout. Letters and arrows may also have to be applied to the photograph to identify specific parts, or the photograph may be accompanied by a line drawing showing the main elements in outline, with identifying letters or abbreviations.

Black-and-White or Color Illustrations

Color printing is far more expensive than black and white, and few journals will publish color illustrations without passing the cost on to the author. If you think color illustrations are needed for your paper, be sure you know the journal's policy on, and charges for, use of color.

Color transparencies (slides) and color negatives (negatives for color prints) are usually preferred by journals over color prints. Because of the problems that might result from loss in the mail of transparencies and color negatives (as with pictures of a patient who subsequently died), you should ask the photographer to take duplicate exposures at the photographic session. Duplicating transparencies and negatives from their originals usually leads to degrading of color quality and image sharpness.

When do you really need color illustrations? Most medical illustrations can make their points as effectively in black and white. Some exceptions are illustrations of some skin lesions (like faint rashes), subtle histologic-stain colors, and multicolor scan images. If photographs you wish to use are in the form of color transparencies or color prints (and the subject cannot be rephotographed for black-and-white prints), ask your photographer to produce black-and-white copies. With appropriate filtering techniques you may get black-and-white equivalents that are almost as effective as the color originals.

SIZE AND FORMAT

An illustration will usually fit within the layout of a journal's page if it has the proportions of a horizontal rectangle, with a longer horizontal than vertical axis. If the details of the illustration (letters, lines, and symbols of a line illustration and features of interest in a continuous-tone illustration) are not too small, and if the journal uses a double-column page format, the illustration will probably be printed as a single-column figure. If the detail is small, it will be printed the full width of the page.

Square-format illustrations should usually have details scaled large enough to enable the journal to use the illustration as a single-column figure on a double-column page. Vertical-rectangle illustrations (vertical axis longer than horizontal axis) may have to be used for specific needs. One example is having to show together the changes of many variables over time. An illustration of the vertical-rectangle type may be acceptable if its detail is large enough to allow for reduction of the illustration to the width of a single column (on a double-column page). This point should be kept in mind by the illustrator or photographer doing your work. If you are drawing your own illustrations, pay careful attention to the sizes of letters and widths of lines and to how small or how large they will be after the illustration is reduced in size for printing (see comments below).

Some illustrations that might seem to need the format of a vertical rectangle at first thought may, with some reflection and ingenuity, be reformatted to the square or horizontal rectangle. An example is a chest roentgenogram. The original film of a chest roentgenogram, for example, has the proportions of a vertical rectangle. Do you really have to show all of the film? Could the feature of interest be shown more clearly if the illustration based on the film shows only a part of the entire field of the film? Can the illustration be made up in a horizontal rectangle, or at least in a square?

Details of Line Illustrations

Because an illustration should be understandable without having to refer to the text it accompanies, all of its features should be identified on it or in its legend. Graphs of numerical data must have their horizontal and vertical axes labeled to indicate the variables plotted and their units. Unless the labeling would crowd the field of a graph, individual lines should be labeled ("control group", "treatment group"; or, to save space, "CG", "TG") with any abbreviations explained in the legend. If most of the field of a graph is too crowded for such labels, they may be grouped in 1 part of the field in a key. An alternative is to use standard symbols in drawing the graph that can be reproduced and explained in the legend.

In drafting line illustrations (graph, family tree, and other types), care must be taken to produce lettering that in publication will not be obtrusively bold or too small. The lettering should be of such a size that after reduction of the illustration for publication the capital letters are approximately 2.0 mm in height. If the original drawing is twice as large as the illustration will be when printed, the capital letters should be drawn 4.0 mm high; at 3 times the size, 6.0 mm high). Lines for the x and y axes and the trend lines should be no wider than the width of the lines making up the letters.

Details of Continuous-Tone Illustrations

The most effective photographs are those that show the points of importance and no more. Hence photographs should be made of only the point of interest or cropped to indicate to the editor and printer the area of interest. In the process do not forget, however, that the orientation of the subject should be apparent. A photograph, for example, of a skin cancer on the upper check should probably include some of the outer corner of the eye or the forward part of the ear to make clear the location.

Wax pencil is often used to mark areas for cropping, but these marks are easily wiped off or smudged. Another procedure is to paste or tape a piece of translucent paper (like tissue paper) to the top of the back of the photograph so that it can be folded over the top of the photograph to lie over its face. On this paper mark (lightly) in pencil the area of the photograph that should be shown in the published illustration. A safer procedure is to mark crop lines with a ball point pen in the white margin of the photograph (if it has white margins) but never on the photograph. You could send with the photograph a sketch on a separate piece of paper indicating desirable cropping. Probably the best method is running off a xerographic copy of the photograph and marking the cropping lines on that copy; the copy will reproduce the photograph well enough for such instructions. Details on a photograph can be emphasized, if necessary, with pressure-sensitive letters and arrows (available in art supply stores). Such identifying letters must be explained, of course, in the legend. Dark areas are best labeled with white letters; light areas, with black letters. If the exact size of the subject of the photograph is important, a short scale line from which dimensions can be judged should be part of the photograph. If the photograph is of a skin tumor, for example, a centimetre-millimetre rule can be laid on the skin so that its edge is seen in the finished photograph. A scale for a photomicrograph will have to be applied to it.

Labeling Illustrations

Each illustration must be labeled on its back to indicate its number (for example, "Figure 2"). Additional identification should include names of authors and a short title for the paper to help prevent loss of the illustration by an editor or a manuscript reviewer. The labeling is best done by typing the needed data onto a pressure-sensitive label. If such labels are not available, write the information on the back with a soft pen while the photograph lies face down on a hard, flat surface; do not write on the back of a photograph with more than minimal pressure lest impressions of the writing show on the front. The labeling should indicate the edge of the photograph that should be regarded as the "top" ; the proper orientation of a roentgenogram, a picture of a skin lesion, or a photomicrograph will not be apparent to the printer, and even the editor may have trouble in deciding what is the "top."

Grouped Illustrations

Photographs of closely related subjects are sometimes more effectively presented as a single, multipart illustration. An example is a general view of the cut surface of a kidney sliced longitudinally accompanied by several close-up photographs of details of the cortex, a pyramid, and the pelvis. Most journals would not want to have such a composite illustration submitted already mounted on cardboard in the arrangement you think best. The better method is to label each component as a part of a single figure—for example, Figure 1A, Figure 1B, and so on. You can then send with the figure a sketch showing the components labeled and in the arrangement you prefer. The editor may not wish to use all of the components and may think of a better arrangement.

LEGENDS

Each illustration must be accompanied by a descriptive legend. A legend must include the figure number indicating the sequence in which the illustration was cited in the text ("Figure 12," for example), the subject of the illustration ("ventral surface of the liver as seen through the laparotomy incision"), any needed technical details such as stains and magnification, and additional description needed by the reader to understand the illustration without referring to the text.

Legends should be typed on a separate page of the manuscript as indicated in Chapter 15.

SUBMITTING ILLUSTRATIONS

Consult the journal's information-for-authors page for instructions on how to submit illustrations. Most clinical journals prefer to receive illustrations as separate photographs on glossy paper, rather than receiving the original art work—a roentgenogram, an electrocardiograph tracing, or a photograph—mounted on illustration board (see Chapter 15). To avoid injury to loose photographs, place them in special envelopes available in standard photographic print sizes. The envelope should be labeled with the authors' names and a short title for the paper.

Be sure to keep any original art work on which the illustrations are based and at least 1 duplicate set of all illustrations in case of loss. Mail does get lost occasionally!

CONCLUSION

Illustrations should be used when the evidence bearing on the conclusions of a paper cannot be adequately presented in a written description or in a table. Emphasis on especially important points to be made is another reasonable justification for their use. Limits set by a journal on the number of illustrations it will accept must be observed; if the journal does not specify the limit, it can be estimated by examining recent issues to calculate the number of illustrations (and tables) used per 1000 words of text.

Illustrations are usually best prepared by professional graphic artists and photographers; numerous details in format, lettering, and labeling call for careful attention. Their legends should be written with a view to ensuring that the illustration can be understood when it is seen by itself.

REFERENCES

1. Scientific Illustration Committee. Illustrating science: standards for publication. Bethesda, Maryland: Council of Biology Editors; 1988.
2. CBE Style Manual Committee. CBE style manual. Bethesda, Maryland: Council of Biology Editors; 1983:196-7.

15

Preparing the Final Manuscript

You have revised your paper thoroughly and carefully. You are now ready to prepare the manuscript to be sent to the journal. The final manuscript is prepared in 3 steps.

Step 1. Review the manuscript requirements of the journal.
Step 2. Review the final version of your paper to be sure that it contains all the needed elements (title page, abstract, text pages, references, and so on) and that these meet the journal's requirements.
Step 3. Get the manuscript typed in accordance with the journal's requirements.

If you read a copy of the journal's information-for-authors page before you began to write the paper and followed the instructions while you worked on the first and later drafts, these 3 steps may not take much time. But even if you proceeded that way, do not shortcut these steps; details in content and format should not be neglected if a final manuscript is to fit the journal's requirements.

Note that *manuscript* should refer only to the physical vehicle for the paper, specifically the sheets of paper, the typing on them, and any photographs and drawings serving as illustrations. The *paper* is the intellectual content carried in the manuscript. A paper is submitted to a journal as a manuscript, but the editor judges and comes to a decision on a paper, not a manuscript.

REVIEW OF THE JOURNAL'S MANUSCRIPT REQUIREMENTS

Journals differ greatly in how much detail they provide in their information-for-authors page. Some do little more than specify the number of copies to be submitted and give the address of the editor.

171

Some provide authors with detailed checklists. If the journal for which you have written your paper does not provide a detailed list, you may find helpful the list below abstracted from "Uniform Requirements for Manuscripts Submitted to Biomedical Journals" (1) with a few details added. This list covers only requirements for content and format; those for typing are given near the end of this chapter.

Manuscripts: Content and Format

1. Title page

- Title
- Author names: First name, middle initial(s), and last name of each author, with highest academic degree(s)
- Department(s) and institution(s) to which paper should be attributed
- Disclaimers, if any
- Author responsible for correspondence about the paper: Name, postal address, telephone number, and any other addresses such as those for a telex, facsimile ("fax"), or electronic-mail terminal
- Author responsible for receiving reprint requests: name and address or statement that reprints will not be available
- Grant support or other type of support, such as provision of study materials, financial assistance
- Running head or footline of no more than 40 characters and spaces (also known as short title)

2. Abstract page

- Abstract not longer than 150 words (but some journals specifically accept longer abstracts, such as the structured abstracts in *Annals of Internal Medicine, British Medical Journal*, and other journals using this innovation)
- Key or indexing terms: 3 to 10 words or short phrases, preferably drawn from the Medical Subject Headings (MeSH) list (2) of *Index Medicus*

3. Text

- Headings appropriate to the type and sequence of the paper (such as Introduction, Methods, Results, and Discussion for research papers)
- Subheadings (within headed sections) in long papers

- Citations of references, as arabic numerals in the order of citation in the text

4. Acknowledgments

- Names of persons who have contributed substantially to the content of the paper and have given you written permission to list their names

5. References

- Listed in order of their first citation in the text
- Verified against original documents
- Content and format based on styles specified in "Uniform Requirements for Manuscripts Submitted to Biomedical Journals" (1); see Appendix 2
- Journal titles abbreviated as in *Index Medicus*
- Unpublished observations and personal communications not to be used as references; papers accepted for publication but not yet published given as references identified as "in press"; research papers submitted to a journal but not yet accepted to be treated as "unpublished observations"

6. Tables

- Each table on a separate page
- Tables numbered (arabic numerals) consecutively in accordance with their order of citation in the text
- Title for each table
- Explanatory text in footnotes, not in title
- Nonstandard abbreviations explained in footnotes

7. Illustrations

- Photographic copies, not original art work or films
- Number of sets of illustrations corresponding to number of manuscript copies
- Photographic prints not larger than 20.3 by 25.4 cm (8 by 10 inches)
- Figures numbered consecutively in accordance with their order of citation in the text
- Each figure identified on back by applied label with figure number, names of authors, and identification of top of figure

- Prints not marred by impressions of writing on their backs or by paper clip marks
- Photomicrographs with an internal scale

8. Legends for illustrations

- Legends on manuscript page(s), not on backs of figures

Although more than 500 journals around the world have agreed to receive manuscripts prepared in accord with these uniform requirements, some of these requirements may not be appropriate for some journals in medicine and related fields. If you use this list, check its details against specific requirements of the journal for which you have written the paper. The section below points out some departures from these uniform requirements.

Note that a few journals in the "Uniform Requirements . . ." agreement change some style details (notably in references) for publication. But journals in the agreement should not ask authors to make such changes.

REVIEW OF THE FINAL VERSION OF THE PAPER

After you have worked on your paper through 2 or more revisions to this final stage, its content and prose style should be beyond need of further reworking. But you may need to correct a few remaining details before you have the final manuscript typed.

Title Page

Title, Running Head, or Footline

Be sure the title describes the content of the paper as specifically as possible. If you drafted the title when you wrote the first version, the title may no longer be fully accurate. Omission of some text when you worked on the first or second revisions may have made the present title inaccurate. Remove such empty phrases as "A Study of . . ." and "Observations on . . .". Shorten an excessively long title by moving some of its content into a subtitle (if the journal allows subtitles; check some recent issues). Titles with more than 100 characters (letters and spaces) usually are too long.

Many journals place highly abbreviated titles representing the content of the paper at the top or foot of each page after the title page to assist readers in orienting themselves. These "running heads" or "footlines" must be much shorter than titles, usually not exceeding 40 characters and spaces. Their terms should be drawn from the paper's title.

Authors

All persons listed as authors must have read and approved this final version. Exceptions can be made if an author has waived this right in advance or will be able either to see the final manuscript just before it is mailed to the journal or to see the paper at the proof stage.

Disclaimers and Acknowledgment of Support

If you have written your paper as part of your duties in a governmental agency or with an industrial employer, you may be required to make a statement in the paper that separates your employer from any responsibility for its content. If you are not sure of how to word the required statement, ask the appropriate person in your organization.

Abstract Page

Abstract

A journal sets a limit on the length of abstracts so they will readily fit into the title pages of papers to serve as opening summaries or fit onto a reference card. Although some journals accept longer abstracts, a 150-word abstract is usually long enough (if not a structured abstract) to reflect accurately a paper's content while being short enough for the needs mentioned above. Be sure that numeric data in the abstract agree with these data as they appear in text and tables.

Key or Indexing Terms

Journals differ in how they select terms under which their papers are listed in the subject section of the volume index. Some use only terms appearing in the titles of papers. Some have an indexer who searches each paper for additional topics under which the paper should be indexed. Some journals use only the Medical Subject Headings (MeSH) terms developed by the US National Library of Medicine for the subject index of *Index Medicus*. This practice prevents the often-confusing use of several synonyms as entry terms in the index for different papers on the same subject. The MeSH terms are recommended in the "Uniform Requirements . . ." document for key words, or indexing terms, to be placed on the abstract page of the manuscript. Authors can find copies of the MeSH compilation (2) in hospital and medical-center libraries.

Text Pages

Text Heading and Subheadings

Unless your paper is short (for example, an editorial or a book review), you have probably divided its text with headings for the main divisions. If it is a paper on experimental findings, for example, the headings probably include Introduction, Methods, Results, and Discussion. The text of a review paper about a disease might carry headings such as Definition, Etiology, Pathogenesis, Pathology, Epidemiology, Diagnosis, Differential Diagnosis, Treatment, and Prognosis. Before the final manuscript is typed, make sure that these headings are at the right divisions in the text. If you have written a very long paper, you have probably divided the text additionally with subheadings appropriate to kinds of headings described above. The section of a review article headed with Diagnosis might carry subheadings such as History, Physical Examination, Laboratory Tests, and Roentgenographic Studies. The main headings are often called *first-order headings*; subheadings at the next level down are *second-order headings* and 2 levels down, *third-order headings*.

In addition to checking all orders of text headings for location and appropriateness, you should, at this point, identify headings as to their levels (first-order, second-order, and so on) so that the typist will use the type conventions corresponding to those in the journal. If the journal prints first-order headings like Results and Discussion in all capital, or "upper case", letters (RESULTS, DISCUSSION), you should write in pencil on the left-hand margin of your manuscript adjacent to each heading the instructions, "first-order heading: all capitals." If second-order headings (the subheadings or next level of headings) are printed in the journal with initial capitals, the pencilled instructions in the margin should be "second-order heading: capitals and lower case." Such instructions can be abbreviated as "1st, all caps" and "2nd, caps and lc". Italicized headings should be typed with an italic typeface (easy to do in many word-processing programs) or underlined in accordance with the manuscript convention for indicating italicization.

Citation of References

Be sure that each reference is cited at the right point in the text. As you read through the text and come to a citation, look back at the references to be sure that the citation is appropriate to the immediately preceding text. Also make sure that every reference is cited at least once in the text, a table, or a legend to a figure.

This is also the time to be sure that the system of citations corresponds to that used in the journal. If you have carried citations through successive versions of the paper as name-and-date designations such as "(Gurwith and Jones, 1978)", as suggested in Chapter 9, and the journal uses citation by numbers, now is the time to assign numbers to the references and place these numbers at the right points in the text, substituting them for the temporary name-and-date citations. Most clinical journals, including those in the "Uniform Requirements . . ." agreement (see Appendix 2), specify that references be arranged in the order in which they are first cited in the paper. For this system (the Vancouver style: see Appendix 2; also see Chapter 15 in *Medical Style and Format* [3]), check the order in which each reference is first cited and be sure that the references are arranged and numbered in the same order. Then replace the name-and-date citations in the text, if you have carried the citations in this form through the successive drafts, with the reference numbers. If a reference is cited only in a table or legend to a figure, and not in the text, treat the first mention of that table or figure as the first mention of the reference.

Some journals in medicine and related fields do not use the citation-and-reference system (Vancouver style) described above but list references in the alphabetic order determined by the family name (surname) of the first author. For these journals you must be sure that your references are in this order. Authors find it easy to arrange most names of European origin in the right alphabetic order, but uncertainties may arise with names carrying definite articles or particles (such as *van* in *Ludwig van Beethoven*) in the family name, with compound family names (such as in Spanish names), or with Oriental names. A thorough guide to alphabetizing author names can be found in Chapter 3 of the *CBE Style Manual* (4). In journals that publish references in alphabetical order by the family name of the first author, the text citations for references are likely to be parenthetic statements of the name of the author (or authors) and the date of the referred-to document's publication, such as "(Huth, 1982)" for the book you are reading. This system, known as the name-and-date system or the Harvard system (3), is widely used among disciplines outside of science. If you have carried name-and-date citations in your text from the first draft and the journal does use the Harvard system, you now need only check those citations to be sure that each is in its right place, that each refers to the reference you intend it to, and that the name-and-date designations correspond to those in each cited reference.

Some journals, notably European journals, publish references in alphabetical order (arranged by first-author family name) but use citation numbers in the text. If your paper is going to such a journal, you now need to check that your references are in correct alphabetical order (see comments above on alphabetization), to number the references, and to replace the name-and-date citations with the newly assigned reference numbers.

Acknowledgments

Many journals allow authors to append an Acknowledgments statement at the end of the text to credit assistance that does not justify authorship. Such assistance should be credited only to persons willing to have it thus acknowledged. Giving the names of persons who may have had some connection with the study or with preparing the paper but who have not consented to mention of their names could be a breach of scientific ethics. A colleague who read your paper in draft and disagreed with some of its content may not wish to be associated with its publication. To acknowledge his or her reading of the paper in draft can imply approval of its content even if your Acknowledgment does not state such approval. For this reason, you should have in hand the written consent of all persons mentioned in an Acknowledgments note before the paper is submitted.

Some journals designate the Acknowledgments section as the place for authors to identify grant support, donors of equipment or supplies, and other kinds of assistance.

References

Order

The section above, "Citation of References", discusses the 2 sequences for references: arrangement by order of first citation in the text and its accompanying tables or figure legends, and alphabetical order based on the family names of first authors. Some other basis for order of references, such as year of publication, is unlikely in medical journals.

Content and Format

Two errors in preparing the final manuscript may lead to its having to be retyped if the paper is accepted: failure to include the data elements expected in references by the journal; failure to place the elements in the specified format. At this point be sure to check the journal's requirements on references. If the journal does not include requirements or formats for references in its information-for-authors page, examine the references in papers in recent issues for guides to the kinds of data required, the arrangement, and the punctuation.

If some of your references are to documents of kinds not frequently cited in clinical journals, such as government reports, newspapers, legal papers, and dissertations, you may be unable to find appropriate example references in recent issues of the journal. Appendix 2 illustrates reference formats for some such documents, as well as the more frequently cited journal articles and books. Additional examples can be found on pages 190 through 209 of *Medical Style and Format* (3). Note that all references should designate an author or authors. The "author" for some kinds of documents may be a committee or government agency. If no organization can be identified as "author" (specifically known as *corporate author* or *collective author*) and the document is likely to have been written by an unnamed person or unnamed persons (but not a corporate group), the author can be designated as "[Anonymous]".

Abbreviations of Journal Titles

The journal for which you are preparing your paper may use the full titles of journals in references, but the odds are that if it uses abbreviated titles those titles are abbreviated in accord with the rules used by *Index Medicus*. Abbreviated titles for most journals likely to be cited in medical papers can be found in each January issue of *Index Medicus*. Abbreviations of journal-title words can be found in *Medical Style and Format* (5). Appendix 2 lists the abbreviated titles (*Index Medicus* style) of journals in the "Uniform Requirements . . ." agreement.

Submitted but Unpublished Papers

Because references should refer only to widely available documents, many journals will not allow references to papers that have been submitted to journals but not yet accepted for publication. In some journals such papers may be cited in the text within parenthesis marks by the author's name and designated as "unpublished".

Most journals will allow references to papers accepted but not yet published because an acceptance can be independently verified with the editorial office of the journal that has issued it. These references should be used in the usual format, with the year given but "[In press]" replacing year, volume number, and page numbers.

Abstracts, Personal Communications, and Unpublished Observations

The acceptability as references of informal documents and of mentions of unpublished observations differs widely among journals.

Most journals will not allow references to such sources; among such journals some will allow citation of them in the text, usually within parenthesis marks. Abstracts are sometimes treated as informal documents (because their content has not passed through formal peer review), and formal reference to them is not allowed; some journals will accept references to them if they are designated as abstracts. As with mention of persons in an Acknowledgments section, personal communications should not be cited in the text (if the journal allows such citations) without written permission from the cited person or persons; the journal may ask for copies of permissions.

Verification of References

The completeness and accuracy of all data elements in all references must be checked against the documents given as the references. You should be able to carry out this verification because you should not cite any documents you have not seen; such citation would be intellectual dishonesty. Your check should include author names, the title of the document and the title of a publication within which it appears (journal title, book title, and so on), and relevant further identification (such as volume and page number, year of publication). Not all of the available identifying data will necessarily have to be carried in your references; some journal articles, for example, have subtitles as well as main titles, and subtitles are rarely included in references. The example references in Appendix 2 illustrate the kinds of data you have to check.

If you find errors in the identifying data in the original document (such as misspelled names of authors), do not correct the errors for your references. The published form of the data element, even if in error, will have to be used by a reader looking for the document; if the search goes through an automated system, the corrected form could obstruct the search. Errors you have identified can be signaled as such by the Latin word sic (meaning *thus*) within square brackets after the error. For example, if you know that "Seabright" in a title with the term, "Seabright bantam syndrome," should be spelled *Sebright*, that error can be indicated as "Seabright [sic] bantam syndrome".

Tables

If in revising your paper through successive drafts you have deleted unneeded text but have not dropped tables or illustrations, the total number of tables and illustrations may be excessive in relation to the length of the text. Too many tables and illustrations can produce difficulties in page layout for the journal. If limits on the number of tables and illustrations are not specified in the journal's information-for-authors page, examine some recent issues to see what number are usually carried in articles with various lengths of text. A useful guide-line to most journals' limits is no more than 1 table or illustration per 1000 words of text (roughly 4 pages of text typed double-spaced).

The title of a table should be complete enough to enable the reader to understand the purpose and content of the table without go-ing to the text for an explanation. Footnotes can explain details that could not be described in the title without making it too long. Be sure that nonstandard abbreviations in the table are explained in footnotes.

Illustrations

Check on whether you have enough photographic copies of all il-lustrations to match the number of copies of the final manuscript you must submit.

TYPING THE FINAL MANUSCRIPT

After you have checked all elements of the paper with attention to the points made above, the final manuscript can be typed. Again, check the journal's information-for-authors page for typing instruc-tions. If it does not provide guidelines for your typist, the points made below may be helpful.

Close attention to a journal's manuscript requirements is most critical for papers going to journals printed from camera-ready copy or manuscripts prepared as magnetic records for direct typesetting.

Manuscripts that are to serve as camera-ready copy (pages to be printed as photographic reproductions of the typed manuscript) must be prepared exactly as specified by the journal. These requirements may include the kind of paper, the kind of typewriter ribbon, and other technical details. The journal will probably provide sheets of pa-per with outlines delineating the area within which typed text must be confined.

Some journals are beginning to use for typesetting by their printer the magnetic records of manuscripts on disks ("floppy disks") generated by word-processing programs. In these systems, the author may be asked to introduce code symbols or words into the text (6); these codes instruct the computer typesetter on choices of typefaces and other details in the page format of the journal. The manuscript will probably be reviewed by the editor and manuscript consultants in the present conventional procedure, with the codes to be inserted into the manuscript only after the journal has accepted the paper and is ready to prepare it for the printer.

Typewriter or Computer-linked Printer

Have the typist use a word-processing program if possible; corrections can be made much more easily and far more rapidly after you and the typist proofread the manuscript. Use a typewriter ribbon producing a black impression. Do not use a typewriter or printer with an unusual typeface, such as one having only capital letters or one imitating handwriting. A dot-matrix printer should be able to produce letter-quality or near letter-quality characters; do not print manuscripts with draft-quality characters (in which individual dots forming the characters are readily visible). Laser printers produce typescripts of substantially better quality than those from typewriters and dot-matrix printers.

Paper

Use a good-quality white bond paper in a standard size: one of the US standard sizes approximating 8.5 by 11 inches (roughly 22 by 28 cm) or, for journals in countries using metric sizes, 212 by 297 mm (ISO A4 size).

Do not use one of the patented bond papers advertised as making erasures easy; type impressions on such papers usually smear readily with handling. Do not use carbon paper for original copies.

Continuous-form papers for computer printers should be of the micro-perforated type so that the manuscript pages do not carry little tufts of paper on their edges.

Spacing

Double-space all typing throughout the manuscript, including not only text pages but also title page, abstract, references, tables, and legends for illustrations. Double-spacing of references means double-spacing between lines of individual references, as well as between adjacent references. Double-spacing is needed for room for instructions to the printer. Do not single-space any part of the manuscript. Avoid the temptation to fool an editor into thinking a paper is shorter than one might guess from the number of pages by typing with 1½ spaces between lines rather than double-spacing or by making the margins excessively narrow. An experienced editor readily catches such ruses and dislikes them.

Numbering Pages

Use arabic numerals and place the page number in a righthand corner (top or bottom) of each page; the righthand bottom corner is preferred. Number pages consecutively, beginning with the title page.

Sequence and Division Sections

Begin each of the sections on a separate page and in this sequence: title page, abstract (with keywords, if requested by the journal), text, acknowledgements, references, tables (no more than one to a page), and legends for illustrations.

Format on Each Page

Type on only 1 side of each sheet of paper. Leave margins of 2.5 to 4 cm (1 to 1.5 inches) at the top, bottom, and sides of each page. Avoid dividing words at the ends of lines. Indent the beginning line of each paragraph.

If the manuscript is prepared with a word-processing program, do not "right-justify" the text at the right margin (vertical alignment of terminal characters of all lines). In many programs, right-justification often produces excessively long spaces between words in each line, which impedes reading.

Other Points

Use normal conventions for capitalizing the title of the paper (7), but use the capitalization style of the journal for text headings and subheadings. Journals prefer xerographic copies to carbon copies (see comments below).

CHECKING AND CORRECTING THE FINAL MANUSCRIPT

The typist should read the completed manuscript first for typing errors. If the manuscript has been typed with a word-processing program, most typing errors can be caught with the program's spelling checker.

You should then read your manuscript twice after typing errors have been corrected, at least once with someone else reading the corrected version from which the final manuscript was typed. In 1 of these 2 readings, pay particular attention to accurate placement of citations in text, accuracy of quotations, and correctness of spelling of names and technical terms. If the manuscript has been typed with a word-processing program, corrections can readily be inserted. With other typewriters insert minor corrections in the space above the line and mark the insertion points in the line with an inverted "vee-mark," also known as a *caret* (see Chapter 18). If long corrections are needed, retype the entire page (and following pages if necessary).

COPIES

Journals expect to receive either original copies of the manuscript or xerographic copies. If the manuscript has been typed on a word-processing program, the additional copies requested by most journals can be provided as typed copies as cheaply as by xerographic copies.

Be sure to retain at least 1 complete copy of the final manuscript, including illustrations, in your own files (as well as the magnetic record of the manuscript if it was prepared with a word-processor). Coauthors should also have complete copies for their files.

CONCLUSION

Before the final version of your paper is typed, review the manuscript requirements of the journal and be sure that your paper contains all the needed elements and that these are in accord with the journal's requirements. Many details will have to be checked on the title page, the abstract page, in the text (especially the citation of references), the references (for data elements and format), and the tables and illustrations. Be sure the final manuscript is typed in accord with the journal's instructions and that the requisite number of copies will be available.

REFERENCES

1. International Committee of Medical Journal Editors. Uniform requirements for manuscripts submitted to biomedical journals. Ann Intern Med. 1982;96:766-71.
   International Committee of Medical Journal Editors. Uniform requirements for manuscripts submitted to biomedical journals. Br Med J. 1982;284:1766-70.
2. National Library of Medicine. Medical subject headings 1987. Bethesda, Maryland: National Library of Medicine; 1987. Published annually as Part 2 of the January issue of *Index Medicus.*
3. Huth EJ. Medical style and format. Philadelphia: ISI Press; 1987:177-210.
4. CBE Style Manual Committee. CBE style manual. 5th ed. Bethesda, Maryland: Council of Biology Editors; 1983:50-3.
5. Huth EJ. Medical style and format. Philadelphia: ISI Press; 1987:321-37.
6. University of Chicago Press. Chicago guide to preparing electronic manuscripts for authors and publishers. Chicago: University of Chicago Press; 1987.
7. Huth EJ. Medical style and format. Philadelphia: ISI Press; 1987:87-9.

16

Submitting the Paper to the Journal

The final version of your paper is ready to be sent to the journal for which you have prepared it. You have in hand the numbers of manuscript copies and illustrations the journal asks for and additional copies for your file and your coauthors.

Four steps remain.

- Preparing the submission letter to accompany the manuscript
- Assembling all other items that also have to be sent with the manuscript
- Packing the letter, manuscript, illustrations, and other documents
- Mailing the manuscript package

THE SUBMISSION LETTER

The editor of the journal to which you are submitting the paper will need some information about you and your paper. You may wish to send additional information that may help the editor in processing the manuscript for review and coming to a decision. All of this information should be in the submission letter, also sometimes called "the covering letter". What should the letter say? What additional information might be included?

Identification of the Paper

The paper should be identified by its full title and the names of all authors. The editor will assume that all of the listed authors have read the final version and agreed to its content. Their institutional affiliations and the name of the institution in which the paper has its origin need not be given in the letter; this information should be carried on the title page (for some journals on the following page).

Description of the Paper

If the title of the paper does not seem to summarize adequately the content of the paper, perhaps because of complexity of its content, you may wish to describe the content more fully.

If the journal publishes various types and formats of papers (such as research reports, brief communications, reviews, editorials), the right category will probably be clear to the editor when he scans the manuscript for a first impression of the paper. You may wish, however, to indicate the category you believe to be appropriate. Presumably you selected the category from the journal's information-for-authors page or a scan of the journal's content before you began to write the paper.

Selection of the Journal

That the content of the paper is relevant to the journal's scope and audience may be clear to the editor from the paper's title, abstract, or quickly scanned text. But if the paper might be appropriate for more than 1 kind of journal, you may wish to explain briefly why you selected the editor's journal. A paper on more efficient procedures for nurses in pediatricians' offices might be submitted to a journal in nursing or one in pediatrics. If the described study finds that the savings in time and costs may benefit the pediatrician more than the nurse, you may decide to prepare the paper for, and send it to, a pediatrics journal. Perhaps you should briefly make this point in your letter lest the editor of the pediatrics journal conclude as soon as he or she looks at the manuscript that it should have been sent to a nursing journal.

Repetitive Publication and Duplicate Submission

Professional journals are expensive to publish, and editors make the best use of their pages by publishing as much as possible only new information. Editors feel ethically obliged to do what they can to prevent clogging bibliographic indexes like *Index Medicus* with references to papers describing the same findings from a single study. For these reasons you should indicate in your letter that the content of your paper has not been published already and is not in any paper already, or about to be, submitted to another journal. A statement this specific is needed because to the editor *repetitive publication* refers not only to exact duplication of a paper (exactly the same title, abstract, text, references, tables, and illustrations) but also to repeated publication of essentially the same information whether or not it is presented in precisely the same way.

If any part of the submitted paper's content has been, or shortly will be, published but you believe that its publication again should not thereby be precluded, you should tell the editor why you believe publication of your submitted paper in his or her journal is justified. The editor may be aided by your including with the manuscript (see below) a copy of any possibly related paper.

A paper should be sent to only 1 journal and not to another until it has been rejected by the first. Editors resent having to spend time and effort in processing papers also submitted to other journals that are subsequently withdrawn because of an acceptance elsewhere. What you might gain through saving time in getting an acceptance more quickly, you may lose in reputation. Your letter should include a statement that the paper is being submitted only to that journal and has not been, or will not shortly be, submitted to another journal.

Conditions on Publication

State in the submission letter any conditions you feel you must place on publication of the paper by the journal if it is accepted. You may wish, for example, to read a version of the paper at a professional society meeting in May and to do so must respect the policy of the society that only papers not already published may be read at its meeting. Hence, you will have to ask of the editor that if the paper is accepted it not be published earlier than June. Or you may wish to have the paper also published in a proceedings of a scientific meeting to be issued at a date far enough in the future so that it will appear after its publication in the journal; you want to be sure that the journal will grant you permission for the re-publication in the proceedings. This situation should be described to the editor so that he or she can decide whether the time needed for review of the manuscript, the journal's backlog (if any), and the press schedule are such that your request could be met. Another example is that of color illustrations; you may wish to have the editor agree to publish the paper, if accepted, only with the color, rather than black-and-white, illustrations.

Whatever condition you may wish to place on publication, be sure that you do need it. The rejection rate is necessarily high in a major journal popular with authors; its editor may not wish to have to deal with conditions that may limit the scope of editorial decisions and the flexibility of schedules. The editor may prefer to reject the paper immediately to avoid possibly being burdened later with the condition asked for.

Copyright

Most professional journals expect to have the copyright on an article to be transferred to the journal by the author when the paper is submitted or when it is accepted. An author will not be free to transfer copyright in 2 circumstances: if he or she has written the paper as a Federal employee, or if the copyright became the property of a private organization at the time of the paper's creation because of the author's acceptance of that arrangement as an employee of the organization. If the author cannot transfer copyright to the journal for 1 of these 2 reasons or any other reason, that constraint should be stated in the submission letter. Some journals will not accept a paper for which copyright cannot be transferred (except papers from Federal employees).

Content for Optional Publication

What if your paper is very long, in part because of an unusually large number of large tables, but you feel that all of its content should be available to at least some readers? You could point out in your letter that you would be willing to have those portions of the paper not critically needed for most readers filed in an archival respository from which interested readers would be able to get copies of the part deleted from the version of the paper published. A journal may be willing to let authors state that they will supply readers with copies of large tables (or other material) that could not be included in the published version of the paper.

Alternatives in Format

A Methods section might be very long because, for example, it includes a detailed description of a statistical method rarely used in medical research. The author might suggest to the editor that that description could be placed at the end of the paper in an appendix, where it would not distract readers interested in the paper but unable to understand the principles and application of the statistical method.

Suggestions on Reviewers

Most editors maintain files with names of potential manuscript reviewers expert in the fields covered by their journals, but these files may not be adequate for some highly specialized topics. If you believe that the topic of your paper is one not frequently covered by the journal, you may wish to suggest experts on the topic who could pass critical judgment on your paper. If you do so, you might assure the editor that the suggested reviewers have not participated in any way in preparing the paper, have not read the paper before its submission, and are not friends who might be uncritically biased toward the paper.

If your research is in a highly competitive field, you may not wish to have your paper reviewed by rivals; you may feel that they might be tempted to hinder or try to block its publication. You can properly ask the editor not to use as reviewers the persons you specify. You should not, however, give the editor such a long list of reviewers to be avoided that he or she will suspect you of eliminating all persons expert enough in the field to find any weaknesses in the paper.

The Responsible Author

The letter must make clear who will be responsible for receiving correspondence and phone calls from the editor or other members of the journal's staff and who will be responsible for revising the paper. Usually, but not always, the two will be the same person, probably you. The letter should include the name(s), postal address(es), and phone number(s). Other useful addresses may include those for an electronic-mail system or a facsimile ("fax") or telex terminal. If the previously agreed-upon responsible author may be away in the near future for a long vacation, business trip abroad, or a sabbatical leave, an alternative responsible author should be designated, also with postal address and phone number.

If your paper is being submitted by an editor in your institution (an "author's editor"), the letter should indicate whether the journal editor is free to correspond with, or telephone, the responsible author for revisions and meeting other requests or should direct all inquiries and requests to the author's editor.

Payment for Manuscript Handling

Some journals charge a fee to cover the costs of processing and reviewing manuscripts. If the journal to which you are sending the paper expects to receive payment with the manuscript, indicate in the letter that payment is enclosed and identify the document of payment (check or money order).

Cost of Color Illustrations

Some journals will take on the cost of publishing color illustrations, which is far higher than for black-and-white illustrations, but many journals expect the author to meet that cost. Indicate in the letter whether you will be willing to pay for this cost if your paper includes color illustrations.

What Not to Include in the Letter

Probably all editors feel that they, their editorial associates, their editorial boards, and their manuscript reviewers are collectively competent enough to judge the importance and validity of papers in the fields their journals cover. You may have doubts about a particular journal, but presumably that is not the journal to which you are sending your paper. Do not risk slurring the editor's competence by including in the letter what the advertising industry calls a "hard sell"; do not claim that the paper reports the greatest breakthrough in medical science since Pasteur demolished the theory of spontaneous generation of life or reports the greatest advance in therapeutics since Fleming stumbled onto penicillin. If your paper is so important, it will be recognized as such. If it is not so recognized, your effusions will probably not change anyone's judgment; the manuscript reviewers will probably not see your letter anyway.

THE NEXT STEP

After you have prepared your submission letter (see Figure 16.1 for an example), you should be ready to prepare the manuscript and accompanying materials for mailing.

The Manuscript Package

Contents

It is clear to you already that more than the manuscript must be mailed to the editor. Here is a checklist that includes items which must be sent and items needed only in some circumstances.

- Submission letter
- Manuscript copies: the number requested by the journal; illustrations in separate envelopes for each set
- Transfer of copyright form (unless letter indicates transfer of copyright)
- Copies of related manuscripts or papers (see above, "Repetitive Publication and Duplicate Submission")
- Reply postal card or letter with self-addressed and stamped envelope for acknowledgment of receipt of the manuscript (not wanted by some journals)

Rosena Happenstance, DM
Editor
Journal of Therapeutic Science
999 Rocky Lane
Butterbush, DN 1001

Dear Dr Happenstance: 31 December 1987

Enclosed are three copies of "Aspirin for Treatment of Headaches: A Double-blind Comparison with a Placebo," by TX Stone, RM Rock, and J Doe. The paper is submitted to be considered for publication as a "research report" in your journal. Neither the entire paper nor any part of its content has been published or has been accepted by another journal. The paper is not being submitted to any other journal.

We believe the paper may be of particular interest to your readers because the study it reports used a new and more precise method of estimating subjective relief of pain.

Correspondence and phone calls about the paper should be directed to me at the following address and phone number:

> Jan Doe, BSN, PhD
> Institute for Analgesic Research
> 4321 Main Road
> Asberdelphia, UZ 12345
> (234) 567-8912

Thank you for your attention to our paper.

Sincerely yours,

Jan Doe, BSN, PhD

Figure 16.1. A typical, but fictional, submission letter.

- Copies of permissions to publish pictures of patients, to cite unpublished communications, to acknowledge help with the paper
- Stiffening cardboard

The items to be sent should be mailed in a sturdy envelope large enough to accommodate them without difficulty but small enough to protect its contents against shifting about. Photographs can be protected against creasing by including cardboard inserts fitting snugly into the envelope.

Addressing the Envelope

Be sure that you have the correct address to which the manuscript package should be mailed; check the journal's information-for-authors page if you are not sure. Occasionally authors erroneously mail manuscripts to the journal's advertising office or its publisher's office, which may not be at the same location as the editorial office.

Mailing

Unless you must meet a very close deadline, the manuscript package can usually be sent to the editorial office within the country by first-class mail; the small gain in time from sending it by one of the express-mail services is rarely worth their greater cost. If you are mailing it to another country and certainly to another continent, use air mail.

Before you mail the package be sure that you, and perhaps your coauthors, have retained copies of all that you are about to mail. Mail service is not flawless anywhere; some manuscripts do get lost.

CONCLUSION

Submitting a paper to a journal calls for preparing a submission letter that will give the editor the information he or she will need about you and the paper, assembling any items that will have to be sent along with the manuscript, packing the manuscript and other items in a suitable envelope, and mailing the package.

17

Responding to the Editor's Decision

You wrote and revised your paper with great care. The manuscript of the final version was typed and assembled with close attention to the journal's requirements. You mailed the manuscript to the editor and received notice of its arrival at the journal's office. What happens next?

EDITORS' DECISIONS

Journals differ greatly in how their editors decide what to accept and what to reject. The chief editors of some journals, notably those in the basic medical services, divide the reading of submitted papers and responsibility for decisions on them among associate editors and members of a large editorial board. Editors of journals in clinical medicine and closely related fields may be aided in assessing papers by 1 or more associate editors but are also likely to ask manuscript consultants to read papers critically, suggest decisions (see Figure 17.1), and recommend revisions the editor may request before acceptance of papers.

Factors Bearing on Decisions

Exactly what procedure is followed by an editor in coming to decisions is less important for authors than the factors the editor may have to take into account in each decision. Most journals receive far more papers than they can carry in the pages allotted by the publisher. For this reason, rejection rates necessarily run at some arbitrary level, which for the better journals is between 50% and 90%. Thus editors must decide on criteria to sort out which papers will be accepted and which will not.

```
ORIGINAL PAPERS ONLY (check one item in each column):

        Scientific Information                      Scientific Validity

        ____ New, major importance                  ____ Valid
        ____ Confirmatory, major importance         ____ Weak in some aspects (comments on
        ____ New, minor importance                       author's sheet)
        ____ Confirmatory, minor importance         ____ Invalid (comments on author's sheet)
        ____ Little value


REVIEWS, EDITORIALS, OPINION PAPERS ONLY (check items that best reflect your judgment):

        ____ Reflects new, important developments    ____ Stale content
        ____ Accurate                                ____ Inaccurate (comments on author's sheet)
        ____ Complete                                ____ Important information missing
        ____ Wide appeal                                  (comments on author's sheet)
                                                     ____ Appeal limited

OVERALL JUDGMENT (check one):

        ____ Accept          ____ Accept after satisfactory revision          ____ Reject


                             ____ Reconsider after major revision
```

Figure 17.1. Example of a form sent to consultants reviewing a manuscript for a peer-review journal. In addition to providing the editor with detailed comments on content of the paper for the editor and for the author, the consultants are asked to indicate with checks on this part of the form their assessment of the overall importance and quality of the paper. (Reproduced by permission of *Annals of Internal Medicine.*)

At least 5 criteria are likely to be applied at some time by most editors.

- Relevance of the paper to the journal's scope and audience
- Importance of the paper's message to most of the journal's audience
- Newness of the paper's message
- Scientific validity of the evidence supporting the paper's conclusions
- Usefulness of the paper to the journal in maintaining a desirable range of topics

Even if a paper is acceptable when judged by these 5 criteria, the editor may have to apply 2 more.

- Effect of acceptance on the journal's backlog of already accepted papers
- Quality of presentation in the manuscript

Editors do not wish to have their journals known as slow to get papers into print, so they have to hold down the backlog of papers accepted but not yet published. The backlog does have to be large enough to ensure an adequate supply of papers for publication in the face of fluctuations from week to week in the numbers of papers submitted. But the backlog also must be kept small enough not to lead to a delay in publishing accepted papers. A paper rejected when the back log is large might have been accepted if the backlog had been small. The quality of presentation may be a decisive factor. Two papers with equal merit in content may compete with each other for acceptance; if one has been poorly written and its manuscript carelessly prepared, it is likely to be the one rejected.

Even though an editor may apply most of these criteria in coming to a decision on your paper, you may never know exactly how your paper was judged. Editors are unlikely to assign exact quantitative judgments to all papers for each criterion. If they did, they would probably not have the time to dictate decision letters that would explain in detail all the criteria applied to each paper and how it ranked for each criterion. The decision letter you receive will almost certainly not explain why your paper was accepted if that is the good news. If the letter brings the bad news of rejection, it is likely to carry at least 1 reason for rejection, but it is not likely to describe all the factors that were assessed by the editor for the decision. Some of them may be apparent in consultants' comments prepared for the author.

Time Needed for a Decision

How soon can you expect to receive a decision? If the editor reads your paper, decides not to send it to consultants, and rejects it, you may receive that decision promptly. But even if the editor decides on rejection as soon as he reads the paper, the typing and mailing of a decision letter take time. So at least 2 or 3 weeks are likely to pass before you hear from the editor.

If the paper is sent to consultants for reading, more time will pass before a decision. Consultants are asked to review papers promptly, often within a specified period such as 10 days or 2 weeks, but even those who agree to a time limit may exceed it because of illness or unanticipated demands on their time. The many differences in editorial-office procedures and consultant response make it hard to predict the time needed for a decision on a consultant-reviewed paper. A fair range of time is 4 to 8 weeks. If you have not received a decision within this period, the editor may have had difficulties in getting adequate consultant critiques or the office staff may have been burdened with an unusually heavy load of work. Sending an inquiry by letter to the editor on the status of your paper after 8 weeks have passed and you have not received a decision is a reasonable step to take.

DECISIONS AND RESPONSES

Acceptances: Immediate and Provisional

Few authors, particularly those whose papers have not been invited, receive immediate and unconditional acceptances. Even authors fortunate enough to have their papers accepted immediately for important and valid content are likely to be asked to revise the paper to improve its presentation: shortening text, restructuring tables, eliminating informal abbreviations, improving illustrations, or other changes. If you do receive an immediate acceptance with such requests for revision, be pleased with your good fortune and carry out the requests. The revisions are, from the editor's point of view, needed for good reasons, such as space available, format limits on number of tables, and other technical problems. If the requests seem unclear, unreasonable, impossible to carry out, or likely to cripple the paper's capacity to carry its message, do not simply refuse to carry out the revisions and return the paper unrevised. Reply by letter to the editor about the difficulties you see in revising the paper along the lines requested and why. The editor may insist on the revisions or, if your objections seem justified, may compromise on the first requests.

Acceptances are often provisional, with final acceptance depending on how well the author can revise the paper to meet criticisms of its content, the requests for revision of its presentation, or both. As with immediate acceptances calling only for technical revisions of the manuscript, do your best to revise the paper without delay along the lines recommended by the consultants and requested by the editor. If recommendations from the consultants are contradictory, you may have to ask the editor for guidance on how to proceed if his letter has not mediated between the conflicting comments. Not all recommendations from consultants may have to be accepted, but you will have to justify to the editor (see below) why you have not made those changes. Before you conclude that revision is not needed because the consultant apparently did not read your paper closely, be sure that the paper does not suffer from faulty presentation, such as unclear writing, conflicting data, or some other defect. If you disagree with most, if not all, of the consultants' recommendations and the editor's requests, you can appeal to the editor for exemptions. Do not simply ignore the consultants' comments and the editor's decision letter and return the paper unchanged. You may prefer withdrawing the paper from further consideration by the journal, but if you take this step, inform the editor so that the journal's records of your paper can be kept up-to-date.

Returning a Revised Paper

Review of your revised paper will be easier for the editor, the journal staff, and consultants who read the new version if you send with it a letter not only identifying it as a new version but also specifying exactly what changes were made, their locations, and their relation to the consultants' recommendations and the editor's requests. Changes asked for and not made should be pointed out, and you should justify having not made them. If each consultant was not identified in some way so that you can link your changes to specific recommendations, you may wish to make copies of the consultants' sheets and mark them for ready reference in your letter, such as "recommendations A1, A3 and recommendations B2, B6, and B7" (from "Consultant A" and "Consultant B").

Rejections

What if the paper is rejected? Do not get angry and take a rash step. The rejection may be fully justified from the editor's point of view. Keep in mind how authors are competing for limited space in journals, especially the most widely read journals. Consider carefully the comments from the consultants, if the paper was sent to consultants. They may point out sound reasons that figured in the editor's decision. If the consultants seem to have misread the paper, the fault may lie in unclear writing, misplaced emphasis, or some other defect in presentation. If the editor's letter simply tells you that the paper could not be given a high enough priority, or that space cannot be made for the paper (another way of stating priorities), you are likely getting the truth. This is a shorthand way to tell you that the paper's information is not new enough or important enough for the journal, at least at this time. That kind of rejection is not a slur on the soundness of the paper's content or on how well it presents its message.

Should you appeal the decision? If you think you can meet major objections to the paper by revising it, the editor may be willing to reconsider a new version but do not send in a new version without getting the editor's consent. If you seek that consent, do it by correspondence. The editor may have reasons not given in the rejection letter as to why the paper was rejected, and you may be able to save yourself time by getting those reasons.

Should you send the paper to another journal? This response is usually the better step, unless you decide not to go on with seeking to get it published. The paper may be readily accepted by a journal of lesser reputation or a more specialized journal. Before you send the paper to a new journal, however, do what you can to improve the odds that it will be accepted. Consider carefully the comments from consultants and from the editor. These may enable you to improve the paper greatly. Do not overlook the possibility that the consultants who will read the paper for the second journal may include one or more of the consultants who read it for the first journal; if so, a failure to revise the paper in response to fair criticism could bias a consultant against the paper in this second submission. Be sure that the manuscript you send is a clean manuscript, bearing no marks from its submission to the first journal, no restapling holes, no other indications to the second journal's editor that he is not the first editor to see it! Be sure, too, that the new manuscript meets all the technical requirements of the second journal. In brief, be sure that the manuscript looks as if it had been prepared specifically for the second journal.

CONCLUSION

Journals differ in some details among the procedures used for review of submitted papers and decisions on which to accept. Most use some variation of the consultant-review system in which experts are asked to give the editor judgments on papers' validity and importance. The editor is likely to apply additional criteria in coming to decisions. If your paper is accepted, some revision is still likely to be needed to meet consultant and editorial requests. If your paper is rejected, consider carefully, not angrily, whether the rejection was justified and whether the paper should be carefully revised again, even if you decide to submit it to another journal rather than give up efforts to get it published.

18

Correcting Proof

The editor has accepted your paper. The letter with that message may also tell you in what issue the paper will be published and when you can expect to receive proof of the paper to read and correct.

Proof, your paper set in type as it will appear in the journal, will show you what changes were made in the paper when the manuscript was prepared for the printer. You will get from the proof some impression of how the paper will look in print, but proof is mainly sent to enable you to catch errors in typesetting the paper and to correct them.

If the editor or publisher has not told you when you can expect to receive proof and you might be away on a business trip or vacation in the months ahead, you should ask when proof is likely to arrive so that, if necessary, you can change the time of your absence or arrange to have a coauthor or another responsible colleague read and correct proof for you. Journals cannot tolerate a delay in return of corrected proof from the author.

FORMS OF PROOF

Proof sent to the author is usually in the form of galley proof, long single-columns of the text of your paper as it has been set in type. A few journals may provide, instead, page proof, which represents the paper set in type arranged in the format it will have in the journal. Some journals send neither galley proof nor page proof but a copy of the manuscript (or a newly typed version) as edited and marked for the printer. Proof of a paper prepared for computer typesetting may include instruction codes for the computer.

Proofs of tables and illustrations are usually sent with the proof of the text.

WHAT NOT TO DO WITH PROOF

Proof is sent for correction, not for rewriting the paper. When the paper was accepted, the editor was accepting that paper and not a new

199

version rewritten at the proof stage. If you have changed your mind about content in the paper you may have to either get permission from the editor to withdraw it from publication or get permission for an addendum at the end of the text with the new material.

Resist the temptation to polish your prose at this last minute. Changes at the proof stage are expensive; the editor will probably disregard changes that have nothing to do with correctness of content.

Unless changes made by the journal's copyeditor have introduced errors, let those changes stand. They probably represent either the journal's policy on details of style or correction of faulty grammar, syntax, or spelling.

Do not treat proof lightly, reading it quickly and casually as if it were sent to you only to have you confirm that yes, this is your paper.

WHAT TO DO WITH PROOF

Read proof to be sure that it says what the accepted manuscript said.

Read proof to be sure that all content of the paper agrees with itself, that the same numbers for the same findings or observations appear in the abstract, the text, the tables, and the illustrations.

Read proof to be sure that nothing has been left out by the printer in the typesetting.

Read proof to detect errors in spelling and mistakes in typesetting.

Mark proof with conventional proofreaders' marks (Table 18.1).

How to Read Proof

Careful and thorough reading of proof calls for 2 readings.

First Reading

For the first reading, enlist the help of someone who will read the manuscript from which type was set while you follow the proof. The reader can be a coauthor or another colleague. The better reader may be someone unfamiliar with the paper and its subject who is more likely to read the manuscript at a properly slow and careful pace. Each word and numeral must be enunciated clearly. Each punctuation sign must be indicated. The beginning and end of each paragraph must be stated. Section headings and subheadings, table titles, figure legends, and other special portions of text must be identified as such. Tables must be read row by row or column by column. As the reader proceeds, you must follow along in the proof at the same location and at the same pace, resisting temptation to scan ahead. Any errors you

Table 18.1. Proofreaders' marks*

(Note that instructions to the printer not to be set in type should be circled.)

Instruction	Marginal mark	In-line mark	Corrected type
		Additions	
Add space	#	the new⎮tumor	the new tumor
Insert in line	new	the˄tumor	the new tumor
Insert as superscript	32✓	[P]AMP	[^{32}P]AMP
Insert as subscript	2	CO˄	CO_2
Restore deletion	(stet)	the new tumor	the new tumor
		Deletions	
Delete	℈	the new tumor	the tumor
Delete and close up	℈	the tumo/r	the tumor
Delete space	⌒	peri⁀natal	perinatal
Reset as superscript	32✓	[32P]AMP	[^{32}P]AMP
Reset as subscript	2	CO2/	CO_2
Substitute in line	new	the old tumor	the new tumor
		Location changes	
Align vertically	‖ or (align)	‖the new ‖ tumor	the new tumor
Align horizontally	= or (straighten)	the ᵉw tumor	the new tumor
Begin new paragraph	¶	¶ The new tumor. . .	The new tumor. . .
Center	(ctr)	] the tumor[	the tumor
Move to left	[	[tumor	tumor
Move to right	]	tumor	tumor
Move up	⌐	⌐tumor⌐	tumor
Move down	⌐	⌐tumor/	tumor
Run paragraphs together	no ¶	The old tumor shrank.⌐ ⌐The new tumor grew.	The old tumor shrank. The new tumor grew.

* A few instructions are duplicated under two headings.

Table 18.1. *Continued*

Instruction	Marginal mark	In-line mark	Corrected type
		Punctuation	
Apostrophe	⌄✓	Cushings syndrome	Cushing's syndrome
Brackets	[/]	﹀tumor﹀	[tumor]
Colon	⦂	Listen﹀ a murmur!	Listen: a murmur!
Comma	⌄?	tumor﹀calor	tumor, calor
Dash, 1-en	⊢N⊣	pages 10﹀12	pages 10–12
Dash, 1-em	⊢M⊣	Listen﹀examine!	Listen—examine!
Hyphen	=	pro﹀abortion	pro-abortion
Parentheses	(/)	. . . study2﹀	. . . study (2)
Period	⊙	The tumor grew﹀	The tumor grew.
Question mark	?	A tumor﹀	A tumor?
Quotation marks, single	⌄/⌄	He admitted, "A ﹀goof﹀."	He admitted, "A 'goof'."
Quotation marks, double	⌄⌄/⌄⌄	He admitted, ﹀A goof﹀. ⌢	He admitted, "A goof."
Semicolon	;	Listen﹀then examine.	Listen; then examine.
Slant line	/	g⌄dL	g/dL
Underline, 3 ems long	Replacement for word	He said, "Dump it."	He said, "___3___ it." M
		Substitutions	
Reset as superscript	32✓	32P	³²P
Reset as subscript	⩘2	CO2	CO₂
Spell out	(SP)	The②tumors	The two tumors
Substitute in line	new	the old tumor	the new tumor
		Type changes	
Capitalize as marked	(cap)	Sle	SLE
Lowercase letter	(lc)	HBR	HBr
Reset broken letter	×	(H)Br	HBr
Set in boldface type	(bf)	TUMOR	**TUMOR**
Set in capitals and small capitals	(c ﹠ sc)	osler	Osler

Table 18.1. *Continued*

Instruction	Marginal mark	In-line mark	Corrected type
Set in italic type	*(ital)*	<u>Proteus</u>	*Proteus*
Set in lightface type	*(lf)*	(tumor)	tumor
Set in roman type	(rom)	(virus)	virus
Wrong font; reset	(wf)	(Osler)	Osler

detect need not be corrected at this time with appropriate marks (see below, "Marking Proof"), but at least penciled notes should be made in the margins of the proof to indicate where corrections will have to be marked after the second reading.

Second Reading

In reading the proof for the second time, read it by yourself. Before starting to read, remind yourself consciously that the reading will have to be slow and deliberate. As you move slowly from word to word, focus attention on each word. The first reading should have caught all errors; the second reading is insurance against missing errors. Do not let your attention wander onto the meaning of text rather than its appearance; try to keep your attention on each and every detail before you. The second reading is also your chance to cross-check data that appear at 2 or more points in the paper.

What to Check

Spelling

Even if you are only slightly uncertain about the correct spelling of a word, verify its spelling in a dictionary. Be especially careful about scientific terms not familiar to you and about personal names. Personal names cited in the text from your references should be checked against those names as they appear in the references; a disagreement should lead to a check against the original document.

Word Division

Some words will have been broken at the end of lines to "justify" the right margin of the text (keeping the right-hand ends of lines of the text evenly aligned). Such divisions are usually in accord with 1 of 2 practices. British practice divides words by etymologic units; American practice divides words by pronunciation units. The newer computer typesetters, in general, divide words according to American practice. Most dictionaries indicate word divisions and can be used to check on the correctness of a break at the end of a line.

Other Details

Focus attention on details readily missed in the first (2-reader) reading, such as correct use of italics for scientific names and proper alignments within equations.

Cross-Checking

Verifying authors' names cited in the text against the references has been mentioned above. Other cross-checks should also be carried out. Do the citation numbers in the text match the right references? Are the same numerical values given for the same data at all points where they are mentioned: abstract, results, text, tables, figures?

Checking Tables

Tables are checked in the first reading for correctness of title, row and column headings, and numeric values for the data in the field. In the second reading, any arithmetic operations represented by data, such as addition for column totals or percentage calculation, should be verified. These checks may have been carried out before the final version of the paper was typed, but a check again at this time is a wise precaution. The correctness of alignment of data under column headings and beside row headings should be checked. Be sure that all footnote symbols in the table have corresponding footnotes and that the footnote symbols are in the proper order: They should read left to right, top to bottom.

Checking Illustrations

Proofs of line illustrations such as graphs and diagrams must be checked closely to be sure that data have not been lost, that lines have not been broken where they should not be, and that no other errors have occurred in reproduction. Continuous-tone illustrations such as roentgenograms and photomicrographs should be checked for defects that might be interpreted by readers as part of the original. Orientation should be checked to be sure that "top" is where the top should be; note, however, that the "top" you designated in a photomicrograph might have become "side" if the editor decided that a change in orientation was needed.

Queries from Editor or Printer

The copy editor in the editor's or publisher's office may have written questions on the manuscript, or in a separate note, asking you to verify some detail in the paper or to check his or her interpretation of it. The printer may have raised a question in the margin of the proof as to whether a detail in the manuscript turned into the right representation of it in type. To these queries you must respond.

MARKING PROOF

Each proof correction needs at least 2 marks: 1 or more at the place in the line to be corrected, and 1 or more in the margin of the proof adjacent to and aligned with the corrected line. For example, in the line

recent studies of myo͜cardial infarction

"myocardial" was set in type with an unneeded space. The sign at the right-hand end is the sign for "close up", and the same sign is applied in the line at the right point. This example would be properly corrected in proof thus:

recent studies of myocardial infarction

The marks should be made in the margin nearest the place in the line to be corrected. If 2 or more marks are adjacent, separate them with slant lines. Make the marks with pencil, for ease in erasure, but be sure that the color of your marks differs from the color of any correction marks already on the proof. Use the standard American marks shown in Table 18.1. British editors and printers use some different marks, but American marks are likely to be readily understood by British printers. Rather different marks are used in some other countries, but the printers are likely to supply a sheet with proof marks.

You may have to write on the proof some instructions or remarks to the printer or to the copy editor who will incorporate your corrections in a master set of corrected proof that will be sent back to the printer. Such notes should be circled to distinguish them clearly from correction marks.

Queries from the editor or printer must be answered. If a suggested change should not be made, draw a line through the query and note within a circle, "OK as set" or "stet."

An extensive change (such as more than a line) should be typed on a narrow slip of paper and taped to the proof at the right location with a circled identification such as "change b for galley 3" on the slip, a similar circled identification in the margin, and a mark for the location of the change.

Figure 18.1. A short sample of text with typesetting errors marked in proof and corrected. Note that instructions to the printer are circled to distinguish them from items to be added. Adjacent marks, instructions, and additions applying to the same line are arranged in the same left-to-right sequence as the errors to which they apply and are separated by slant lines (also known as slashes). The points of insertion of corrections are indicated by insertion marks (also known as carets).

Figure 18.1 illustrates the use of proof-correction marks on a small sample of text.

================ **CONCLUSION** ================

Proof—a paper as first set into type—is sent to authors not for rewriting of the paper but solely for correction of errors made by the copy editor in marking the manuscript for the printer or in typesetting by the printer. Two readings of proof, the first with 2 persons, will sharply reduce the chances that any errors will go uncorrected. Proofreading should look not only for errors committed after the paper was accepted but also for errors that might have escaped attention when the final manuscript was read before being sent to the journal, such as disagreement between data in the abstract and in the main body of the paper. Errors should be corrected with standard proofreaders' marks, in the margin of the proof and within the line where the error appears.

19

Between Proof and Publication

After you have received proof, corrected it, and returned it to the journal, you can be reasonably sure that the paper will appear in the journal in a few weeks to a few months. The proof probably carried a note indicating the date of the issue in which your paper will appear. Between the date on which you returned the proof and the publication date, some questions may come up that merit comment here.

REPRINTS AND PREPRINTS

Reprint order forms are usually sent with proof. If the order form did not arrive with your proof, request the form from the publisher. Reprints may be more expensive if ordered after publication of the issue with your paper. Some authors may wish to provide colleagues elsewhere with copies of a paper in advance of publication by mailing them copies of the manuscript or of the proof rather than sending reprints. They should remember that after a paper is accepted and its copyright transferred to the journal by the author, the journal acquires by that copyright the legal right to decide how the paper is handled up to its publication. The journal may not wish to have copies of the paper circulated before the issue for which it is scheduled appears. If the journal wishes, for example, to have no mention of the content of the paper appear in another journal or in a newspaper before its own publication date, that wish may have been stated in the acceptance letter as a condition of acceptance. If no such condition of acceptance was stated, the journal may wish, nevertheless, that the paper not circulate before it appears in print. The prudent author who wants to send out preprint copies will consult the journal's editor before doing so; the journal may be willing to let you send out preprints.

PREPUBLICATION DISCLOSURES

If your paper is reporting new scientific information likely to be of interest to a much wider audience than that of the journal, your institution or the journal itself may wish to send out press releases about it in advance of its publication. Journals are unlikely to send out such releases without the consent of authors, but if you do not wish to have a press release go out and the journal has not queried you on this point, you should notify the editor of your wish. Presumably, your institution likewise would not prepare and mail press releases without your consent.

If you read your paper (or a shorter version of it) at a scientific meeting, you may face the risk that a reporter will prepare a news story about your findings. If the reporter has been invited to the meeting by the society or association running it, you will probably be asked to meet the reporter to facilitate preparation of an accurate story. When you meet the reporter, indicate the publication ("release") date of the paper. A scrupulous reporter will hold the story until the release date if he or she is going to report your findings on the basis of the published version. If the reporter's assignment is specifically to cover the meeting, the reporter may ignore the date.

You or the journal editor may be approached by other parties for information about the content of the paper. Stock-market analysts may get wind of a drug trial and wish to know the details of the findings; a favorable outcome could lead to a big price rise in the stock of the firm marketing the drug. A pharmaceutical firm may hear of a new serious adverse effect of one of its drugs and wish to get details about your findings before the paper reporting the effect is published. In circumstances like these you may be visited or telephoned by someone seeking information about your paper but not known to you as a professional colleague. Do not forget that as soon as your paper was accepted and your copyright passed to the journal, the paper and any of its content became the property of the journal, with the right to decide whether any preprint disclosure of content should be allowed. Hence, any inquiries to you about the paper should be referred to the editor or the publisher. If the editor is approached for similar prepublication release of information and believes such release is acceptable from the journal's point of view, you are likely to be contacted by the editor for permission for the release despite the journal's holding the copyright.

CITING ACCEPTED PAPERS

Chapter 15 points out that in deciding which references could be used in the formal list of references at the end of the paper, cited papers could be identified as "in press" after they had been accepted (finally, not only provisionally) by a journal. If you have written or are writing another paper that cites the paper you have "in press", references to your paper "in press" can now be changed to give more precise identification. At least you should be able to add the journal's volume number, or publication date, or both in place of "in press". The editorial office may be able to give you the page numbers if you have returned the proof.

PUBLICATION

In a few weeks or months your paper will appear in print, probably touching off in you a well-justified pride. But do not be surprised if on reading the paper in the journal you are hit by a wave of nausea or some similarly unpleasant sensation. You may suddenly see a defect you did not catch in the last revision. You may see how you could have said something better. Hold on; do not flog yourself. You will do better in your next paper!

Keep in mind that a serious error undetected before publication can be corrected in many journals by your sending the journal a letter-to-the-editor for publication describing the error and giving the correction.

Appendix 1

Twenty Steps in Planning, Writing, and Publishing a Paper

1. Decide on the message of the paper. Can you state it in a single sentence? With case reports and reviews, you may not be sure of the exact message until you have searched the literature. (Chapters 1 and 2)

2. Decide whether the paper is worth writing. Have similar findings been reported? Is there a need for another report? With case reports and reviews, has your literature search turned up similar cases or reviews? (Chapters 1 and 2)

3. Decide on the importance of your paper. Apply the "so-what" test; how would the paper change concept or practice? (Chapter 1)

4. Decide on the audience for the paper; apply the "who-cares" test. (Chapter 1)

5. Select the journal for which you will prepare the paper. (Chapter 1)

6. Search the literature: For a firm decision on writing the paper and on its message; for documentary materials. (Chapter 2)

7. Decide on authorship. (Chapter 3)

8. Assemble the materials needed to write and eventually publish the paper. If you are writing an invited review paper or editorial, make sure you know the conditions accompanying the invitation and request any you feel should be met before you accept it. (Chapter 3)

9. Look up the manuscript requirements for the journal. (Chapter 3)

10. Consider the proper structure for the paper before you begin to outline it and write the first draft. (Chapters 4-8)

11. Develop a sketch or outline for the first draft. (Chapter 9)

12. Write the first draft. (Chapter 9)

13. Revise the first draft and subsequent drafts (with any coauthors) until you are fully satisfied with the content of the paper. (Chapter 10)

14. Revise your prose for fluency, clarity, accuracy, economy, and grace. (Chapter 11)

15. Make sure that the details of scientific style are correct. (Chapter 12)

16. Prepare the final choices and right presentations for tables and illustrations. (Chapters 13 and 14)

17. Review, and revise if necessary, the last complete draft and get it typed for the final manuscript. (Chapter 15)

18. Assemble the manuscript copies and accompanying materials to send to the journal's editor with a submission letter. (Chapter 16)

19. Respond to the editor's decision: Revise a provisionally accepted paper as requested; send a rejected paper to another journal after making needed revisions; or give up trying to get the paper published. (Chapter 17)

20. If the paper is accepted, correct proof carefully as soon as it arrives, return it promptly, and await publication of the paper. (Chapters 18 and 19)

Appendix 2

Formats for References

The formats for references illustrated below have been recommended to the International Committee of Medical Journal Editors by the National Library of Medicine. These formats can be expected to be acceptable in manuscripts submitted to the more than 500 journals around the world subscribing to the Committee's "Uniform Requirements" agreement; some of these journals may change some details in style of references for publication but all have agreed not to require authors to make those changes. The journals are listed below under "Journals in the 'Uniform Requirements . . .' Agreement as of September 1989". The Committee's original formats were described in "Uniform Requirements for Manuscripts Submitted to Biomedical Journals", published in *Annals of Internal Medicine* 1982;96(Part 1):766–71 and *British Medical Journal* 1982;284:1766–70. The formats set forth here differ in some details from the original formats, and new examples for various kinds of documents have been added.

Note that the formats of some of the references in this book, prepared before these recommendations were available, may differ from those recommended here.

REFERENCES FORMATS

Journals

1. Standard Journal Article
   List all authors when 6 or less; when 7 or more, list the first 6 and add et al. If the journal carries continuous pagination throughout a volume, the issue number may be omitted, as in the second example.

   You CH, Lee KY, Chey WY, Menguy R. Electrogastric study of patients with unexplained nausea, bloating and vomiting. Gastroenterology 1980 Aug;79(2):311–4.
   You CH, Lee KY, Chey WY, Menguy R. Electrogastric study of patients with unexplained nausea, bloating and vomiting. Gastroenterology 1980 Aug;79:311–4.

Goate AM, Haynes AR, Owen MJ, Farrall M, James LA, Lai LY, et al. Predisposing locus for Alzheimer's disease on chromosome 21. Lancet 1989 Feb 18;1(8634):352–5.

2. Organization as Author

The Royal Marsden Hospital Bone-Marrow Transplantation Team. Failure of syngeneic bone-marrow graft without preconditioning in post-hepatitis marrow aplasia. Lancet 1977 Oct 8;2(8041):742–4.

3. No Author Given

Note that when the title is followed by an explanatory element within square brackets the period (full stop) that usually closes the title is omitted.

Coffee drinking and cancer of the pancreas [editorial] Br Med J [Clin Res] 1981 Sep 5;283(6292):628.

4. Article in a Foreign Language

Massone L, Borghi S, Pestarino A, Piccini R, Gambini C. Localisations palmaires purpurique de la dermatite herpetiforme. Ann Dermatol Venereol 1987;114(12):1545–7.

5. Volume with Supplement

Magni F, Rossoni G, Berti F. BN-52021 protects guinea-pig from heart anaphylaxis. Pharm Res Commun 1988 Dec;20 Suppl 5:75–8.

6. Issue with Supplement

Complete page numbers used with the alphanumeric designator for pages when the letter follows the numeral(s); if the letter precedes the numeral, follow the general rule for page numbers, for example, S31-7.

Gardos G, Cole JO, Haskell D, Marby D, Paine SS, Moore P. The natural history of tardive dyskinesia. J Clin Psychopharmacol 1988 Aug;8(4 Suppl):31S–37S.

7. Volume with Part

Hanly C. Metaphysics and innateness: a psychoanalytic perspective. Int J Psychoanal 1988;69(Pt 3):389–99.

8. Issue with Part

Edwards L, Meyskens F, Levine N. Effect of oral isotretinoin on dysplastic nevi. J Am Acad Dermatol 1989 Feb;20(2 Pt 1):257–60.

9. Issue with No Volume

Baumeister AA. Origins and control of stereotyped movements. Monogr Am Assoc Ment Defic 1978;(3):353–84.

10. No Issue or Volume

Danoek K. Skiing in and through the history of medicine. Nord Medicinhist Arsb 1982:86–100.

11. Pagination in Roman Numerals
Use uppercase or lowercase numerals, as in the source.

Ronne Y. Ansvarfall. Blodtransfusion till fel patient. Vardfacket 1989 Jan 26;13(2):XXVI–XXVII.

12. Type of Article Indicated as Needed
See Example 3 above on omission of the period (full stop) at the end of the title when it closes with a square-bracketed explanatory term or phrase.

Spargo PM, Manners JM. DDAVP and open heart surgery [letter] Anaesthesia 1989 Apr;44(4):363–4.
Fuhrman SA, Joiner KA. Binding of the third component of complement C3 by Toxoplasma gondii [abstract] Clin Res 1987;35(3):475A.

13. Article Containing Retraction
See Example 3 above on omission of the period (full stop) at the end of the title when it closes with a square-bracketed explanatory term or phrase.

Shishido A. Retraction notice: effect of platinum compounds on murine lymphocyte mitogenesis [Retraction of Alsabti EA, Ghalib ON, Salem MH. In: Jpn J Med Sci Biol 1979 Apr;32(2):53-65] Jpn J Med Sci Biol 1980 Aug;33(4):235–7.

14. Article Retracted
    See Example 3 above on omission of the period (full stop) at the
    end of the title when it closes with a square-bracketed explanatory
    term or phrase.

    Alsabati EA, Ghalib ON, Salem MH. Effect of platinum compounds on
    murine lymphocyte mitogenesis [Retracted by Shishido A. In: Jpn J
    Med Sci Biol 1980 Aug;33(4):235–7] Jpn J Med Sci Biol 1979
    Apr;32(2):53–65.

15. Article Containing Comment
    See Example 3 above on omission of the period (full stop) at the
    end of the title when it closes with a square-bracketed explanatory
    term or phrase.

    Piccoli A, Bossatti A. Early steroid therapy in IgA neuropathy: still an
    open question [comment] Nephron 1989;51(2):289-91. Comment
    on: Nephron 1988;48(1):12–7.

16. Article Commented Upon
    See Example 3 above on omission of the period (full stop) at the
    end of the title when it closes with a square-bracketed explanatory
    term or phrase.

    Kobayashi Y, Fujii K, Hiki Y, Tateno S, Kurokawa A, Kamiyama M.
    Steroid therapy in IgA neuropathy: a retrospective study in heavy pro-
    teinuric cases [see comments] Nephron 1988;48(1):12–7. Comment
    in: Nephron 1989;51(2):289–91.

17. Article with Published Erratum
    See Example 3 above on omission of the period (full stop) at the
    end of the title when it closes with a square-bracketed explanatory
    term or phrase.

    Schofield A. The CAGE questionnaire and psychological health [pub-
    lished erratum appears in Br J Addict 1989 Jun;84(6):701] Br J Addict
    Jul;83:761–4.

BOOKS AND OTHER MONOGRAPHS

1. Personal Author(s)

    Colson JH, Armor WJ. Sports injuries and their treatment. 2nd rev. ed.
    London: S. Paul; 1986.

2. Editor(s), Compiler as Author

Diener HC, Wilkinson M, editors. Drug-induced headache. New York: Springer-Verlag; 1988.

3. Organization as Author and Publisher

Virginia Law Foundation. The medical and legal implications of AIDS. Charlottesville: The Virginia Law Foundation; 1987.

4. Chapter in a Book

Weinstein L, Swartz MN. Pathologic properties of invading microorganisms. In: Sodeman WA Jr, Sodeman WA, editors. Pathologic physiology: mechanisms of disease. Philadelphia: Saunders; 1974:457–72.

5. Conference Proceedings

Vivian VL, editor. Child abuse and neglect: a medical community response. Proceedings of the First AMA National Conference on Child Abuse and Neglect; 1984 Mar 30-31; Chicago. Chicago: American Medical Association; 1985.

6. Conference Paper

Harley NH. Comparing radon daughter dosimetric and risk models. In: Gammage RB, Kaye SV, editors. Indoor air and human health. Proceedings of the Seventh Life Sciences Symposium; 1984 Oct 29-31; Knoxville (TN). Chelsea (MI): Lewis; 1985:69–78.

7. Scientific and Technical Report

Akutsu T. Total heart replacement device. Bethesda, Maryland: National Institutes of Health, National Heart and Lung Institute; 1974 Apr. Report No.:NIH-NHLI-69-2185:4.

8. Dissertation
See Example 3 above on omission of the period (full stop) at the end of the title when it closes with a square-bracketed explanatory term or phrase.

Youssef NM. School adjustment of children with congenital heart disease [dissertation] Pittsburgh (PA): Univ. of Pittsburgh; 1988.

9. Patent

Harred JF, Knight AR, McIntyre JS, inventors. Dow Chemical Company, assignee. Epoxidation process. US patent 3,654,317. 1972 Apr 4.

Other Published Material

1. Newspaper Article

Rensberger B, Specter B. CFCs may be destroyed by natural process. The Washington Post 1989 Aug 7;Sect. A:2 (col. 5).

2. Audiovisual Items
   See Example 3 above on omission of the period (full stop) at the end of the title when it closes with a square-bracketed explanatory term.

   AIDS epidemic: the physician's role [videorecording] Cleveland (OH): Academy of Medicine of Cleveland; 1987.

3. Computer File
   See Example 3 above on omission of the period (full stop) at the end of the title when it closes with a square-bracketed explanatory term.

   Renal system [computer program] MS-DOS version. Edwardsville (KS): Medi-Sim; 1988.

4. Legal Material
   Note that this format is based on the authority on legal citations, *A Uniform System of Citation*, 13th edition. Cambridge (MA): Harvard Law Review Association; 1981.

   Toxic Substances Control Act: Hearing on S.776 Before the Subcomm. on the Environment of the Senate Comm. on Commerce, 94th Congr., 1st Sess. 343 (1975).

5. Map
   See Example 3 above on omission of the period (full stop) at the end of the title when it closes with a square-bracketed explanatory term or phrase.

Scotland [topographic map Washington: National Geographic Society (US); 1981.]

6. Book of *The Bible*

Ruth 3:1-18. The Holy Bible. Authorized King James Version. New York: Oxford Univ. Press; 1972.

7. Dictionary and Similar Reference Books

Ectasia. Dorland's illustrated medical dictionary. 27th ed. Philadelphia: Saunders; 1988:527.

8. Classical Material

The Winter's Tale: act 5, scene 1, lines 13–16. The complete works of William Shakespeare. London: Rex; 1973.

Unpublished Material

1. In Press

Lillywhite HB, Donald JA. Pulmonary blood flow regulation in an aquatic snake. Science. In press.

2. Paper Presented at a Meeting but Not Published

Jenicek M, Demirjian A, Dubuc MB. Relations between recommended basic measurements in nutritional anthropometry during growth. Paper presented at the 9th International Congress of Nutrition; 1972 Sep; Mexico City.

3. Poster Presented at a Meeting

Morse DF. Application of two-bath development processing to transmission electron films. Poster presented at the 20th Annual Meeting of the Electron Microscopy Society; 1988 Jun; Kansas City (MO).

4. Personal Communication

Carson PC. Letter to Jon P. Adams. 1989 May 10.

JOURNALS IN THE "UNIFORM REQUIREMENTS . . . ." AGREEMENT AS OF SEPTEMBER 1989

ACTA ANATOMICA
ACTA CHIRURGICA HELLENICA
ACTA HAEMATOLOGICA
ACTA MEDICA COLOMBIANA
ACTA MEDICA HELLENICA—*see* HELLINIKIIATRIKI
ACTA MEDICA SCANDINAVICA—*see* JOURNAL OF INTERNAL MEDICINE
ACTA ORTHOPAEDICA SCANDINAVICA
ACTA PAEDIATRICA JAPONICA
ACTA PAEDIATRICA SCANDINAVICA
ACTA PHARMACOLOGICA SINICA
ACTIVOX
ACUTE CARE
AIDS: AN INTERNATIONAL BIMONTHLY JOURNAL
AMERICAN FAMILY PHYSICIAN
AMERICAN HEART JOURNAL
THE AMERICAN JOURNAL OF CARDIOLOGY
THE AMERICAN JOURNAL OF CHIROPRACTIC MEDICINE
THE AMERICAN JOURNAL OF CLINICAL NUTRITION
AMERICAN JOURNAL OF DISEASES OF CHILDREN
THE AMERICAN JOURNAL OF EMERGENCY MEDICINE
AMERICAN JOURNAL OF EPIDEMIOLOGY
AMERICAN JOURNAL OF HOSPITAL PHARMACY
THE AMERICAN JOURNAL OF HUMAN GENETICS
THE AMERICAN JOURNAL OF INFECTION CONTROL
THE AMERICAN JOURNAL OF MEDICINE
AMERICAN JOURNAL OF NEPHROLOGY
AMERICAN JOURNAL OF OBSTETRICS AND GYNECOLOGY
AMERICAN JOURNAL OF NONINVASIVE CARDIOLOGY
AMERICAN JOURNAL OF OPTOMETRY AND PHYSIOLOGICAL OPTICS
AMERICAN JOURNAL OF ORTHODONTICS AND DENTOFACIAL
    ORTHOPEDICS
THE AMERICAN JOURNAL OF PATHOLOGY
THE AMERICAN JOURNAL OF PSYCHIATRY
THE AMERICAN JOURNAL OF PUBLIC HEALTH
AJR: AMERICAN JOURNAL OF ROENTGENOLOGY
THE AMERICAN JOURNAL OF SURGERY
AMERICAN REVIEW OF RESPIRATORY DISEASE
THE AMERICAN SOCIETY FOR ARTIFICIAL INTERNAL ORGANS (ASAIO)
    TRANSACTIONS
THE AMERICAN SURGEON
ANALYTISCHE PSYCHOLOGIE
ANAESTHESIA
ANAESTHESIA AND INTENSIVE CARE
ANESTHESIA AND ANALGESIA
ANNALS OF CLINICAL BIOCHEMISTRY
ANNALS OF CLINICAL AND LABORATORY SCIENCE
ANNALS OF EMERGENCY MEDICINE

ANNALS OF INTERNAL MEDICINE
ANNALS OF NUTRITION AND METABOLISM
THE ANNALS OF OTOLOGY, RHINOLOGY AND LARYNGOLOGY
ANNALS OF THE RHEUMATIC DISEASES
THE ANNALS OF THE ROYAL COLLEGE OF PHYSICIANS AND SURGEONS OF
    CANADA
ANNALS OF THE ROYAL COLLEGE OF SURGEONS OF ENGLAND
ANNALS OF SURGERY
THE ANNALS OF THORACIC SURGERY
ANNALS OF TROPICAL PAEDIATRICS
APPLIED NEUROPHYSIOLOGY
APPLIED PATHOLOGY
ARCHIVES OF DERMATOLOGY
ARCHIVES OF DISEASE IN CHILDHOOD
ARCHIVES OF GENERAL PSYCHIATRY
ARCHIVES OF INTERNAL MEDICINE
ARCHIVES OF NEUROLOGY
ARCHIVES OF OPHTHALMOLOGY
ARCHIVES OF OTOLARYNGOLOGY—HEAD AND NECK SURGERY
ARCHIVES OF PATHOLOGY AND LABORATORY MEDICINE
ARCHIVES OF PHYSICAL MEDICINE AND REHABILITATION
ARCHIVES OF SURGERY
ARCHIVOS DE BRONCONEUMOLOGIA
ARCHIVOS DE INVESTIGACION MEDICA
ARCHIVOS DE NEUROBIOLOGIA
ARIZONA MEDICINE
ARTERIOSCLEROSIS
AUDIOLOGY
AUSTRALASIAN JOURNAL OF DERMATOLOGY
AUSTRALIAN AND NEW ZEALAND JOURNAL OF MEDICINE
AUSTRALIAN AND NEW ZEALAND JOURNAL OF OPHTHALMOLOGY
THE AUSTRALIAN AND NEW ZEALAND JOURNAL OF SURGERY
AUSTRALIAN FAMILY PHYSICIAN
AUSTRALIAN JOURNAL OF HOSPITAL PHARMACY
AUSTRALIAN JOURNAL OF OPHTHALMOLOGY—see AUSTRALIAN AND NEW
    ZEALAND JOURNAL OF OPHTHALMOLOGY
AUSTRALIAN JOURNAL OF OPTOMETRY—see CLINICAL AND EXPERIMENTAL
    OPTOMETRY
AUSTRALIAN ORTHOPTIC JOURNAL
AUSTRALIAN PAEDIATRIC JOURNAL
BANGLADESH PAEDIATRICS
BIBLIOTEK FOR LAEGER
BIOLOGY OF THE NEONATE
BIOMEDICAL BULLETIN
BLOOD PURIFICATION
BLOOD VESSELS
BOLETIN DE LA ASOCIACION MEDICA DE PUERTO RICO
BOLETIN MEDICO DEL HOSPITAL INFANTIL DE MEXICO
BORDEAUX MEDICAL
BRAIN & DEVELOPMENT
BRAIN, BEHAVIOR AND EVOLUTION

BRAIN DYSFUNCTION
BRITISH DENTAL JOURNAL
BRITISH HEART JOURNAL
BRITISH HOMOEOPATHIC JOURNAL
BRITISH JOURNAL OF ANAESTHESIA
BRITISH JOURNAL OF INDUSTRIAL MEDICINE
BRITISH JOURNAL OF OCCUPATIONAL THERAPY
BRITISH JOURNAL OF OPHTHALMOLOGY
BRITISH JOURNAL OF PAIN
BRITISH JOURNAL OF RHEUMATOLOGY
BRITISH JOURNAL OF SURGERY
BRITISH JOURNAL OF VENEREAL DISEASES—*see* GENITOURINARY
  MEDICINE
BRITISH MEDICAL BULLETIN
BRITISH MEDICAL JOURNAL
BULLETIN OF THE MEDICAL LIBRARY ASSOCIATION
BRITISH OSTEOPATHIC JOURNAL
BULLETIN OF THE WORLD HEALTH ORGANIZATION
CANADIAN ANAESTHETISTS' SOCIETY JOURNAL—*see* CANADIAN JOURNAL
  OF ANAESTHESIA
CANADIAN FAMILY PHYSICIAN
CANADIAN JOURNAL OF ANAESTHESIA
CANADIAN JOURNAL OF COMPARATIVE MEDICINE
CANADIAN JOURNAL OF HOSPITAL PHARMACY
CANADA JOURNAL OF PUBLIC HEALTH
CANADIAN JOURNAL OF SURGERY
CANADIAN JOURNAL OF OPHTHALMOLOGY
CANADIAN MEDICAL ASSOCIATION JOURNAL
CANADIAN VETERINARY JOURNAL
CARDIOLOGY
CARDIOVASCULAR PHARMACOLOGY & THERAPEUTICS
CARDIOVASCULAR RESEARCH
CARIES RESEARCH
CENTRAL AFRICAN JOURNAL OF MEDICINE
CEPHALALGIA
THE CERVIX AND THE LOWER FEMALE GENITAL TRACT
THE CEYLON MEDICAL JOURNAL
CHEMOTHERAPY
CHEST
CHINESE JOURNAL OF ANESTHESIOLOGY
CHINESE JOURNAL OF CARDIOVASCULAR DISEASE
CHINESE JOURNAL OF DERMATOLOGY
CHINESE JOURNAL OF DIGESTION
CHINESE JOURNAL OF ENDOCRINOLOGY AND METABOLISM
CHINESE JOURNAL OF EPIDEMIOLOGY
CHINESE JOURNAL OF EXPERIMENTAL SURGERY
CHINESE JOURNAL OF GERIATOLOGY
CHINESE JOURNAL OF HEMATOLOGY
CHINESE JOURNAL OF HOSPITAL ADMINISTRATION
CHINESE JOURNAL OF INDUSTRIAL HYGIENE AND OCCUPATIONAL
  DISEASE

CHINESE JOURNAL OF INFECTIOUS DISEASES
CHINESE JOURNAL OF INTERNAL MEDICINE
CHINESE JOURNAL OF MEDICAL HISTORY
CHINESE JOURNAL OF MEDICAL LABORATORY TECHNOLOGY
CHINESE JOURNAL OF MICROBIOLOGY AND IMMUNOLOGY
CHINESE JOURNAL OF NEPHROLOGY
CHINESE JOURNAL OF NEUROLOGY AND PSYCHIATRY
CHINESE JOURNAL OF NEUROSURGERY
CHINESE JOURNAL OF NUCLEAR MEDICINE
CHINESE JOURNAL OF OBSTETRICS AND GYNECOLOGY
CHINESE JOURNAL OF ONCOLOGY
CHINESE JOURNAL OF OPHTHALMOLOGY
CHINESE JOURNAL OF ORGAN TRANSPLANTATION
CHINESE JOURNAL OF ORTHOPEDICS
CHINESE JOURNAL OF OTORHINOLARYNGOLOGY
CHINESE JOURNAL OF PATHOLOGY
CHINESE JOURNAL OF PEDIATRIC SURGERY
CHINESE JOURNAL OF PEDIATRICS
CHINESE JOURNAL OF PHYSICAL MEDICINE
CHINESE JOURNAL OF PHYSICAL THERAPY
CHINESE JOURNAL OF PLASTIC SURGERY AND BURNS
CHINESE JOURNAL OF PREVENTIVE MEDICINE
CHINESE JOURNAL OF RADIOLOGICAL MEDICINE AND PROTECTION
CHINESE JOURNAL OF RADIOLOGY
CHINESE JOURNAL OF STOMATOLOGY
CHINESE JOURNAL OF SURGERY
CHINESE JOURNAL OF TUBERCULOSIS AND RESPIRATORY DISEASES
CHINESE JOURNAL OF UROLOGY
CHINESE MEDICAL JOURNAL
CHRONIC DISEASES IN CANADA (Quarterly Bulletin)
CIRCULATION
CLINICA CHIMICA ACTA
CLINICAL AND EXPERIMENTAL OPTOMETRY
CLINICAL BIOCHEMISTRY
CLINICAL CHEMISTRY
CLINICAL DIABETES
CLINICAL NUTRITION
CLINICAL PEDIATRICS
CLINICAL PHARMACOLOGY AND THERAPEUTICS
CLINICAL PHARMACY
CLINICAL PHYSIOLOGY AND BIOCHEMISTRY
CLINICAL PREVENTIVE DENTISTRY
COMMUNITY DENTISTRY AND ORAL EPIDEMIOLOGY
COMMUNITY MEDICINE
COMPLEMENT
CORNELL VETERINARIAN
CORONARY ARTERY DISEASE
CUADERNOS DEL HOSPITAL DE CLINICAS
DANISH DENTAL JOURNAL
DANISH MEDICAL BULLETIN
DASEINSANALYSE

DENTAL ABSTRACTS
DENTAL TEAMWORK
DERMATOLOGICA
DEVELOPMENTAL NEUROSCIENCE
DEVELOPMENTAL PHARMACOLOGY AND THERAPEUTICS
DIABETES
DIABETES CARE
DIABETES JOURNAL
DIABETOLOGIA
DIABETIC NEPHROPATHY—*see* THE JOURNAL OF DIABETIC
    COMPLICATIONS
DIAGNOSTIC CYTOPATHOLOGY
DIGESTION
DIGESTIVE DISEASES
DIGESTIVE SURGERY
DRUG INTELLIGENCE & CLINICAL PHARMACY
EDIZIONI MINERVA MEDICA
ENVIRONMENTAL MEDICINE
ENZYME
EUROPEAN HEART JOURNAL
EUROPEAN JOURNAL OF CANCER AND CLINICAL ONCOLOGY
EUROPEAN JOURNAL OF CLINICAL INVESTIGATION
EUROPEAN JOURNAL OF GASTROENTEROLOGY AND HEPATOLOGY
EUROPEAN JOURNAL OF RHEUMATOLOGY AND INFLAMMATION
EUROPEAN NEUROLOGY
THE EUROPEAN RESPIRATORY JOURNAL
EUROPEAN SURGICAL RESEARCH
EUROPEAN UROLOGY
EXPERIMENTAL AND CLINICAL IMMUNOGENETICS
EXPERIMENTAL CELL BIOLOGY
FAMILY MEDICINE
FAMILY PRACTICE RESEARCH JOURNAL
FETAL THERAPY
THE FINNISH MEDICAL JOURNAL
FOCUS ON CRITICAL CARE
FOLIA PHONIATRICA
FOLIO PRIMATOLOGICA
GASTROENTEROLOGY
GASTROINTESTINAL ENDOSCOPY
GENITOURINARY MEDICINE
GERIATRIC CARDIOVASCULAR MEDICINE
GERIATRICS
GERONTOLOGY
GUT
GYNAKOLOGISCHE RUNDSCHAU
GYNECOLOGIC AND OBSTETRIC INVESTIGATION
HAEMOSTASIS
HAWAII MEDICAL JOURNAL
HEALTH TRENDS
HEART AND LUNG: THE JOURNAL OF CRITICAL CARE
HELLINIKI IATRIKI

HEPATOLOGY
HORMONE RESEARCH
HOSPITAL CHRONICLES—see NOSOKOMIAKA CHRONICA
HOSPITAL PHARMACY
HUMAN DEVELOPMENT
HUMAN HEREDITY
IATRIKI
IMMUNOLOGIC RESEARCH
INDIAN JOURNAL OF DERMATOLOGY, VENEREOLOGY AND LEPROLOGY
INDIAN JOURNAL OF GASTROENTEROLOGY
INDIAN JOURNAL OF UROLOGY
INTERNATIONAL ARCHIVES OF ALLERGY AND APPLIED IMMUNOLOGY
INTERNATIONAL DISABILITY STUDIES
INTERNATIONAL JOURNAL OF EPIDEMIOLOGY
INTERNATIONAL JOURNAL OF PEDIATRIC NEPHROLOGY
INTERNATIONAL REHABILITATION MEDICINE—*see* INTERNATIONAL
　DISABILITY STUDIES
INTERNATIONAL SURGERY
INTERVIROLOGY
INVASION AND METASTASIS
INVESTIGATIVE RADIOLOGY
IRISH JOURNAL OF PSYCHOLOGICAL MEDICINE
ISRAEL JOURNAL OF PSYCHIATRY AND RELATED SCIENCES
THE JOURNAL OF ALLERGY AND CLINICAL IMMUNOLOGY
JOURNAL OF THE AMERICAN ACADEMY OF DERMATOLOGY
JOURNAL OF THE AMERICAN ACADEMY OF PHYSICIAN ASSISTANTS
JOURNAL OF THE AMERICAN COLLEGE OF CARDIOLOGY
JADA—JOURNAL OF THE AMERICAN DENTAL ASSOCIATION
JOURNAL OF THE AMERICAN MEDICAL ASSOCIATION
JOURNAL OF THE AMERICAN SOCIETY OF ECHOCARDIOGRAPHY
THE JOURNAL OF APPLIED NUTRITION
JOURNAL OF BIOLOGICAL STANDARDIZATION
JOURNAL OF THE BRITISH ASSOCIATION FOR IMMEDIATE CARE
JOURNAL OF THE CANADIAN ASSOCIATION OF RADIOLOGISTS
JOURNAL OF THE CANADIAN CHIROPRACTIC ASSOCIATION
THE JOURNAL OF CARDIOVASCULAR SURGERY
JOURNAL OF CHRONIC DISEASES
JOURNAL OF CHEMOTHERAPY
JOURNAL OF CLINICAL ENDOCRINOLOGY AND METABOLISM
JOURNAL OF CLINICAL GASTROENTEROLOGY
JOURNAL OF CLINICAL PATHOLOGY
JOURNAL OF THE DANISH MEDICAL ASSOCIATION
JOURNAL OF DENTAL EDUCATION
THE JOURNAL OF DIABETIC COMPLICATIONS
JOURNAL OF DIARRHOEAL DISEASE RESEARCH
JOURNAL OF EMERGENCY NURSING
JOURNAL OF ENTEROSTOMAL THERAPY
JOURNAL OF EPIDEMIOLOGY AND COMMUNITY HEALTH
JOURNAL OF THE FACULTY OF MEDICINE BAGHDAD
JOURNAL OF GENERAL INTERNAL MEDICINE
JOURNAL OF HAND SURGERY

THE JOURNAL OF HEART TRANSPLANTATION
JOURNAL OF HONG KONG MEDICAL TECHNOLOGY ASSOCIATION
JOURNAL OF HYPERTENSION
JOURNAL OF THE INSTITUTE OF MEDICINE
JOURNAL OF INTERNAL MEDICINE
JOURNAL OF THE IRISH COLLEGES OF PHYSICIANS AND SURGEONS
THE JOURNAL OF LABORATORY AND CLINICAL MEDICINE
THE JOURNAL OF MATERNAL AND CHILD HEALTH
JOURNAL OF MANIPULATIVE AND PHYSIOLOGICAL THERAPEUTICS
JOURNAL OF MEDICAL ETHICS
JOURNAL OF MEDICAL GENETICS
JNCI. JOURNAL OF THE NATIONAL CANCER INSTITUTE
JOURNAL OF NEUROLOGY, NEUROSURGERY AND PSYCHIATRY
JOURNAL OF NEUROPATHOLOGY AND EXPERIMENTAL NEUROLOGY
JOURNAL OF THE NORWEGIAN MEDICAL ASSOCIATION—*see* TIDSSKRIFT
    FOR DEN NORSKE LAEGEFORENING
THE JOURNAL OF NUCLEAR MEDICINE
JOURNAL OF NUCLEAR MEDICINE TECHNOLOGY
THE JOURNAL OF PALLIATIVE CARE
JOURNAL OF PATHOLOGY
JOURNAL OF PEDIATRIC NEPHROLOGY
JOURNAL OF PEDIATRICS
JOURNAL OF PERIODONTOLOGY
JOURNAL OF PHARMACY TECHNOLOGY
JOURNAL OF PROSTHETIC DENTISTRY
JOURNAL OF PSYCHOSOMATIC RESEARCH
JOURNAL OF THE ROYAL ARMY MEDICAL CORPS
JOURNAL OF THE ROYAL COLLEGE OF PHYSICIANS OF LONDON
JOURNAL OF THE ROYAL COLLEGE OF SURGEONS OF EDINBURGH
JOURNAL OF THE ROYAL NAVAL MEDICAL SERVICE
JOURNAL OF THE ROYAL SOCIETY OF MEDICINE
THE JOURNAL OF THE SWEDISH MEDICAL ASSOCIATION—*see*
    LAKARTIDNINGEN
JOURNAL OF THORACIC AND CARDIOVASCULAR SURGERY
JOURNAL OF VASCULAR SURGERY
JOURNAL OF THE VIVEKANANDA INSTITUTE OF MEDICAL SCIENCES
LAKARTIDNINGEN
THE LANCET
LEPROSY REVIEW
LIJECNICKI VJESNIK
MACEDONIAN STOMATOLOGICAL REVIEW
MAGNESIUM
MALADIES CHRONIQUE EN CANADA—*see* CHRONIC DISEASES IN CANADA
MALAYSIAN JOURNAL OF PATHOLOGY
MANEDSSKRIFT FOR PRAKTK LAEGEGERNING
MEDICINA INTENSIVA
MEDICAL CARE
MEDICAL AND PEDIATRIC ONCOLOGY
THE MEDICAL JOURNAL OF AUSTRALIA
MEDICAL LABORATORY SCIENCES
MEDICINA CLINICA

MEDICINE (OXFORD)
MILITARY MEDICINE
MINERAL AND ELECTROLYTE METABOLISM
THE MOUNT SINAI JOURNAL OF MEDICINE
NATIONAL MEDICAL JOURNAL OF CHINA
NATURAL IMMUNITY AND CELL GROWTH REGULATION
NEDERLANDS TIJDSCHRIFT VOOR GENEESKUNDE
NEPHRON
THE NETHERLANDS JOURNAL OF MEDICINE
NEUROENDOCRINOLOGY
NEUROEPIDEMIOLOGY
NEUROFIBROMATOSIS
NEUROLOGY (CLEVELAND)
NEUROPSYCHOLOGY
NEW DOCTOR
THE NEW ENGLAND JOURNAL OF MEDICINE
NEW YORK STATE JOURNAL OF MEDICINE
NEW ZEALAND FAMILY PHYSICIAN
NEW ZEALAND JOURNAL OF MEDICAL LABORATORY TECHNOLOGY
NEW ZEALAND JOURNAL OF OPHTHALMOLOGY
NEW ZEALAND MEDICAL JOURNAL
NEWFOUNDLAND MEDICAL ASSOCIATION JOURNAL
NIGERIAN MEDICAL JOURNAL
NO TO HATTATSU
NORDISK MEDICINE
NORTH CAROLINA MEDICAL JOURNAL
NOSOKOMIAKA CHRONICA
NURSING
OBSTETRICS AND GYNECOLOGY
ONCOLOGY
OPHTHALMIC RESEARCH
OPHTHALMOLOGICA
OPHTHALMOLOGY
ORAL SURGERY, ORAL MEDICINE AND ORAL PATHOLOGY
ORL; JOURNAL OF OTO-RHINO-LARYNGOLOGY AND ITS RELATED
   SPECIALTIES
ORTHOPTIC JOURNAL OF AUSTRALIA
OTOLARYNGOLOGY AND HEAD AND NECK SURGERY
PM. PHARMACY MANAGEMENT
PAKISTAN JOURNAL OF MEDICAL RESEARCH
PAPUA NEW GUINEA MEDICAL JOURNAL
PATHOLOGY
PATHOLOGY AND IMMUNOPATHOLOGY RESEARCH
PEDIATRIC EMERGENCY CARE
PEDIATRIC INFECTIOUS DISEASE JOURNAL
PEDIATRIC NEUROSCIENCE
PEDIATRICIAN
PERITONEAL DIALYSIS BULLETIN
PHARMACEUTISCH WEEKBLAD
PHARMACEUTISCH WEEKBLAD SCIENTIFIC EDITION
PHARMACOLOGICAL RESEARCH COMMUNICATIONS

PHARMACOLOGY
PHARMACOTHERAPY
PHONETICA
THE PHYSICIAN AND SPORTS MEDICINE
POSTGRADUATE DOCTOR—AFRICA
POSTGRADUATE DOCTOR—ASIA
POSTGRADUATE DOCTOR—MIDDLE EAST
POSTGRADUATE MEDICAL JOURNAL
POSTGRADUATE MEDICINE
PSYCHIATRIA FENNICA
PSYCHOPATHOLOGY
PSYCHOTHERAPY AND PSYCHOSOMATICS
PUBLIC HEALTH
PUERTO RICO HEALTH SCIENCES JOURNAL
QUARTERLY JOURNAL OF MEDICINE
RADIOLOGY
RENAL PHYSIOLOGY
RESPIRATION
REVISTA CHILENA DE PEDIATRIA
REVISTA CLINICA ESPANOLA
REVISTA DE GASTOENTEROLOGIA DE MEXICO
REVISTA DE INVESTIGACION CLINICA
REVISTA ESPANOLA DE REUMATOLOGIA
REVISTA ESPANOLA DE ANESTESIOLOGIA Y REANIMACION
REVISTA MEDICA DE CHILE
REVISTA MEDICA DEL IMSS
REVISTA MEXICANA DE ANESTESIOLOGIA
REVISTA MEXICANA DE PEDIATRIA
REVISTA MEXICANA DE RADIOLOGIA
SALUD PUBLICA DE MEXICO
SANGRE
SAUDI MEDICAL JOURNAL
SCANDINAVIAN JOURNAL OF DENTAL RESEARCH
SCANDINAVIAN JOURNAL OF HAEMATOLOGY
SCANDINAVIAN JOURNAL OF RESPIRATORY DISEASES—*see* EUROPEAN
    JOURNAL OF RESPIRATORY DISEASES
SCANDINAVIAN JOURNAL OF SOCIAL MEDICINE
SCHUMPERT MEDICAL QUARTERLY
SCHWEIZERISCHE MEDIZINISCHE WOCHENSCHRIFT
SEXUALLY TRANSMITTED DISEASES
SHINKEI BYORIGAKU (NEUROPATHOLOGY)
SKIN PHARMACOLOGY
SOUTH AFRICAN MEDICAL JOURNAL
SOUTHERN MEDICAL JOURNAL
SPECIAL CARE DENTISTRY
THE SPRINGFIELD CLINIC
SRI LANKAN FAMILY PHYSICIAN
SURGERY
SWEDISH MEDICAL JOURNAL—*see* THE JOURNAL OF THE SWEDISH
    MEDICAL ASSOCIATION
THEORETICAL MEDICINE

THORAX
THROMBOSIS AND HAEMOSTASIS
TIDSSKRIFT FOR DEN NORSKE LAEGEFORENING
TRANSFUSION
TROPICAL GASTROENTEROLOGY
TUMOR BIOLOGY
UGESKRIFT FOR LAEGER
ULSTER MEDICAL JOURNAL
UNDERSEA BIOMEDICAL RESEARCH
UROLOGIA INTERNATIONALIS
VETERINARY RADIOLOGY
VOX SANGUINIS
THE WEST VIRGINIA MEDICAL JOURNAL
THE WESTERN JOURNAL OF MEDICINE
WHO CHRONICLE
WORLD HEALTH ORGANIZATION JOURNALS
WORLD HEALTH ORGANIZATION MONOGRAPH SERIES
WORLD HEALTH ORGANIZATION TECHNICAL REPORT SERIES
WORLD HEALTH STATISTICS QUARTERLY
WORLD MEDICAL JOURNAL
THE YALE JOURNAL OF BIOLOGY AND MEDICINE

Appendix 3

*Guidelines on Authorship**

. . . PRINCIPLES FOR AUTHORSHIP

Principle 1. Each author should have participated sufficiently in the work represented by the article to take public responsibility for the content.

Investigators in the sciences and others who use scientific information must have confidence in its accuracy and validity. Such confidence rests in part on knowing that at least one person has taken public responsibility for the information, and for published information the responsible persons are authors . . . . "Public responsibility" means that an author can defend the content of the article, including the data and other evidence and the conclusions based on them. Such ability can come only from having participated closely in the work represented by the article and in preparing the article for publication . . . . This responsibility also requires that the author be willing to concede publicly errors of fact or interpretation discovered after publication of the article and to state reasons for error.

In the case of fraud or other kinds of deception attributable to one or more of the authors, the other authors must be willing to state publicly the nature and extent of deception and to account as far as possible for its occurrence.

Principle 2. Participation must include three steps: (1) conception or design of the work represented by the article, or analysis and interpretation of the data, or both; (2) drafting the article or revising it for critically important content; and (3) final approval of the version to be published.

The work represented by a scientific article includes forming the hypothesis tested by the research it reports or forming the question it answers, developing the means of gathering the reported data or other evidence, collecting the data or other evidence, critically analyzing the evidence and any counter-evidence, and writing the article so that it

*This appendix is an excerpt from "Guidelines on Authorship of Medical Papers" (Huth EJ. Ann Intern Med. 1986;104:269-74),which draws on principles developed by the International Committee of Medical Journal Editors and represented in its 1985 statement on authorship (Brit Med J. 1985;291:722).

229

accurately reports all of these steps and their products in the structure of critical argument . . . . Authors could not publicly defend the intellectual content of an article unless they understand thoroughly the basis for its origin (conception) and can testify to the validity of its argument (critical analysis of evidence). Authors must also have sufficient involvement in writing the [article], either in drafting the initial version or revising subsequent versions to insure validity of the argument and conclusions, to be able to defend the article as an accurate report . . . of the work that led to it.

Principle 3. Participation solely in the collection of data (or other evidence) does not justify authorship.

Data and other evidence bearing on the conclusions and validity of a scientific article may be gathered by persons who know little or nothing of the steps critical to its main intellectual substance: the genesis, design of the work, and the critical analysis of evidence. Such persons could not take public responsibility for the main elements of an article and could testify only to the validity of elements of evidence and not to how they support the argument and its conclusion. Contributions of data by persons for whom authorship is not justified can be acknowledged by other means (see Principle 5).

Principle 4. Each part of the content of an article critical to its main conclusions and each step in the work that led to its publication (steps 1, 2, and 3 in Principle 2) must be attributable to at least one author.

. . . Each element of a scientific article vital to its conclusions . . . must be publicly defensible or its validity is open to question. Therefore, the authorship of [an article] must include one or more persons able to defend any of its critically vital elements . . . .

Principle 5. Persons who have contributed intellectually to the article but whose contributions do not justify authorship may be named and their contribution described—for example, "advice", "critical review of study proposal", "data collection", "participation in clinical trial". Such persons must have given their permission to be named. Technical help must be acknowledged in a separate paragraph.

Contemporary research can involve persons whose contributions are not vital to the argument and conclusions of the article but that have been supportive for authors. Lest authors misrepresent themselves as being solely responsible for all that the article represents, they should indicate who provided intellectual assistance and its nature. Purely technical assistance includes building equipment, collecting data (specimen gathering and laboratory measurements), locating and abstracting literature, and work in preparing a manuscript that is not intellectual work on its scientific content.

GUIDELINES FOR SPECIFIC KINDS OF ARTICLES

Principle 2 defines participation in three steps as a requirement for authorship:

Step 1. Conception of the work represented by the article, design of the work, analysis and interpretation of data or other evidence presented in the article, or all of these.

Step 2. Drafting the article or revising it for critically important content.

Step 3. Approving the final version of the article for publication.

Steps 2 and 3 necessarily apply to all types of articles. Specific contributions in Step 1 may differ for the various types of articles written for a clinical journal.

Step 1 for Articles Reporting Clinical, Epidemiologic, or Laboratory Research

Conception: Framing a specific hypothesis to be tested or specific question to be answered.

Design of the work: Drafting and deciding on the structure and methods for the research.

Analysis and interpretation of the data: This function includes assessing the precision, accuracy, and relevance of data, and statistical analysis. It also includes reviewing the literature for supportive evidence and counter-evidence.

Participation solely in study design or in data analysis or in both may represent adequate participation in Step 1 to justify authorship. Providing technical help, simple referral of patients, or collecting data do not by themselves represent adequate participation in Step 1. In epidemiologic studies the referral of a problem for study does not by itself represent adequate participation in Step 1, but recognizing in the problem an hypothesis to be tested or a specific question to be answered may be adequate.

Step 1 for Articles Reporting a Case-Series Analysis

Conception: Framing the specific question or questions the analysis is expected to answer.

Design of the work: Defining the characteristics of the cases to be analyzed and the scope of the literature to be considered for supportive evidence and counter-evidence.

Analysis and interpretation of the case data and literature evidence: Critical assessment; structuring and presentation; statistical analysis.

Locating and abstracting case data or literature do not by themselves represent adequate participation in Step 1 for this kind of article. Providing case data ("routine examination and tests") that would have been obtained even if the case-series analysis was not to be carried out is not participation justifying authorship (see Principle 3).

Step 1 for Individual Case Reports

Conception: Recognizing and defining the case characteristics that appear to justify further study of the case and eventually the report.
Design of the work: Deciding on and securing additional case data and relevant literature evidence that support the importance identified in "Conception".
Analysis and interpretation of the case data and literature evidence: Critical assessment and selection of case data and literature evidence.

Providing case data (such as "routine tests", laboratory estimations, roentgenographic or other imaging studies, cardiac studies) does not by itself represent adequate participation in Step 1 to justify authorship. Just the referral of the patient (case) to the person or persons responsible for "Conception" does not justify authorship.

Step 1 for Review Articles, Editorials, and Similar Articles Based on Critical Assessment of the Literature and Personal Experience

Conception: Framing the specific question or questions to be answered.
Design of the work: Defining the characteristics of the literature to be reviewed.
Analysis and interpretation of the evidence considered: Selection of evidence through critical assessment.

Locating and abstracting the literature are not by themselves participation in Step 1. . . .

Appendix 4

References and Reading: An Annotated Bibliography

Careful authors need guides to usage in the many details that make up prose style. Authors in the medical sciences have to be able to verify the spelling, definition, or correct use of scientific terms. Skills in writing are built largely through self-training, with the help of books that give insights into the characteristics of prose style and into ways of writing more easily and effectively. But medical writing also almost invariably depends on thorough knowledge of the literature relevant to the author's topic. How to find that literature is an indispensable skill. The books described below will help authors meet these various needs. The titles of the books are given first, rather than the authors' names, to emphasize the subjects of the books.

DICTIONARIES

The American Heritage Dictionary: 2nd College Edition. Boston: Houghton Mifflin; 1984.

This dictionary is, for me at its price, the best of the English-language dictionaries published in the United States. Its usage notes, a generous part of many of its entries, make more clear than in other dictionaries the proper level of usage for a word and the nuances among synonyms. The "Guide to the Dictionary" in the opening pages should be digested by all who are not regular users of any dictionary.

The Random House Dictionary of the English Language: 2nd Edition, Unabridged. New York: Random House; 1987.

Much more comprehensive than the "desktop" dictionaries. Includes highly useful appendixes on style and usage, many biographic and geographic entries, and 4 short foreign language-to-English dictionaries (French, German, Italian, Spanish). Rich in new words and technical terms.

Blakiston's Gould Medical Dictionary. 4th ed. New York: McGraw-Hill; 1979.

Butterworths Medical Dictionary. 2nd ed. Boston: Butterworths; 1980.

Churchill's Medical Dictionary. New York: Churchill; 1989.

Dorland's Illustrated Medical Dictionary. 26th ed. Philadelphia: W. B. Saunders; 1981.

International Dictionary of Medicine and Biology. New York: John S. Wiley; 1986.

Stedman's Medical Dictionary. 25th ed. Baltimore: Williams & Wilkins, 1990.

Five of these six major English-language dictionaries of medicine differ little. *Butterworths* is a distinctly British dictionary and thus is less fitted to North American needs than the four American dictionaries. The *International Dictionary* is a big 3-volume work particularly useful for its following the proper conventions for italicization of taxonomic terms when they are entry terms and for its wide coverage of biology outside of medicine. *Churchill's* is based on the database compiled for the *International Dictionary* but provides pronunciations and definitions for new terms. The remaining 3 American dictionaries are much the same in their qualities; the new edition of *Stedman's* has a greatly improved page design.

McGraw-Hill Dictionary of Scientific and Technical Terms. 4th ed. New York: McGraw-Hill; 1988.

A valuable supplementary reference source for terms outside of medicine and biology.

GUIDES TO GRAMMAR AND USAGE

American Usage and Style: The Consensus. RH Copperud. New York: Van Nostrand Reinhold; 1979.

Notes, arranged alphabetically by entry term, on word usage, punctuation, grammar, and defects in prose style. Weighs differences in views of presumed authorities and compares American and British usage. Often witty.

A Dictionary of Modern English Usage. HW Fowler. Revised and edited by E Gowers. 2nd ed. New York: Oxford University Press; 1983.

A classic guide, widely known as "Fowler", to myriad details of prose style. Some of Fowler's positions may seem too fastidious, even precious, but his keen judgments rarely fail to make one think more about judgments in writing.

Modern American Usage: A Guide. W Follett. Edited and completed by J Barzun. New York: Hill & Wang; 1966.

The American equivalent to Fowler's *A Dictionary of Modern English Usage;* not as witty as "Fowler" but the introductory and closing essays offer a well-reasoned argument on the value of careful distinctions in all details of style.

The Nonsexist Word Finder: A Dictionary of Gender-Free Usage. R Maggio. Phoenix, Arizona: Oryx; 1987.

A detailed, thorough survey of formal and informal words and terms that properly or improperly convey connotations of gender. The body of the text is a dictionary; entries include useful synonyms or substitute terms. The first appendix offers wide-ranging guidelines; the second, selected short readings on gender distinctions in writing.

Webster's Dictionary of English Usage. Springfield, Massachusetts: Merriam-Webster; 1989.

An exhaustive survey of historical and contemporary American and English usage in vocabulary, grammar, and syntax. Tends to avoid firm positions but offers thorough discussions and a wealth of examples. Its analyses of possible variations in usage might be regarded as pedantic and indecisive but they have the value of giving its users adequate rationalizations for preferences that can be based on personal values. Probably now the best single source for style decisions in all kinds of American-English prose.

The Words Between: A Handbook for Scientists Needing English, with Examples Mainly from Biology and Medicine. 2nd ed. JM Perttunen. Helsinki: Kustannus oy Duodecim; 1986.

An exhaustive survey of a great number of details in English prose style often not known to non-anglophone writers in biology and medicine (and even to anglophone writers). Although 1 chapter focuses on difficulties in Finnish-to-English translation, most of the text will be useful any place in the world of medical and biologic writing.

Usage and Abusage: A Guide to Good English. E Partridge. Baltimore: Penguin Books; 1963.

Much like "Fowler" but with longer discussions of some topics, such as the articles on jargon and punctuation. More generous use of illustrative quotations. References to other standard works on grammar, punctuation, and usage.

You Have a Point There. E Partridge. Boston: Routledge & Kegan Paul; 1977.

If you want punctuation discussed more thoroughly than what you find in the broader manuals on usage, this is the book to get. The British terms ("full stop" rather than "period," for example) will be unfamiliar to some American readers. Includes discussion of other type conventions like capitalization, italics, and other related devices; a chapter by JW Clark distinguishes American usage. My reference is to the paperback edition.

STYLE MANUALS

Council of Biology Editors Style Manual: A Guide for Authors, Editors, and Publishers in the Biological Sciences. CBE Style Manual Committee. 5th ed. Council of Biology Editors, 1983.

An authoritative guide to manuscript and publication styles. Particularly valuable for help with the style conventions for plant sciences, microbiology, animal sciences (including the medical sciences), and chemistry and biochemistry. Ethics for authors. Copyright. Indexing. Comprehensive list of abbreviations and symbols, with notes on the authorities for their use.

Medical Style and Format: An International Manual for Authors, Editors, and Publishers. EJ Huth. Philadelphia: ISI Press; 1987. Distribution by Williams & Wilkins.

A detailed guide to punctuation, quotation and ellipsis, capitalization, type conventions, word structure, American and British differences in English-language usage, nomenclature, addresses, symbols and abbreviations, degrees and honorific terms, numbers and units of measurement, mathematics, statistics, and style in specific medical fields. Thorough presentation of bibliographic references for a wide range of document types, with principles of reference construction. An appendix on SI units in clinical chemistry and hematology.

The ACS Style Guide: A Manual for Authors and Editors. JS Dodd, ed. Washington: American Chemical Society; 1986.

A basic and clear manual of style for all fields of chemistry.

American Medical Association Manual of Style. 8th ed. C Iverson and others. Baltimore: Williams & Wilkins; 1988.

The comprehensive style manual for the journals of the American Medical Association. Some of its conventions depart from standard usage in other medical journals.

ASM Style Manual for Journals and Books. Washington: American Society for Microbiology; 1985.

Details of style for bacteriology, mycology, virology, and genetic aspects of these fields.

Publication Manual of the American Psychological Association. 3rd ed. Washington: American Psychological Association, 1983.

A guide for authors preparing papers for publication in journals of the American Psychological Association: organization of manuscripts; prose style; details of manuscript style; procedure for typing and submitting manuscripts; proofreading. Describes the APA journals and their publication process. Lists non-APA journals that use its style specifications. Helpful discussions of ethics in scholarly publishing.

The Chicago Manual of Style. 13th ed. Chicago: University of Chicago Press, 1982.

The standard manual for many fields of scholarly publishing. Useful to authors of scientific papers for details of style not set forth in some of the more specialized manuals described above. Discussions of copyright, preparation of tables, mathematics in type, and documentation that supplement related sections in the scientific style manuals.

Webster's Standard American Style Manual. Springfield, Massachusetts: Merriam-Webster; 1985.

A comprehensive general manual. Some of its recommended conventions are not standard in the medical sciences.

SCIENTIFIC DATA AND NOMENCLATURE

American Drug Index. Philadelphia: J. B. Lippincott. Annual editions.

A dictionary of chemical, generic, and trade names for drugs. Identifies drug vehicles and components of multi-drug preparations.

The Merck Index: An Encyclopedia of Chemicals and Drugs. 11th ed. Rahway, New Jersey: Merck and Company, 1989.

Entry articles include synonymous common names, chemical names, molecular formulas and weights, brief descriptions of uses and properties, and other details.

Pharmacological and Chemical Synonyms. 8th ed. EEJ Marler. Amsterdam: Excerpta Medica, 1984.

A dictionary of generic, chemical, and trade names for drugs, pesticides, and other compounds of importance in pharmacology and biochemistry. Draws on International Non-proprietary Names (World Health Organization) and on other nationally approved systems of nomenclature such as United States Adopted Names (USAN; see below).

USAN and the USP Dictionary of Drug Names. Rockville, Maryland: United States Pharmacopeial Convention. Published annually.

Entries for US Adopted Names, current USP and NF names, international and other non-proprietary names, brand names, code designations, Chemical Abstracts Service registry numbers, cross-references, and categories of pharmacologic activity. The articles on US Adopted Names typically include year of publication of the USAN, pronunciation, designation of official compendium such as USP, molecular formula, chemical names, CAS registry number, pharmacologic (including therapeutic) activity, brand names, manufacturer or distributor name, code designation, and graphic formula.

GUIDES TO WRITING

Arguing from Sources: Exploring Issues through Reading and Writing. DS Kaufer, C Geisler, CM Neuwirth. San Diego: Harcourt Brace Jovanovich; 1989.

Notably helpful in its sections on the development of argument in expository writing.

Communicating in Science: Writing and Speaking. V Booth. Cambridge, England: Cambridge University Press; 1985.

Pithy advice on how to write and what faults to avoid. Not a full and systematic discussion.

The New Writer: Techniques for Writing Well with a Computer. JP Mitchell. Redmond, Washington: Microsoft Press; 1987.

How to use word-processing programs on microcomputers for efficient and effective writing, both content and procedure. Includes attention to drafting early versions, writer's block, problems in prose style.

The Nurse's Guide to Writing for Publication. SK Mirin. Wakefield, Massachusetts: Nursing Resources, 1981.

Includes a short section on information resources and an 89-page appendix with tabulated characteristics of journals in nursing.

Problem-Solving Strategies for Writing. 2nd ed. L Flower. New York: Harcourt Brace Jovanovich; 1985.

Among the various strategies discussed by the author, from those for planning of a paper to those for editing a final version, is use of the "issue tree", a graphic device for diagramming one's ideas and how they relate to each other.

Writing Research Papers: An Easy Guide for Non-Native-English Speakers. P Stapleton. Canberra: Australian Centre for International Agricultural Research; 1987.

Although not specifically written for medical authors, serves as a clear short introduction to organizing the materials for a paper, getting it written, submitting it to a journal, and cleaning up prose style.

PROSE STYLE AND STRUCTURE

The Elements of Style. W Strunk Jr, EB White. 3rd ed. New York: The Macmillan Company, 1979.

The short classic on principles of clear writing widely known as "Strunk and White". If you can afford only 1 book on style, this is the one to buy.

English Prose Style. H Read. New York: Pantheon Books; 1983.

Elegant essays on composition (words, epithets, metaphor, the sentence, the paragraph, arrangement) and rhetoric. Of the 8 essays on aspects of rhetoric, that most pertinent to scientific writing is the essay on exposition.

The Reader over Your Shoulder: A Handbook for Writers of English Prose. R Graves, A Hodge. 2nd ed. New York: Random House; 1979.

Twenty-five principles for clear statement and sixteen for graceful prose, sharply applied to samples of prose from eminent English writers. This second, abridged edition is not as good as the long out-of-print first, which included chapters on the history of English prose style as well as more examinations of prose samples.

Revising Prose. 2nd ed. RA Lanham. New York: Charles Scribner; 1987.

How to analyze one's prose for the "lard factor" and apply the "paramedic treatment" to rid it of the vices of the "official and school" styles. The appendix reviews the elements of grammar and sentence structure, describes basic sentence patterns, and briefly analyzes the "noun style" and the "verb style."

Simple & Direct: A Rhetoric for Writers. J Barzun. New York: Harper & Row; 1985.

In clear essays Barzun works from the smallest elements of style, words, through the elements of linking, tone, and meaning, to paragraphs and the entire composition. The last chapter is on revision. As he goes along, he sets forth 20 principles of clear writing.

Style: Ten Lessons in Clarity and Grace. 2nd ed. JM Williams. Glenview, Illinois: Scott, Foresman; 1985.

A classic didactic text on how to give your prose the qualities of clarity, coherence, emphasis, and concision (economy). Particular attention to rhythm and to punctuation.

ILLUSTRATIONS

Charts & Graphs: Guidelines for the Visual Presentation of Statistical Data in the Life Sciences. D Simmonds, ed. Baltimore: MTP Press; 1981.

Illustrates methods of graphic presentation for publication, slide presentation, and television; briefly discusses principles behind these methods. Presents the conventions for genealogic diagrams. Includes a glossary of terms and a compilation of abbreviations and symbols.

Graphics Simplified: How to Plan and Prepare Effective Charts, Graphs, Illustrations, and Other Visual Aids. AJ MacGregor. Toronto: University of Toronto Press; 1979.

Principles of illustration, with examples of various formats. Not as comprehensive as Charts & Graphs described above.

Handbook of Graphic Presentation. CF Schmid, SE Schmid. 2nd ed. New York: John S. Wiley; 1979.

A comprehensive, heavily illustrated guide to the design of many kinds of charts: rectilinear coordinate, bar and column, semilogarithmic, frequency, and pictorial. Chapters on drafting and projection techniques, computer methods. The chapter on statistical maps should be useful to epidemiologists.

Illustrating Science: Standards for Publication. Scientific Illustration Committee. Bethesda, Maryland: Council of Biology Editors; 1988.

A thorough presentation of illustration principles, aesthetic considerations, and technical methods for drawings, photographs, and graphs. Chapter IV, "Graphs and Maps", will be the most useful section for most medical authors.

Semiology of Graphics: Diagrams, Networks, Maps. J Bertin. WJ Berg, trans. Madison, Wisconsin: University of Wisconsin Press; 1983.

An exhaustive and thorough analysis of the problems and methods in graphic representation of complexly related variables. Particularly valuable for possibilities in representing complex relations of epidemiologic data.

GUIDES TO MEDICAL LITERATURE, DATABASES, AND OTHER SOURCES OF INFORMATION

A Basic Guide to Online Information Systems for Health Care Professionals. RG Albright. Arlington, Virginia: Information Resource Press; 1988.

The main online information resources relevant to clinical and research medicine, with details of their contents and search methods: Compuserve; The National Library of Medicine's MEDLINE and other MEDLARS databases (with attention to Grateful Med, the Library's low-cost, easy-access search program); PaperChase (a proprietary gateway to MEDLINE); the DIALOG databases; BRS/Colleague; MEDIS; and AMA/NET. Some description of the technical basis for online searching. Not a good introduction for computer-naive persons but should be helpful to those already comfortable with using a microcomputer for communications.

Databases: A Primer for Retrieving Information by Computer. SM Humphrey, BJ Melloni. Englewood Cliffs, New Jersey: Prentice-Hall; 1986.

A general, broad, but remarkably detailed introduction to search methods and strategies. A long appendix on major computerized information-retrieval services and databases.

Encyclopedia of Health Information Sources. P Wasserman, ed. Detroit: Gale; 1987.

A detailed compilation of information sources, with entries arranged under subject headings such as nephrology, orthopedics, physicians, psychosomatic disorders: abstract services and indexes; annuals, reviews, and yearbooks; associations and professional societies; bibliographies; directories and biographic sources; handbooks and manuals; online databases; periodicals; popular works and patient education; research centers, institutes, and clearinghouses; standards; statistic sources; textbooks and general works.

Information Sources in the Medical Sciences. 3rd ed. LT Morton, S Godbolt, eds. London: Butterworths; 1984.

A survey, first, of the main kinds of information sources (libraries; primary sources such as journals; indexes, abstracts, bibliographies, reviews; reference works, computerized services) and, second, of the sources most useful in the main medical sciences and clinical disciplines.

Introduction to Reference Sources in the Health Sciences. FW Roper, JA Boorkman. Chicago: Medical Library Association; 1980.

An authoritative guide to bibliographic sources (including computerized data bases) and information sources (terminology, data handbooks, drug information, audiovisual materials, statistics, directories, biographical material, history sources). Prepared for librarians but will be useful to authors not fully familiar with how to find the literature of their fields.

MEDLINE: A Basic Guide to Searching. SJ Feinglos. Chicago: Medical Library Association; 1985.

A detailed primer on search terms, operators, and methods. Aimed at the professional searcher but would be helpful to others who wish to improve the efficiency of their online searches in any system.

Online Databases in the Medical and Life Sciences. New York: Cuadra/Elsevier; 1987.

An exhaustive catalog of databases in the United States, Canada, and other countries. Each entry describes type of database, its subjects, the producer, the vendors of online access, special conditions for use, content, language, geographic coverage in its content, time span of coverage, and frequency of updating. Includes a compilation of addresses for services and gateway systems. Subject, vendor, and title indexes.

Searching the Medical Literature: A Guide to Printed and Online Sources. J Welch, TA King. London: Chapman & Hall; 1985.

Akin to *Information Sources in the Medical Sciences* described above but shorter and less comprehensive.

Index